Contents

ABOVE: The Ffestiniog Railway's replica Lynton & Barnstaple Railway Manning Wardle-type
-2T *Lyd* making its debut at Wood Bay in 2010. The wreath on the smokebox recalls
one made of bronze chrysanthemums famously left at the Barnstaple Town stop block
r the original line closed in 1935, with a card which read 'perchance it is not dead, but
peth'. *Lyd's* debut showed that the line is now very much awake again!

ER PICTURE: The king of the new-build steam locomotives, £3 million Peppercorn
acific No. 60163 *Tornado*, in British Railways apple green livery, storms away from
ghborough Central on the Great Central Railway. BRIAN SHARPE

ETS (LEFT TO RIGHT): Ffestiniog Railway double Fairlie No. 12 *David Lloyd George* heads a
bound for Porthmadog. FR
Patriot 4-6-0 No. 45551 The Unknown Warrior, the National Memorial Engine, takes shape
seley Locomotive Works in February 2016. LMS-PATRIOT PROJECT
R steam railmotor No. 93 running on the Llangollen Railway in March 2011, before its
ial launch at Didcot Railway Centre. ROBIN JONES

Steam FROM SCRATCH
Building new British steam locomotives today

AUTHOR: Robin Jones

DESIGN: atg-media.com

PRODUCTION EDITOR: Sarah Palmer

COVER DESIGN: Michael Baumber

REPROGRAPHICS: Jonathan Schofield

PUBLISHER: Tim Hartley

COMMERCIAL DIRECTOR: Nigel Hole

PUBLISHING DIRECTOR: Dan Savage

PUBLISHED BY: Mortons Media Group Ltd, Media Centre,
Morton Way, Horncastle, Lincolnshire, LN9 6JR
Tel: 01507 529529

PRINTED BY: William Gibbons And Sons, Wolverhampton

MORTONS
MEDIA GROUP LTD

Introduction

S ince the Talyllyn Railway at Tywyn in central Wales because the world's first steam line to be taken over by volunteers in 1951, the railway preservation movement has worked wonders to save and reopen others. Not only that, it has saved hundreds of historically priceless locomotives, carriages and wagons from the cutters' torches as the steam era gave way to that of diesel and electric traction.

Britain's railway system came into being as a result of the amalgamations of myriad smaller companies, before the Grouping of 1923, which created the GWR, LNER, LMS and Southern Railway, and Nationalisation of 1948 that left us with British Railways.

Each merged company often found itself with an arbitrary collection of rolling stock, no more so than British Railways, which began withdrawals of non-standard class steam locomotive types en masse in the Fifties.

Had they managed to linger on another 10 years, the preservation movement may have been sufficiently advanced and resourced to have saved them. Sadly, it was not to be.

Once superseded by diesel or electric traction, or declared surplus to requirements both by the closing of branch lines before as well as during the Beeching cuts, steam locomotives would within weeks be despatched to the nearest breaker's yard. The breaker, anxious to make a quick profit, would reduce them to piles of scrap within days, and what we now view as priceless pieces of British transport history were lost, seemingly forever.

There was one glaring exception to this rule. Dai Woodham, owner of Barry scrapyard in South Wales, took a commercial decision in the mid-Sixties to focus on the more lucrative business of scrapping wagons while leaving his rusting steam engines 'for a rainy day'.

That rainy day lasted for years, long after the last steam locomotive ran in revenue-earning BR traffic in 1968, and the breathing space allowed heritage railways and enthusiast groups time to mature to the point where they were ready to buy a scrap engine and begin the long and costly process of restoring it.

In fairness, some of the locomotives at Barry had been out of traffic for only a handful of

years, having been rendered obsolete not by their condition but by dieselisation, and were returned to steam in a fairly short space of time. Altogether, 213 would be saved for preservation purposes from the Woodham scrapyard.

However, they never came close to representing a reasonably representative cross-section of the 20th century steam era. Because Barry scrapyard had taken delivery of redundant locomotives, primarily from the Southern and Western regions, certain classes were over-represented, such as Bulleid Pacifics and GWR Manors and Halls, while others were noticeably absent, such as GWR 47XXs and Hawksworth County 4-6-0s.

There was but one LNER locomotive, B1 No. 61264, which was saved and restored to main line condition, but there were not A1 Pacifics, LMS Patriots or a BR Clan 4-6-2.

On January 9, 2016, *Flying Scotsman*, the world's most famous steam locomotive, hauled its first passenger trains on the East Lancashire Railway at the end of a marathon £4.2 million overhaul lasting more than a decade. Yet had it not been for Ffestiniog Railway saviour our

ABOVE: In BR express passenger blue livery, *Tornado* storms through Gleneagles on February 8, 2013. The A1 Steam Locomotive Trust has kept its pledge that, during the first 10 years of its operation, *Tornado* will be painted in all four liveries carried by the original Peppercorn A1s. BRIAN SHARPE

LEFT: Back in apple green livery, Peppercorn A1 Pacific No. 60163 *Tornado* passes Borthwick as it makes its debut on the newly opened Borders Railway on September 13, 2015. JONATHAN GOURLAY

ABOVE: The production line at Brunel's Great Western Railway works at Swindon in the early Fifties. Britain's great steam building plants have long since closed, but the building of new GWR locomotives continues at workshops at Didcot Railway Centre and on the Llangollen Railway, thanks to an army of enthusiasts who are overcoming great difficulties, not least of all the dedicated locomotive building facilities of the past, to plug missing gaps in the British heritage fleet. BRITISH RAILWAYS

the late Alan Pegler, who bought it straight out of BR service in 1963, it may well have ended up as a distant memory rather than a machine capable of enthralling millions today. So nearly lost, it was not taken back into public ownership until a nationwide appeal raised £2.31 million in 2004 to buy it for the National Railway Museum. Thanks to Alan, we have an A3 Pacific, but it too so nearly missed the boat.

MISSION IMPOSSIBLE?

Many of the short-trousered school boys of the Fifties who could do nothing to save their beloved locomotives as they were replaced by diesels eventually laid down their Ian Allan ABC Locospotters books and went home. Others, however, did not concede their places on the lineside so easily, and set about saving redundant branch lines as heritage railways.

Some managed to buy steam locomotives straight out of BR service, but once steam vanished from the national network in 1968, Dai Woodham was not only the best bet as a source of motive power but the only choice available.

The preservation sector, fueled by the nation's love of steam and pride in Britain's glorious railway history, grew to the point where it became a major player in the tourist economy.

As the nascent heritage lines found themselves able to sit back and consolidate, thoughts of many enthusiasts turned to "the ones that got away".

Even the Talyllyn pioneers of 1951 would have probably thought it would be beyond anyone's wildest dreams that new steam locomotives could be built to fill missing gaps in our collection. Yet recent history has shown that has become a natural progression of the preservation movement.

Of course, the manufacture of steam locomotives never died out in Britain, even though from the Sixties onwards it was kept alive mainly by miniature engineering societies. It is often held that the first new-build project was to be found in the Sixties at Lakeland's Ravenglass & Eskdale Railway, which in broad terms uses freelance types loosely based on full-size main line locomotives but a fraction of the size.

Fast forward to 2009, and one of the greatest achievements of the heritage railway sector was the launch of an all-new Peppercorn A1 Pacific, No. 60163 *Tornado*, by Prince Charles and the Duchess of Cornwall at York. Those who began the project effectively on the back of a beermat nearly two decades earlier were often laughed at, yet their efforts ended in a full-size steam locomotive hauling trains in regular service on the modern national network, attracting the crowds wherever it goes. Not only that, but we can now again savour the sights and sounds of an A1, a locomotive believed to have been consigned to history.

Tornado is the epitome of the concept of steam from scratch, and remains the market leader in the field.

WHY SO EXPENSIVE?

As this book highlights, there are now many new-build projects, either completed, nearly completed or making steady progress. However, what made The A1 Steam Locomotive Trust's project stand out from the ▶

rest was the immense fundraising machine that swung into operation to raise the necessary £3 million.

Selling souvenir badges, biros and notebooks, a mainstay of the early rail revival sector, would never have raised even a miniscule fraction of that amount. The trust realised early on that what was needed was a regular donation scheme, launched with resounding success as "the price of a pint of beer a week".

I make no apology in the chapter detailing with the history of *Tornado* for going into detail on The A1 Trust's fundraising scheme, because the lack of financial planning is the primary reason as to why similar projects stall or become slow burners.

Love and enthusiasm for a particular lost locomotive class are fine energisers for a new-build project, but they don't pay the bills. If you can't work out how to raise sufficient finance to keep a steam from scratch project making steady progress with the completion of components at regular intervals and inspire supporters and recruit more along the way, don't start one. Make a model of your favourite locomotive instead.

Of course, the cost of building a locomotive from new today, inflation apart, is far greater than what it would have been in the steam era. Then, there were major railway companies and outside builders like Hunslet, North British and Robert Stephenson & Hawthorns who had their dedicated locomotive building plants with production lines and the resulting economies of scale. Those works are now gone: if you want to build a new steam locomotive, sooner or later you will need fully-equipped premises in which to do so. The A1 Trust has its base in the former Hopetown carriage works at Darlington, while the Great Western Society has been undertaking its projects in the former steam shed at Didcot.

Other groups have slowly built up their collection of components at an assortment of locations: the builders of new BR Clan Hengist even assembled their cab in a member's bedroom!

It is not only the lack of established premises, but the absence of essential components such as patterns, which have to be expensively made new from drawings, often just for a single batch of castings.

ABOVE: The original LBSCR Atlantic No. 32424 *Beachy Head* heading a Railway Correspondence & Travel Society special on October 5, 1952. Sadly it was scrapped along with all other members of its class, but we eagerly await the completion of a replica at the Bluebell Railway, maybe in 2018. ATLANTIC GROUP

ABOVE: The Ffestiniog Railway's Boston Lodge Works is the oldest railway workshops in the world still in continuous use as such. It built two of the line's famous double Fairlies in Victorian times, and has turned out four new steam locomotives in the heritage era. ROBIN JONES

MIX AND MATCH

The other way to recreate an extinct locomotive is a 'steam halfway from scratch' principle and use secondhand parts from ones that did survive.

The method is possible, at least in terms of GWR types, because of the policy of Locomotive Superintendent George Jackson Churchward, who after his appointment in 1902 introduced standardised parts such as wheels, cylinders and connecting rods to the Swindon production line. In theory, a bogie wheel from a main line express locomotive could also be used for a humble workaday tank engine, for instance.

The last 10 of the 213 steam locomotives saved from Barry scrapyard were the ones least wanted by enthusiasts. They either duplicated existing preserved engines, had parts missing or were deemed too costly to restore.

In 1990, these last occupants of the site were bought by the now-defunct South Glamorgan Council with just over £85,000 of grant aid from the former National Heritage Memorial Fund, for an abortive project to develop a Welsh National Railway Museum at Butetown station in the docklands area of Cardiff. In 1979, the Butetown Historic Railway Society had been formed to restore the then derelict Taff Vale Railway station, and establish a steam-hauled passenger service to Cardiff Queen Street. By 1994, a short section of track existed, over which Peckett 0-6-0ST 1859 of 1932 *Sir Gomer*, which had worked at the National Coal Board's Mountain Ash Colliery, hauled short passenger trains.

However, when the Cardiff Bay Development Corporation indicated in the late Nineties that it did not want a preserved railway in the redeveloped former dockland, the society was welcomed by the Vale of Glamorgan County Council, which helped it relocate to Barry Island, as the Vale of Glamorgan Railway. It was seen an important attraction to further the council's plans to restore the port of Barry to its former glory as a major tourist resort on the Bristol Channel.

The museum plans were dropped, and the Butetown stock including the 'Barry 10', as the last rusting hulks from the scrapyard became known, were moved back to Barry Island, where they had rusted in the Severnside air at Dai's scrapyard for so long.

The 10 comprised GWR 2-8-0 No. 2861, 2-6-2Ts Nos. 4115, and 5539, 2-8-0T No. 5227, 0-6-2T No. 6686, 4-6-0 No. 7927 Willington Hall, LMS 'Black Five' 4-6-0 No. 44901, LMS Stanier 8F 2-8-0 No. 48518; BR Standard 2-6-4T No. 80150 and BR Standard 9F 2-10-0 No. 92245 No. 5538 was added to the 'Barry 10' at a later date.

The enthusiast fraternity was, of course, aware of them, and also that no examples of numerous major classes had survived in the preservation era. Eventually, the idea was mooted that while there was no incentive to restore yet another example of a surviving type in its own right, what if they could be transformed into a new example of an extinct one?

Churchward's standardised parts policy came into play big time here. Dismantle two locomotives, build a few new parts, buy some secondhand spares elsewhere, and you could create three new ones, so the theory ran. It was like having a giant box of Lego bricks; take one

ABOVE: Transport historian and author Tom Rolt founded the modern-day operation railway heritage movement. Thanks to him, in 1951, the Talyllyn Railway became the world's first to be taken over by volunteers, a small acorn from which mighty oaks grew, with more than 120 heritage lines in Britain today. Tom is seen waving off an early privatisation-era train. However, when the little line in mid-Wales was saved, there was no immediate threat to steam traction: main line diesels were a rarity and the recently nationalised British Railways still had many classic pre-Grouping steam types in regular serviced. All that changed with the BR 1955 Modernisation Plan, which called for the elimination of steam and its replacement with diesel and electric traction, even though main line steam locomotives would continue to be built for another five years. The saving of the Talyllyn was a magnificent start, but it would be many years before the British preservation movement developed such muscle as to be able to prevent many classic steam types being rendered extinct at scrapyards, but now new-build groups are aiming to slowly but surely go some way to making good those losses. TR ARCHIVES

ABOVE: One of the greatest achievements of the new-build sector has been the restoration by the Great Western Society of GWR steam railmotor No. 93. The original carriage body survived, but the new-build element was the steam motor bogie. The railmotor concept is the 'missing link' between steam locomotives and modern diesel and electric multiple units. When the GWR introduced them in Edwardian times, they produced a mini transport revolution for local stopping services, but within three decades had disappeared from the Swindon empire. The rebuilding of No. 93 is now not only a major addition to the UK heritage fleet but a priceless education asset. It is seen passing Garth-y-Dwr on a runpast at the Llangollen Railway on March 22, 2011, since when it has acquired a matching trailer, making it Britain's only operational Steam Multiple Unit. ROBIN JONES

ABOVE: The Prince of Wales takes the controls of market-leading new-build project A1 Peppercorn Pacific No. 60163 Tornado after officially launching it into traffic at York on February 19, 2009, when it first hauled the Royal Train. Prince Charles has since given permission for builder The A1 Steam Locomotive Trust to use his title Prince of Wales as the name for the seventh Gresley P2 Mikado No. 2007, now the world's fastest-growing standard gauge new-build project. ROB MORELAND/A1SLT

model apart, and you could use them to build an entirely new one.

In late 2003, the Vale of Glamorgan Council voted in favour of a report for the release of several of the locomotives for use in such projects, and permission was obtained from the Lottery, which had financed their original purchase, to allow it to happen. Much, much more on this in the chapters ahead.

A SHINY NEW STEAMY FUTURE!

So, new-build may be a costly and time-consuming process, but it is certainly considered a worthwhile cause not only by the enthusiasts

involved, but the general public who turnout in droves to see new locomotives, photograph them and ride behind them.

It has been said that the number of people willing to freely give their weekends to volunteer on heritage railways is dropping off. Not so visitor numbers, with many of the lines reporting regular year-by-year increases in passenger numbers.

There are still many Barry hulks waiting to be restored, but will there in years to come still be the volunteers to finish them?

It is now being asked – rather than keep repairing historic locomotives with expensive

mandatory overhauls every 10 years, might it not be cheaper to obtain a bank loan and build new locomotives from scratch?

Furthermore, it has long been suggested that batch building of ideal types to work heritage lines of the average eight to 10-mile lengths might be a way forward to bring down the costs by virtue of economies of scale. Two of the projects in this book chose to replicate a BR Standard 3MT 82XXX 2-6-2T, and a NER G5 0-4-4T, which are considered as such 'ideal' types.

Britain invented the steam locomotive more than two centuries ago, and there is certainly no sign of us ever giving up building yet more. •

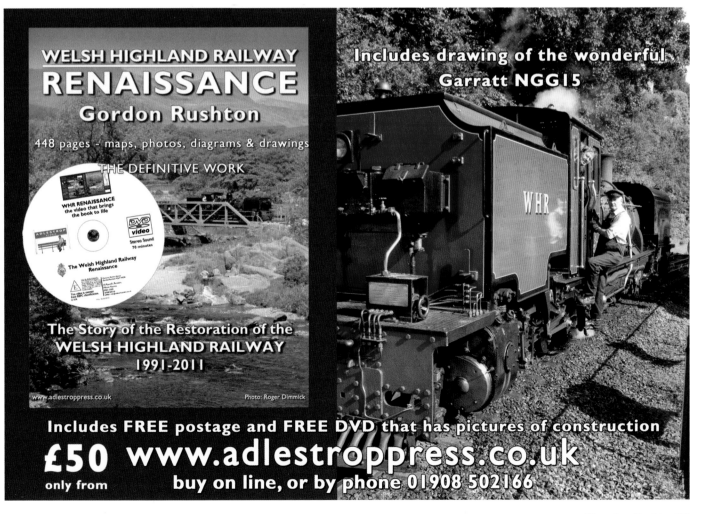

Chapter 1

The first enthusiast
new-build

The first heritage-era new-build steam locomotive owed much to the miniature railway engineering tradition that began in the mid-Victorian era.

ABOVE: The Ravenglass & Eskdale Railway's 2-8-2 *River Mite* was built in 1966 and lays claim to being the first new-build locomotive of Britain's heritage railway era. RER

The impetus for building replicas of lost steam locomotives originated with the enthusiast fraternity. Indeed, as long as there have been railway enthusiasts, there have been those who were not just content to watch and ride on steam trains, but wanted one of their own. Especially one pulled by their favourite locomotive.

Decades before mass-market model railways from the likes of Hornby and Marklin appeared in high street stores; one particularly well-heeled Victorian enthusiast built his own live steam locomotives.

Sir Arthur Percival Heywood, 3rd Baronet, was born on December 25, 1849. He grew up in the family home of Dove Leys

at Denstone in Staffordshire. The house overlooked the valley through which the North Staffordshire Railway's line from Rocester to Ashbourne ran.

The Heywood family travelled by train to visit relatives in Manchester and to holiday in Inveran in the Scottish Highlands. Like many of the short-trousered schoolboy trainspotters

ABOVE: Arthur Heywood and the first 15in gauge locomotive, *Effie*, on his pioneering Duffield Bank Railway.

of the 20th century, who were also inspired by the fact that steam trains took them to their annual summer seaside holiday, young Arthur developed a passion for the railway.

He assisted his father with his hobby of ornamental metalwork, using a Holtzapffel lathe, and in his late teenage years, built a 4in gauge model railway with a steam locomotive.

Wanting something on which his younger siblings could ride, he built a 9in gauge locomotive and train. The experience set him on a path that one day would have resounding consequences.

He attended school at Eton and then Trinity College, Cambridge, where he made friends with local railwaymen, taking trips on locomotive footplates. He graduated in 1872 with a degree in Applied Science and in the same year married his cousin, Margaret Effie, daughter of Rev George Sumner, rector of Alresford in Hampshire and set up home at Duffield Bank in Duffield near Derby; the headquarters of the Midland Railway. Many of the directors lived in the area, and Arthur soon developed an interest in Derby Works.

He became aware of unsuccessful experiments by the Royal Engineers in building railways for use in warfare. He began experimenting himself, and developed what he called the "minimum gauge railway" with an optimum gauge of 15in, as his 9in gauge locomotive had proved too small to carry passengers. His first locomotive on his Duffield Bank Railway was an 0-4-0T named *Effie*.

Built on a steep hillside, the line was an ideal testing ground and, to gain the adhesion for steep gradients and the ability to negotiate

ABOVE: Belgrave engine shed on the Eaton Hall Railway.

small-radius curves, he built six coupled locomotives with what he called his radiating axle.

Arthur hoped to market his minimum gauge railway and the expanding Duffield line was used as a showcase; there were many potential visitors but few buyers.

One big customer was the Duke of Westminster, for whom Arthur built the Eaton Hall Railway. Arthur was working on it in 1916 when he became unwell and died at home that year.

The 4½-mile 15in gauge Eaton Hall Railway linked the hall to the GWR station sidings at Balderton on the Shrewsbury to Chester line.

The first engine was 0-4-0T *Katie*, followed by two identical 0-6-0Ts, *Shelagh* and *Ursula*. *Katie* proved capable of handling loads of up to 40 tons at a speed of around 10mph, with twice that speed being achieved in tests.

The Eaton Hall Railway closed in 1946 and the line was lifted two years later. A new 15in gauge Eaton Park Railway, which follows a small part of the original route, was built in 1994 along with a replica of *Katie*, but is only accessible to the public on open days.

The Duke's railway paved the way for hundreds of miniature railways, with many locomotives and carriages run on them being built in the 20th century, including the Romney, Hythe & Dymchurch Railway in Kent, the Fairbourne Railway in central

Wales and the Ravenglass & Eskdale Railway in the Lake District – not to mention hundreds of miniature railways at seaside resorts around Britain and private lines that the public never saw.

The British Railways Modernisation Plan of 1955 marked a watershed in UK railway history. After the country had pulled out of the years of wartime austerity, it was time to modernise the nation's railways; steam locomotives were to be phased out in favour of diesel and electric traction. The final locomotive to be built for British Railways was Standard 9F 2-10-0 No. 92220 *Evening Star*, which emerged from Swindon Works on March 20, 1960, however, steam locomotives continued to be built by British manufacturers for another 11 years. It is widely accepted that the steam railway era, which began with Richard Trevithick, ended in 1971, when Hunslet turned out the last steam locomotive to be built for commercial use (as opposed to tourist, enthusiast or heritage purposes) at the Jack Lane Works in Leeds, as 0-4-0ST works No. 3902.

The 2ft 6in gauge locomotive was exported to Indonesia for use on the Trangkil sugar mill estate system in Java. It worked there for 33 years as Trangkil No. 4 until made redundant by rationalisation of the system.

Graham Lee, who then owned Hunslet, had been steadily developing an impressive private multi-gauge system on his farm near Tamworth, Staffordshire as the Statfold Barn Railway, and he acquired the locomotive along with several others from the region.

Trangkil No 4, which was originally built to 750mm gauge, returned to England in 2004 to become part of the Statfold collection. During overhaul it was regauged to 2ft, and returned to steam.

Although British manufacturers ceased full-size steam locomotive production, the technology never went away.

Model engineers continued to build miniature steam engines in their sheds, garages and private workshops, and many societies were formed with their own dedicated running lines. Also, several firms continued building miniature steam locomotives for pleasure lines.

However, building a new full-size steam locomotive would be a world apart from such activities. Well, almost.

ABOVE: One of the miniature railways operating at Skegness in the middle of the 20th century. ROBIN JONES COLLECTION

LAKELAND ADVENTURE

ABOVE: New-build *Northern Rock* heads through the Lakeland pastures alongside the Ravenglass & Eskdale Railway. RER

The term 'toy train' was a term frequently applied to narrow gauge railways for a century or more, even though they are full-size concerns and not models.

Today's 15in gauge Ravenglass & Eskdale Railway – popularly known locally as La'al Ratty – might be more accurately described as a 'toy train' than any of the above, as it uses locomotives based, if loosely, on quarter-scale versions of main line types, and sits on the boundary between narrow gauge and miniature railways, such as the Romney Hythe & Dymchurch, Fairbourne, Cleethorpes Coast Light and Rhyl Miniature railways.

It was not always the case, however. For when a railway was first built along the route, it was a full-size 3ft gauge narrow gauge line.

Promoted by the Whitehaven Iron Mines Company to carry haematite iron ore from its mines in Eskdale for use in the blast furnaces of the booming steelworks town of Barrow-in-Furness, in 1873, the Ravenglass & Eskdale Railway was authorised by an Act of Parliament. The first public narrow gauge railway in England, it opened for goods on May 27, 1875, using Manning Wardle 0-6-0T *Devon*; opening to passengers on November 20, 1876, with the train decorated with flags and Lord Muncaster riding on the engine.

It was a commercial failure all but overnight, for six months later, the contractor who built the line forced the railway company into receivership after not being paid.

Isolated iron ore mines along the railway could not make it pay, and became unprofitable after iron prices slumped, but the passenger services continued, with the line managed by a receiver.

However, the railway cashed in on the new generations of late-Victorian tourists by becoming a tourist attraction, advertising a journey into the 'English Alps'. On bank holidays, trains were packed, and wagons had to be pressed into service, fitted with benches from Ravenglass public hall.

ABOVE: Boot station on the original 3ft gauge Ravenglass & Eskdale Railway. Common in Ireland and the Isle of Man, 3ft gauge was a rarity on the British mainland.
RER PRESERVATION SOCIETY

However, as the financial situation worsened, nobody could be found to buy the line to pay the creditors off. The track and locomotives were neglected and the passenger service was finally stopped in 1908. A new company was formed to take it over, but all traffic had ceased by 1913.

It was then that the Duffield Bank/Eaton Hall concept came into play.

Wenman Joseph Bassett-Lowke, the most famous modelmaker of the early 20th century, was already familiar with a passenger-carrying miniature line at Blakesley Hall near Towcester, which linked the mansion to the local station, using two imported Cagney Brothers US outline 4-4-0s. Aided by engineer Henry Greenly, Bassett-Lowke formed a company, Miniature Railways of Great Britain, in 1904 and the firm acquired an existing 10¼in gauge line, the Bricket Wood Railway at St Albans, which was moved next to Northampton's Abington Park, opening at Easter 1905, and so the principle of a railway line, albeit a very small one, owned, managed and driven by enthusiasts, was established.

While the senseless carnage on the Western Front continued unabated in 1915, Bassett-Lowke spotted an advertisement for the derelict Ravenglass & Eskdale Railway. He and his friend R Proctor-Mitchell bought the line for their firm, Narrow Gauge Railways Ltd, and halved the gauge, relaying it to 15in gauge as a base for testing their miniature versions of main line locomotive types under fairly harsh operating conditions.

Sans Pariel, a 4-4-2, began running trains to Muncaster on August 28, 1915, and tracks reached Eskdale Green by Easter 1916. Despite the First World War, the trains were busier than they had been at any time during the 3ft gauge years. The line also advertised itself as the smallest public railway in the world.

The locomotives and rolling stock from 15in gauge pioneer Sir Arthur Heywood's Duffield Bank line, were brought in following his death. These included *Muriel*, which dated from 1894, and whose frames and running gear were rebuilt as 0-8-2 *River Irt*.

By 1917, the entire line had been converted and trains were running along the whole length. A new locomotive, Davey Paxman 2-8-2 *River Esk*, was built in 1923, and by the mid-Twenties, the line had been extended to its present terminus at Dalegarth station.

The original *Katie* from Eaton Hall was sold to the newly built line, was resold in 1922, and effectively scrapped in 1926. Surviving parts now form the basis of a long-term rebuild project at Ravenglass.

As well as passengers, the line transported granite between Beckfoot Quarry and Murthwaite crushing plant. From Murthwaite to Ravenglass, a third rail was laid to accommodate standard gauge trains too.

The railway closed during the Second World War and was bought by the Keswick Granite Company, which closed the quarries in 1953, the standard gauge line being subsequently lifted.

In the Fifties, passenger services continued to lose money and after to attempts to place it on the market, it was put up for sale by auction in 1960.

ABOVE: *Northern Rock*, the second steam locomotive built by the Ravenglass & Eskdale Railway in the 'modern' era. ANDREW BOWDEN*
LEFT: Resplendent in Furness Railway maroon, *River Mite* heads another service through spectacular Lakeland scenery. RER

SAVED AGAIN

Enthusiasts came to the rescue for a second time, with Midland stockbroker, Colin Gilbert, his associate, Douglas Robinson, and local landowner, Sir Wavell Wakefield, forming a new railway company backed by a preservation society formed by local people.

They stepped in on the day of the auction and paid the balance of the purchase price.

The society's task was to return the railway to profitability. It soon became apparent that a new locomotive was needed, and Clarkson of York was contracted to build it.

To be named *River Mite*, the locomotive part was all new, but the old eight-wheeled steam tender from the Davey Paxman 1923-built 2-8-2 *River Esk* was used.

River Mite was built to a design based on a miniature version of an LNER Gresley P1 2-8-2 locomotive and an LMS Stanier tender. Volunteers raised around £8000 to build it.

It arrived in style in December 1966, having been hauled from York to Ravenglass by traction engine *Providence*, and was commissioned into traffic on May 20, 1967.

The new locomotive gave the railway the capacity to operate a longer and more intensive summer service.

The Ravenglass & Eskdale then built a new steam locomotive by itself in the railway's own workshops at Ravenglass.

After taking the Romney, Hythe & Dymchurch Railway's Davey Paxman 4-6-2 No. 2 *Northern Chief* on trial in 1972, it was decided to build a new 2-6-2 tender locomotive.

The original idea was to name it Sir Arthur Heywood after the legendary miniature railway pioneer, but the project was funded by the Northern Rock building society.

It was therefore named *Northern Rock*, and entered traffic in 1976.

It has since visited railways as far afield as Dresden to act as an ambassador for the Lakeland line. Its design proved to be so successful that two similar locomotives were built at Ravenglass for Japan's Shuzenji Romney Railway, *Northern Rock II* in 1989 and *Cumbria* in 1992.

Despite Northern Rock having transformed itself into a bank, and then been taken into public ownership during the credit crisis in 2007, the locomotive has kept the name of the institution that was its benefactor.

Locomotive building at Ravenglass continued with the building in 1978-80 of Bo-Bo diesel *Lady Wakefield*, named after the wife of the former chairman of the railway company.

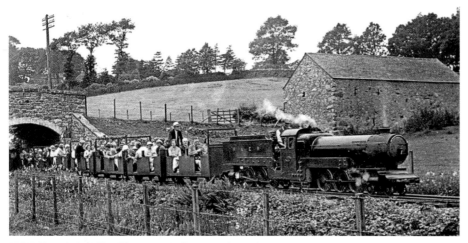

ABOVE: The 1967-built *River Mite* was not the first locomotive bearing that name to run on the Ravenglass & Eskdale Railway, or to be built there. Constructed at Murthwaite with a new boiler and the running gear of two other locomotives in 1927, the first *River Mite* was an unsuccessful four-cylinder articulated locomotive of the railway's own design. It lasted a decade in traffic before being scrapped, being too lightly built for the amount of work and the steep gradients of the line. It is pictured in the Thirties. ROBIN JONES COLLECTION

ABOVE: *Northern Rock* arrives at Irton Road, with a train for Ravenglass. PETER TRIMMING*

THE PRESERVATION QUANDARY

ABOVE: *River Mite* on the turntable. ANDREW BOWDEN*

So was the 1966 *River Mite* the first new-build steam locomotive of the British heritage or preservation era?

In terms of being built to run regular services on a public passenger-carrying railway, the answer must be yes.

However, are the likes of the Ravenglass & Eskdale, Romney, Hythe & Dymchurch and Fairbourne railways 'preserved' lines in the true sense of the world, or are they oversized seaside miniature railways, for which steam locomotive building has been with us since the Heywood era?

It is generally held that the first preserved railway was the Talyllyn, which enthusiasts largely from the West Midlands under the leadership of transport author Tom Rolt took over in time for the 1951 season, and as we know, the global railway revival movement snowballed in its wake.

However, the three above-mentioned miniature railways pre-date it by several decades.

While the Talyllyn was built to serve slate quarries and local villages and farms, by contrast the Romney, Hythe & Dymchurch was an out-and-and enthusiast railway (the "main line in miniature") from day one (although it did run armoured troop trains during the Second World War and has operated school services in modern times).

Both the Ravenglass and Fairbourne lines were in industrial use before their conversion to 'miniature' steam operations. Indeed, the Fairbourne (which was converted from a 2ft gauge horse-drawn tramway to a 15in gauge steam line by Bassett Lowke in 1916) was regauged from 15in to 12¼in in 1984, when new miniature steam locomotives and stock were brought in.

All three are today counted as heritage lines, but are they really 'preserved' in the traditional or colloquial sense of the word, any more than a seafront miniature line, as opposed to, say, a revived part of the British Rail network such as the Bluebell or Severn Valley railways?

Herein lies a philosophical question, which presents a real conundrum to the historian. When and where exactly does 'heritage', and new-build for heritage, begin ?

Are *River Mite* and *Northern Rock* the true predecessors of the likes of A1 Pacific *Tornado*, or just another two miniature locomotives built to fulfil the needs of a commercial enterprise?

The fact that 15in gauge hovers on the border between what is generally accepted as the miniature railway sector and 'true' narrow gauge does not help answer that question.

I would say that just because a fully fledged timetabled public railway uses locomotives based on reduced scale freelance versions of main line types, it does not diminish its status when measured against other narrow gauge lines that use full-size engines. In this case, *River Mite* was a first. ●

ABOVE: Seaside and holiday camp miniature railways reached the height of their popularity in the middle of the 20th century, but went into decline somewhat when the novelty wore off as steam haulage ended on the national network. However, there are still many to be found in Britain's traditional resorts. A modern example dating from 1975 is the Beer Heights Light Railway 7¼in gauge system at Pecorama, the headquarters of model railway manufacturer Peco at Beer in east Devon, which has a fleet of eight steam locomotives. In a surprise March snowfall miniature Penrhyn Quarry Hunslet 2-4-0T *Linda* is seen being steam tested before the annual boiler inspection as well as performing essential winter works on the track. BHLR

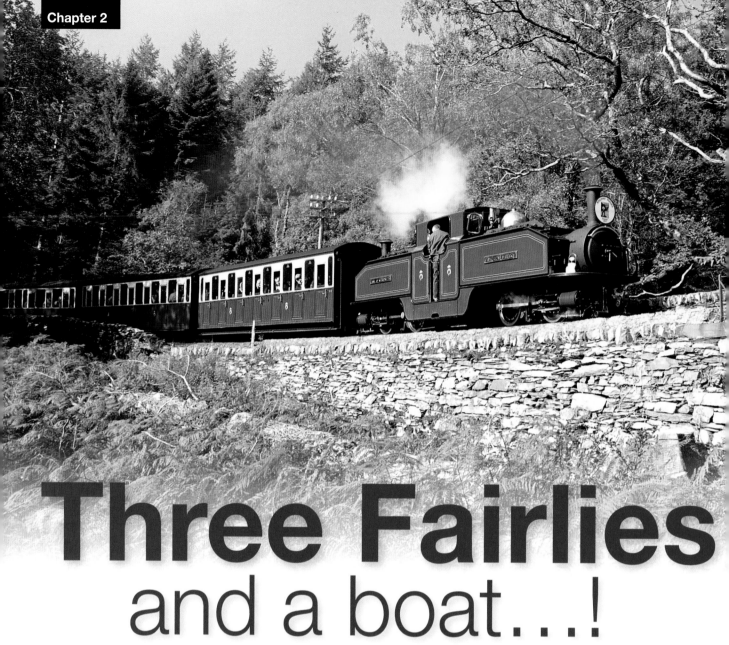

Chapter 2

Three Fairlies
and a boat…!

Building miniature or demonstration locomotives is a world apart from constructing a new full-size engine, but that was the threshold passed by the Ffestiniog Railway in 1979.

1979 was a landmark year in the history of Britain's new-build locomotives. For it was then that the first new full-size locomotive on a full-size railway for regular passenger traffic was turned out.

The 11ft 11½in gauge Ffestiniog Railway proudly unveiled a new double Fairlie 0-4-4-0+0-4-4-0T *Earl of Merioneth*, built at the line's Boston Lodge Works, the oldest railway works in the world still in use as such.

It was built under the Fairlie patent, to which the Ffestiniog has a licence in perpetuity to use.

It may be claimed that new locomotives built previously for the 15in gauge Ravenglass & Eskdale Railway might have beaten *Earl of Merioneth* in respect of this claim to be a 'first'. The counter argument is that locomotives on that line and the similar Romney, Hythe & Dymchurch Railway are poised halfway between miniature railways and narrow gauge, and are broadly reduced-scale replicas of main line types.

However, *Earl of Merioneth* is not a replica of any previous double Fairlie, but one built

to a modern updated design of the Victorian concept, with sloping square tanks.

Engineer Robert Francis Fairlie devised a simple solution to the problem of having to turn an engine when it reached its destination – build one with two ends. The cabs are joined back to back to make one, and there are two articulated power bogies – much the same as on a modern diesel locomotive with two ends.

Earl of Merioneth was the latest in a lineage beginning with Little Wonder, built by London builder George England to Fairlie's design in 1869 for the Ffestiniog.

In February 1870, Fairlie hosted locomotive engineers from as far afield as Russia, Mexico, Turkey and Sweden at the Ffestiniog where he gave demonstration runs of *Little Wonder*.

Orders for this startlingly new and revolutionary locomotive type flooded in, to Fairlie's great delight. He was so pleased that he gave the Ffestiniog Railway Company a permanent licence to use his locomotive patent without restriction in return for using the line to demonstrate *Little Wonder*, which was successful in that it could travel around

the line's tight curves at a respectable speed, meaning that expensive plans to double the track were rendered redundant.

By 1876, 43 different railways around the world had operated Fairlie's distinctive double-ended engines.

However, Mexico, New Zealand and the Ffestiniog apart, the bubble soon burst. Fairlie received complaints about the limited capacity for fuel and water, the flexible steam pipes being prone to leakage and wasting of power and the absence of unpowered wheels, which on 'normal' steam locomotives act as stabilisers.

Never mind, thought Fairlie, the customer is always right – and so he created a more traditional version of his locomotive, cut the design in half – and created a 'single Fairlie'.

Little Wonder was scrapped in 1882. A second Ffestiniog double Fairlie, No. 8 *James Spooner* of 1889, lasted until 1933 when it met the same fate. The railway's third double Fairlie, No. 10 *Merddin Emrys*, was built at the line's own Boston Lodge Works in 1879 – and is still in service today.

ABOVE: *Earl of Merioneth* at Porthmadog in February 2013. ANDREW THOMAS

LEFT: *Earl of Merioneth* continued the locomotive building tradition at Boston Lodge Works and became the third double Fairlie to be built there. It is seen heading towards Blaenau Ffestiniog on October 9, 2010. FR

ABOVE: In 1869, *Little Wonder* became the Festiniog (then spelled with one f) Railway's first double Fairlie. FR

ABOVE: *Livingston Thompson*, the oldest surviving Ffestiniog Railway double Fairlie, in the National Railway Museum at York. ROBIN JONES

THE 'OLDEST' LOCOMOTIVE WORKS

Boston Lodge Works has its origins in barracks provided for many of the 150 men working from the Merioneth side on the building of the great embankment across Traeth Mawr known as the Cob. Stables and smithies for the horses and wagons used to carry the stone were erected on site.

With the coming of the initially horsedrawn Festiniog Railway in 1836, the stables and smithies were brought back into use and there has been almost continuous development of the site for railway purposes since that time.

Between 1847 and 1851 the works was considerably developed by the construction of ferrous and non-ferrous foundries, a pattern-making shop, a blacksmith's shop, a carpenter's shop, and an engine house in which a steam engine provided power for machinery in a sawmill, pattern shop and machine shops.

In the 1870s further construction provided a paint shop, joiner's shop and erecting shop. The second locomotive to be built there was another double Fairlie, *Livingston Thompson*, in 1885. During the First World War, most of the works was used as a munitions factory, largely staffed by women, from September 1915 until early in 1919.

However, the works was closed along with the railway from March 1947 until September 20, 1954. Since then, many of the original buildings have been extensively repaired as they were brought back into use to serve a growing heritage railway, following the revival of the line begun by the late Alan Pegler, the man, who in 1963, bought LNER A3 Pacific No. 4472 *Flying Scotsman* from British Railways.

Works machinery has been updated and modern materials and techniques have been introduced. Additional workshops have been built as well as new locomotive servicing facilities and carriage storage depots.

In 1977, the works undertook the design and installation of oil-firing equipment on the Vale of Rheidol Railways 2-6-2T No.7 *Owain Glyndwr*. It the first of numerous outside contracts that the works has undertaken over the years, included restoration of steam engines and the construction of narrow gauge coaches.

Now, however, the revival had reached the point when the works was set to outshop an all-new steam locomotive again.

ABOVE: New-build double Fairlie *Earl of Merioneth* on shed at Boston Lodge Works on July 17, 2012. ROBIN JONES

ABOVE: *Earl of Merioneth* arrives at Porthmadog with the 3.10pm service from Blaenau Ffestiniog on April 4, 2010. Station pilot *Vale of Ffestiniog* awaits the arrival of a Welsh Highland Railway service from Caernarfon. ANDREW THOMAS

While volunteers were rebuilding the line to the eastern terminus of Blaenau Ffestiniog, Ffestiniog officials were looking at future motive power needs. The rebuilding was a monumental task involving building a spiral loop and hacking through a slate mountainside to create a deviation around the Central Electricity Generating Board's Llyn Ystradau hydro-electric reservoir, which had flooded part of the original route.

If trains were once again to run over the full 13½ miles between Porthmadog and Blaenau Ffestiniog, extra motive power was needed, and what better than to build a traditional double Fairlie in Ffestiniog's own workshops.

Earl of Merioneth was also built to replace *Livingston Thompson*, which is now on static display in the Great Hall of the National Railway Museum in York.

It would be the second locomotive to carry the name *Earl of Merioneth*. The first, originally named No. 3 *Livingston Thompson*, subsequently *Taliesin*, was renamed *Earl of Merioneth* in 1961. It reverted to its original name after its 'successor' was outshopped in 1979.

Building work for the new double Fairlie – the third locomotive to be constructed at Boston Lodge – began in 1972 following delivery of the boiler. Designed like the original Fairlies for coal burning, oil tanks and oil burning equipment were fitted in 1978 before the boiler was first steamed.

It incorporated the power bogies and some other parts from *Livingston Thompson*, while Hunslet of Leeds made the superheated boiler. New steel wheels were cast by British Rail Engineering at Crewe and the axles and wheels were machined by JIP Engineering Ltd of Willenhall, Staffordshire, for assembly at Boston Lodge.

Carrying the name *Earl of Merioneth* in English on one side and in Welsh *Iarll Meirionnydd* on the other, it made its first trip out of the works and across the Cob on June 12, 1979.

On June 23 that year, the railway's late general manager, Allan Garraway, formally named it at Porthmadog Harbour station, with older sister *Merddin Emrys* alongside carrying an 1879-1979 headboard. Five days later, the new locomotive hauled a 12-coach test train to Tanygrisiau.

The new locomotive hauled its first passenger train on July 19, 1979, and was then rostered for two trips a day. It showed exactly what it could do on August 12, when following the failure of another locomotive, it hauled 12 trains up the line without any difficulty.

The new *Earl of Merioneth* was not to everyone's liking. Its angular appearance led to it being nicknamed 'The Square'. Accordingly, at its first 10-year overhaul in 1989, the opportunity was taken to attempt to soften its appearance by fitting brass dome covers and copper-capped chimneys – both of which had been fitted to *Merddin Emrys* before that locomotive's 1988 rebuild. The livery was also adjusted to include more traditional lining.

In 1992 *Earl of Merioneth* was found to have serious cracks around the boiler throatplate, because, it was said, of a design-flaw in the two 1971-built Hunslet boilers.

At the same time, the railway was building a second new double Fairlie, No. 12 *David Lloyd George*. It was decided to withdraw *Earl of Merioneth* and use its bogies and other components to complete the new locomotive.

Earl of Merioneth was then stored as a kit of parts until 1995-96, while repairs were made

ABOVE: *Earl of Merioneth* in traffic on August 24, 2009. FR

ABOVE: *Earl of Merioneth* approaches Boston Lodge with a Santa special on a snowbound December 19, 2010. CHRIS PARRY

ABOVE: The box-like design of *Earl of Merioneth* earned it the nickname of 'The Square'. FR

to the boiler. However, the same problems were also being experienced with the boiler on *Merddin Emrys*, which resulted in it being withdrawn in 1996.

So as to keep two double Fairlies running *Earl of Merioneth* reappeared in 1997 with bogies and burners from *Merddin Emrys*, and also new round smokeboxes, which further 'smoothed' its appearance.

Despite being built as an oil burner – the Ffestiniog started converting its engines to oil firing in the early 1970s in a bid to reduce lineside fires in the Snowdonia National Park – *Earl of Merioneth* was converted to coal firing in 2007, owing to the by-then significant difference in the prices of oil and coal. As a coal burner, it re-entered traffic on May 27 that year.

ABOVE: Then outshopped in black livery, *Earl of Merioneth* heads round the UK's only railway spiral at Dduallt with a train to Blaenau Ffestiniog on September 27, 2007. FR

A SECOND NEW DOUBLE FAIRLIE

The *David Lloyd George* project began as a proposal to build a new boiler for *Earl of Merioneth* – but got carried away with itself so much that a new locomotive appeared.

In 1989 the railway successfully gained grant funding for a development programme known as the INcreased CApacity or INCA project. The grant aid package included the construction of a new double Fairlie locomotive to a new design, but having a more traditional outline than *Earl of Merioneth*. The locomotive was designed to match the appearance of the 1880s Fairlies but with many improvements to performance and range, including a completely new tapered boiler design with higher degree of superheat.

The boiler is designed to operate at a higher pressure and has a greater degree of superheat than any other double Fairlie example, making *David Lloyd George* the most powerful steam locomotive ever to run in normal service on the Ffestiniog, able to haul 12 coaches efficiently and economically.

It was designed from the outset to be oil fired, and was completely new with the exception of the power bogies, which came from under *Earl Of Merioneth*, and had been withdrawn for overhaul as described above.

The engine carries its name *David Lloyd George*, after the Liberal prime minister who was brought up locally and travelled on the railway in English on one side and in Welsh as Dafydd Lloyd George on the other.

In its first decade of operation, No. 12 was so reliable that it did not miss a single season. However, its use declined in the 21st century, one factor being the fact it was still oil fired, and another being the age of the power bogies, the oldest still in use on the line. In 2012, it ran just two round trips over the line, one being a special to carry the Olympic torch on May 28.

In 2010 an appeal had been launched to build two new bogies to fit beneath No. 12. Its bogies were removed in February 2013 and fitted to *Earl of Merioneth*, and the boiler was stripped, retubed and converted from oil firing to coal.

During the winter of 2013 and early 2014, the locomotive was reassembled with both its bogies on their wheels with valve gear fitted, and new taller chimneys installed. *David Lloyd George* returned to service in May 2014, temporarily painted in grey to imitate the early state of *Taliesin* (*Livingston Thompson*) in 1956.

In 2015, No. 12 was repainted back into the familiar red and relaunched at the May Day bank holiday gala.

ABOVE: Deep in the heart of Snowdonia slate mining country, new-build double Fairlie No. 12 *David Lloyd George* climbs up the steep gradient towards the railway's summit, as it heads a train bound for Porthmadog. FR

ABOVE: On May 28, 2012, double Fairlie No. 12 *David Lloyd George* hauls a special train to carry the Olympic torch during its around-Britain relay for the London 2012 Games. FR

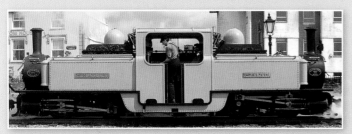

ABOVE: *David Lloyd George* in works grey livery on May 6, 2014, following a major rebuild. ANDREW THOMAS

RIGHT: Double Fairlie *David Lloyd George* rolled out for the cameras at Pen Cob on April 29, 2015, following its repaint, as sister *Earl of Merioneth* passes with a service train. NSREW THOMAS

HALF A DOUBLE IT IS

Just as the designer of the double Fairlies had produced a single version to satisfy Victorian traditionalists, so the heritage railway decided to build one to fill a historic gap in its fleet.

Built by the Vulcan Foundry in 1876, and named after a Welsh folk hero, the original 0-4-4-T *Taliesin* entered service on August 10 that year.

It was dismantled in preparation for a new boiler in 1924, but the railway board refused to buy one. Records of what happened to the single Fairlie after this are sketchy, but the maintenance records log indicates that what was left of it was scrapped in 1937.

The only parts of this locomotive known to have survived are the reversing lever and the eccentrics. However, a historic set of Fairlie wheels survives and might be from the original *Taliesin*.

A replica was built by the Taliesin 2000 project at Boston Lodge between 1996-99, the new Taliesin first steaming on April 11 that year. It was the fifth locomotive built by the railway and the third in the heritage era.

Funds for the replica were raised by an appeal whereby 250 people gave £10 or more a month for 12 years.

I say replica, but is it just as original as *Flying Scotsman*, which has but a handful of components remaining from the original locomotive that emerged from Doncaster in 1923, but incorporates the reversing lever from the original locomotive. Does that make it new-build or a 'heavy general repair', I wonder?

The toolbox on the rear bufferbeam is a replica built from the original found in the stores.

The new *Taliesin* locomotive can run as either a coal or an oil burner, the conversion between one or the other taking a day. A popular engine with crews, it is currently running on coal.

In 2012, following adjustments to the valve timing, the boiler pressure was raised to 200psi and its haulage capacity on the Ffestiniog raised to seven coaches.

ABOVE: *Taliesin* at Porthmadog on January 19, 2011. ANDREW THOMAS

ABOVE: The original single Fairlie *Taliesin* in 1887. FR

LEFT: *Taliesin* crosses Britannia Bridge on January 20, 2011, with a train for Hafod y Llyn. ANDREW THOMAS

ABOVE: *Taliesin* runs round at Minffordd on October 15, 2015. ANDREW THOMAS

ABOVE: *Taliesin* crosses the Cob with an eastbound service on October 9, 2015. CHRIS PARRY

SAIL AWAY!

Finally, there needs to be mention of another replica of an original Ffestiniog Railway form of traction – a sail-powered boat on rail wheels.

James Spooner, together with his sons James Swinton and Charles Easton and other members of their family, constructed and managed the Ffestiniog Railway for more than 50 years.

The family had the sailboat built partly as an inspection vehicle and partly as a private vehicle almost certainly before the arrival of steam locomotives in 1863.

It is recorded as being demonstrated in 1876, achieving a speed of 27mph and able to stop from this within 30 yards. Its demise came when Charles Easton Spooner disobeyed the rules for train staff working and crashed into an Up train in February 1886.

Ffestiniog Railway Heritage Group chairman, Michael Seymour, came up with an idea of building a working replica, and left money in his will for such a project. He died in 1999, and the late David Newham spent many hours researching the details of the boat, having only an engraving and written descriptions to work with.

His friend Stuart Baker produced a drawing as the basis of a project plan.

A contract for construction of the body and mast was awarded to local boatbuilder Bill Piper, and the body was delivered in time for the FR50 weekend in September 2004, with the mast and yard following afterwards.

The metal underframe, including specially cast wheels, bigger than any others on the railway, were then manufactured, and the new Spooner's Boat, assembled at Boston Lodge was ready in time for the October 2005 Victorian-themed vintage weekend.

On July 18, 2007, the boat ran under sail across the Cob using an engineer's possession, and on the way back it achieved a speed of 15.4mph. ●

ABOVE: The boat sails into Porthmadog Harbour station on October 15, 2005 during the annual Victorian weekend. CHRIS PARRY

LEFT: The replica of Spooner's Boat. FR

Chapter 3

Going back to Sainthood

The Great Western Society has, for nearly a third of a century, harboured a dream to build a new example of Churchward's legendary Saint class – but has done it by retro-converting an example of its Collett successor type.

It is now 61 years since No. 2920 *Saint David*, the last GWR 29XX Saint, was withdrawn – at the time many people felt it was a travesty that it was not preserved since it was the last example of Locomotive Superintendent George Jackson Churchward's (at the time) revolutionary two-cylinder 4-6-0; a design that went on to influence all two-cylinder 4-6-0 designs in the UK right up to the end of steam.

Indeed, the Saints are now acknowledged to have had a profound influence on almost every aspect of subsequent steam locomotive

development, and their absence from today's heritage steam fleet is a gaping hole – one that is now being filled.

Introduced in Edwardian times by Churchward, a total of 77 Saints were built, but were withdrawn between 1931 and 1953.

Churchward is widely regarded as the finest and arguably the most influential of all British locomotive engineers.

An enormous step forward came with the production of the company's first 4-6-0s, after Churchward imported French-built De Glehn compound No, 102 *La France* in 1903 to carry out comparison trials.

It had two high-pressure cylinders between the frames, with pistons linked to the front driving wheels, and two lower pressure cylinders visible on the outside of the frames and wheels, acting on the second set of wheels making a total of four cylinders. Churchward, who believed that simple, as opposed to compound, expansion as embraced by the LNWR and others could still win the day, worked out that the smoother riding of the four-cylinder engine gave massive potential for more power.

Swindon built a trio of prototypes during 1902-03, the first numbered 100, which

ABOVE: George Jackson Churchward, who developed the Saint class 4-6-0s and is considered by many to be Britain's finest steam locomotive engineer.

ABOVE: GWR Saint 4-6-0 No. 2902 *Lady of the Lake* heads through Acton with a Birmingham express as depicted on an Edwardian hand-coloured postcard. GWS

looked radically different to anything that had gone before on the GWR. It became the blueprint for the Saint class of 4-6-0 medium-size express passenger engines, and became No. 2900 *William Dean*, honouring Churchward's mentor.

A second Saint prototype, No. 171, designed to compete with the De Glehn compound, was built as a 4-6-0 with two-cylinder simple steam expansion, but briefly converted to a 4-4-2. Churchward ordered another 19, with 13 initially running as 4-4-2s, the rest as 4-6-0s from the start.

However, by the early Twenties, a great potential existed for a large mixed-traffic locomotive that could work any type of train from an express passenger to a slow goods.

Churchward's successor, Charles Benjamin Collett, was no inventor in the traditional sense of the word. He was instead the GWR's greatest innovator, a man who reassessed the world-beating designs that he had inherited from his predecessor, and evolved them to their next logical stages.

Ordered to produce an all-round locomotive to replace Churchward's 43XX 2-6-0s, in 1924, he decided to rebuild a Saint, No. 2925 ▶

BELOW: Great Western Saint 4-6-0 No. 2902 *Lady of the Lake*, pictured in 1928. NATIONAL RAILWAY MUSEUM

ABOVE: Saint No. 2904 *Lady Godiva* heads through Kensal Green at speed. GWS

Saint Martin, as an experimental locomotive, with smaller 6ft diameter driving wheels and a more enclosed cab.

This rebuild, numbered 4900, formed the prototype of the hugely successful Hall class locomotives, brilliant do-anything versatile mixed-traffic 4-6-0s, of which a total of 259 were built from 1928, and constituted the most numerous GWR tender locomotive. Collett's successor, Fredrick Hawksworth, improved the design and built 71 Modified Halls from 1944-50.

In 1936, Collett developed the Hall design to produce a smaller version, the Grange or 6880 class, of which 80 were built. His 30-strong 7800 Manor class was a lighter version of the Hall; the first appearing in 1930.

AN EARLY LOSS

At the time when the last Saint was withdrawn, the railway preservation movement was in its infancy and The Titfield Thunderbolt, a 1953 Ealing comedy that told the Talyllyn Railway-inspired story of villagers saving their local branch line from closure had only just been released.

Steam locomotives were then commonplace: there were not mass calls for examples to be preserved, and even if there were, there would be few with the money to do so at a time when Britain was pulling out of postwar austerity.

The first section of British Railways' standard gauge line to be saved by preservationists was the Horsted Keynes to Sheffield Park section of the East Grinstead to Lewes line. It reopened as

the Bluebell Railway in 1960, and in the 55 years that followed, grew to become a world leader in railway preservation. Its early success also provided a template for others across Britain.

The Great Western Society originated with the publication of a list of locomotives elected for the new National Collection, in the April 1961 edition of Railway Modeller magazine. Out of 71 locomotives chosen, there were only 10 from the GWR/WR – and there was no Collett 14XX, no Hall and no Manor.

The list was the catalyst that prompted four schoolboys to launch a fund to preserve a 14XX locomotive. Angus Davis said to his friends Graham Perry, Jon Barlow and Mike Peart that if a 14XX was not to be preserved officially, they must try to buy one themselves.

As he was the only one with a typewriter, Jon Barlow wrote to The Railway Magazine to publicise their 14XX appeal fund and their letter was published in the August 1961 edition.

The cost of launching the society was a three-penny stamp and this initial tiny investment resulted in an organisation that 50 years later is responsible for assets in excess of £12 million, including the biggest collection of GWR/WR locomotives and stock anywhere.

An inaugural meeting was held at Southall Community Centre in May 1962, and the formation of the Great Western Society was the result the following year.

As pressure mounted during the Beeching years for more steam locomotives to be purchased before they disappeared, the society was offered the use of the redundant engine shed at Didcot, and moved in during 1967. Didcot Railway Centre has since gone from strength to strength.

Having acquired a selection of working locomotives, the society turned to types at Barry scrapyard, which would improve the collection, in particular 1917-built GWR 2-6-0 No. 5322 and a four-cylinder 4-6-0, in the form of No. 5051 *Earl Bathurst*.

WE NEED A SAINT TOO!

People's minds kept going back to 1953 and the uncomfortable fact that Saint No. 2920 should not have been lost.

It was this that inspired Peter Lemar, Peter Rich and Peter Chatman to conceive the ground breaking idea that it should be possible to take a two-cylinder Hall 4-6-0 and convert it back to two-cylinder Saint 4-6-0. Such a move would reverse Collett's conversion of No. 2925 *Saint Martin* to become the pioneer Hall.

For this purpose, No. 4942 *Maindy Hall* was acquired in 1974 with the express intention of back-converting it to a Saint.

ABOVE: In very much ex-Barry scrapyard condition, before dismantling, GWR 4-6-0 No. 4942 *Maindy Hall* in storage at Didcot Railway Centre, ironically its final shed in its Western Region days. BARRY LEWIS*

Built at Swindon in July 1929, *Maindy Hall* was shedded at Newton Abbot, Goodwick (Fishguard), Swansea (Landore), Llanelli, Carmarthen, Weymouth, Swindon, Westbury, Bristol (St Philip's Marsh and Bath Road), Exeter, Banbury, Cardiff East Dock… and finally Didcot, from where it was withdrawn in December 1963, arriving at Barry the following June.

Maindy Hall was the 51st out of 213 locomotives bought from Barry for preservation purposes. The preservation movement was still in its infancy, and nobody had yet attempted to convert one standard gauge locomotive into another for heritage purposes. The society certainly did not have the resources at the time.

However, the three Peters said that it did not matter if the rebuild did not take place for many years, having the basis for the rebuild was the important thing. Looking back now, it is possible to conclude that this was visionary stuff, but the society had to endure a considerable amount of criticism.

When *Maindy Hall* was bought, Barry scrapyard was still fairly full. It has now been empty for more than 25 years. To scrap a steam engine today would be sacrilege.

There were critics who said that a Hall would be dismembered and lost. Backers of the scheme said that you would lose one locomotive to get another, and there were 11 GWR Halls in preservation, plus seven of the later Modified Halls, yet no Saint. How much would such abundance of Halls, several of them still to be restored, contribute to the preservation of GWR history, when there was not a single example of a Saint?

The original plan to rebuild No. 4942 to the Saint/Court style with Holcroft curves was launched in 1982. However, although there was a good initial response it was decided that it was insufficient to continue and the plan was quietly shelved.

Another decade or more was to pass before the Saint Project was to see the light of day again, but this time there had been a change of mind.

The project was relaunched in 1995; this time it was decided that the new Saint should be the straight frame version with the square drop ends from the Lady 290X design.

Going for the straight frames also gave the society the

ABOVE: Churchward Atlantic No. 187 *Bride of Lammermoor* pictured in 1909. The new Saint will be convertible to a Churchward 4-4-2. GWS

opportunity to run the locomotive as a Churchward Atlantic, just like many of the early class members as stated previously. This time the proposal was well received and work has been progressing steadily ever since.

Following a national competition to find a suitable name, the late Peter Bird's suggestion of *Lady of Legend* was chosen.

The name was considered especially appropriate, as the original 'Lady' series was the first of the straight-framers. The number 2999 was the next available number in the straight-frame series, coming after No. 2998 *Ernest Cunard*. Some people argued that the new locomotive should be numbered 2956 as this was the lowest Saint number never to have been used, but that would have placed it in the curved-frame series.

ABOVE: GWR 4-6-0 No. 4942 *Maindy Hall* at Bristol Temple Meads in June 1961. This locomotive is still with us, but will never be seen in this form again, having undergone a retro-conversion to its predecessor type, Churchward's Saint. A DRAKE/COLOUR-RAIL brw1602

SECOND BITE AT THE CHERRY

ABOVE: GWR 4-6-0 No. 2999 *Lady of Legend*, formerly No. 4942 *Maindy Hall*, outside Didcot Railway Centre on July 13, 2013. GWS

In the years between the two project proposals, a considerable amount of background work had been undertaken to prove the ability to deliver.

Among other landmarks in the wider preservation movement, new cylinders had been cast for unique BR 8P Pacific No. 71000 *Duke of Gloucester* while closer to home, the society had manufactured a new driving wheel set for its GWR 4-6-0 No. 6023 *King Edward II*, both locomotives having been rescued from Barry. Wheels and cylinders were major components, which would be needed for the Saint project to succeed.

Initial work was concentrated on the new wheelsets and new cylinder block. The society had in its possession a 6ft 8½in wheel pattern that had been retrieved from Swindon Works around 1972 but unfortunately this was not suitable for use with modern casting methods and so a new pattern had to be made.

The centre boss for the central driving wheels is one inch greater in diameter than those for the other four wheels and so the pattern was initially made to the larger diameter for the two centre driving wheels to be cast first and then taken back and altered to allow the other four to be cast.

The bogie wheels are 3ft 2in; a GW standard, and the society knew that there were eight ex-Castle bogie wheels under the

telescope at Jodrell Bank. The society hoped that it would be able to reuse them and thus save the time and cost of casting new ones.

To fit the circular railway on which the telescope sat, the axles had been cut but despite the society's best efforts these were not considered acceptable and a new pattern had to be made and four wheels cast.

Completing the new wheelsets took several years; however, this meant that the project team could use the Churchward rather than the Collett design used on the Castles in the same way it had done for the driving wheels.

With regard to the cylinder block, the team was fortunate to receive a major bequest that allowed it to make the pattern and cast and machine the new block; this was completed around the same time as the new wheelsets.

As a result work to prepare the donor locomotive for the rebuild did not start until the end of the Nineties.

The biggest job was removing the extension frame and cylinder block from the main frame. This is still at Didcot and available for anyone who has a 49XX Class 4-6-0 in need of a replacement cylinder block. It is believed that No. 4942 may well have received a new block towards the end of its life.

Once the frames had been dismantled, they were shipped to Riley & Son at Bury, which

carried out the rebuild. New extension frame forgings were supplied by Heskeths and fitted while work was carried out on the main frames to allow for the 4¼in difference in the height between the Halls and the Saints. To give extra rigidity to the frames above the axleboxes and hornguides, the extra height in the Hall frame has been retained, hidden by the splashers.

The opportunity was also taken at the same time to construct and fit the trailing wheel subframes so that No. 2999 can run as an Atlantic and these are currently stored behind the locomotive works at Didcot.

Alterations to the bogie centre pin and bogie itself were also made to compensate for the extra height of the driving wheels. Work started on the frame alterations before the wheelsets were completed and once the latter had been done these were delivered to Bury so that No. 2999 could become a rolling chassis.

The intention was for No. 2999 to return to Didcot as a rolling chassis and be towed in over Network Rail metals. Before this was allowed it was necessary to ship the boiler to Bury so that it could be placed in the frames. The society had been told that it would not be allowed to move over part of the national network without the boiler in place.

The chassis finally returned at the end of 2006 and restoration work got under way at Didcot and has continued ever since.

TWO NEW LOCOMOTIVES IN ONE!

When complete, No. 2999 will carry the tall safety bonnet with top feed and be painted in 1913 GWR livery complete with the brass beading in which both the Stars and Saints ran before it was removed during the First World War.

The majority of the work below the running plate on No. 2999 is now complete. Restoration of the boiler is also proceeding well. When the smokebox is installed, it will have flush rivets in the original style. Over the years, project members have gathered together all the fittings needed.

Work will proceed to pipe up GWR 28XX 2-8-0 No. 2861's boiler, which is currently sitting in No. 2999's frames while the remaining work on No. 2999's boiler is completed. It is a major boost to completing No. 2999 that the team has been able to sit No. 2861's No. 1 boiler in the frames allowing work to progress on completing No. 2999's boiler and allow it to steam out of the frames, before a quick substitution.

At the time of writing, work is also progressing on restoring and rebuilding the 3000-gallon tender that will run with No. 2999. Most of the items below the running plate have been restored although not all have yet been fitted and a new tank is almost complete. The running gear has still to be fitted.

The boiler overhaul is also at an advanced stage and has been tubed; the project team also has the superheater elements in its possession but members will not do the final test on the boiler until it has the pipework fitted up. The cladding and insulating material have still to be ordered. The crinolines to take the cladding have been made and fitted.

The rebuild/restoration of No. 2999 is now nearing the final stages, with 2017 given by society officials as the latest-hoped for date for it to run.

Regarding the Atlantic option, the plan is to run No. 2999 as a 4-6-0 for a suitable length of time and then convert it into a 4-4-2; for this to happen it will be necessary to lift the boiler out of the frames so fundraising will continue after No. 2999 takes to the rails to acquire the remaining items required to transform it from one type to another.

The team already has a set of wheels for the trailing axle as the diameter is the same as those under Great Western tenders, although it may be necessary to fit new tyres. It will also have to manufacture two coupling rods, springs and axleboxes.

When the locomotive runs as an Atlantic, it will carry the number 191 and the name *Churchward*.

So, this has turned out to be a case of losing one old locomotive, of a type more than well represented in the heritage sector, and gaining two new ones, which are not.

Another, longer-term society aim is to restore and assemble a complete rake of Edwardian coaches to run behind the Saint, with several candidates for restoration and inclusion identified, although it remains very unlikely that such a train would be permitted to run on today's national network.

ABOVE: The rear of *Lady of Legend* as seen on July 13, 2013. GWS

ABOVE: The superheater elements for the new Saint at Didcot on October 17, 2015. ADRIAN KNOWLES

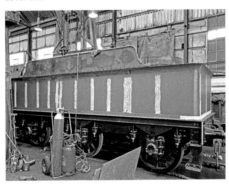

ABOVE: The tender being prepared for *Lady of Legend*, as seen on October 17, 2015. ADRIAN KNOWLES

ABOVE: One of the driving wheels cast for No. 2999 *Lady of Legend*. PETER CHATMAN

For more details of how you can help make the new Saint a reality, contact Richard Croucher at chairman@didcotrailwaycentre.org.uk or visit www.didcotrailwaycentre.org.uk

Donations may be sent to Richard Croucher, Appeal Co-ordinator (Saint Project), Great Western Society Limited, Didcot Railway Centre, Didcot, Oxfordshire, OX11 7NJ. ●

ABOVE: The first and last of the GWR two-cylinder 4-6-0s together: GWR 4-6-0 No. 2999 *Lady of Legend* (right) stands next to the frames of another Great Western Society new-build project, Hawksworth County 4-6-0 No. 1014 *County of Glamorgan*, at Didcot Railway Centre on October 15, 2015. FRANK DUMBLETON/GWR.

Chapter 4

Home on the **Grange!**

One of the classic GWR classes to slip through the preservation net at the end of British Railways steam as the Grange, but a new one is now rapidly taking shape at Llangollen.

Some years ago, when cutting up an old sofa at my parents' house I came across an Ian Allan locospotters' book from 1960, which had all the engines I had seen underlined in blue.

This indicated to me that in my infant years, when taken by my elder brother Stewart trainspotting to Widney Manor station on the Solihull to Leamington line – that I had seen most of the members of the soon-to-be extinct GWR 6800 or Grange class.

Here was a class that did not have the good fortune of ending up at Dai Woodham's scrapyard, and while there were multiple examples of other GWR types there for the fledgling railway preservation movement, the Granges ended up elsewhere, in other words, dismembered within days.

The Llangollen Railway-based 6880 Society (registered charity, No. 1100537) was formed in 1998 with the sole intention of recreating a Grange in the form of No. 6880 *Betton Grange*, which, when completed will become the 81st example of the class.

The origins of the class date back to 1901 when George Jackson Churchward drew up his scheme for six types of engine that would fulfill the needs of the GWR, all using a series of standard or similar components. The 2800s, 5500s, 4200s and the Collett version of the large prairies were all built combining the use of a No. 1 Boiler and 5ft 8in driving wheels. Granges were not built at this time owing to weight limits, light traffic and the 4300 moguls appearing to fill the gap.

When Collett replaced Churchward, increased traffic saw the resurrection of the plans for a 4-6-0 mixed-traffic locomotive.

The first batch of 20 Granges was built in 1936 with the first, No. 6800 *Arlington Grange*, completed in August that year at a cost of £4965. In 1937 a further 40 were turned out, finishing with another 20 in 1939, the last, No. 6879 *Overton Grange*, completed in May 1939 at a cost of £4939. If not for the outbreak of war, more Granges would have been built as the next batch of 20 names had been allocated with a further 150 set aside… including what would have been the next in line, *Betton Grange*.

Nearly half of the names were taken from the granges that were destroyed by King Henry VIII following the Dissolution of the Monasteries in the 1530s.

The Granges were fitted with the versatile Swindon No. 1 Boiler designated AH, with a maximum pressure of 225lbs and a two-row superheater, a proven unit as fitted to the Saints, Stars, Halls and 2800s.

BELOW: GWR 4-6-0 No. 6832 *Brockton Grange* is seen piloting No. 7813 *Freshford Manor* crossing the (now) Grade II listed 151ft high St Pinnock Viaduct at Trago Mills in Cornwall, on a Newquay to Paddington train on September 13, 1958. TB OWEN/6880 SOCIETY

The wheels were of 5ft 8in diameter, again from 4300s with modifications to the crankpins and centre balance weights in order to work with the longer connecting rods used by the new locomotives. The bogie was a standard design as fitted to the Halls with 3ft diameter wheels. Braking was achieved by a four-cone ejector as fitted to the larger 4-6-0s, running down the driver's side of the boiler.

The total engine weight with tender was 114 tons, of which 74 tons was the engine. This gave the Granges a Red route availability, which barred them from the Cambrian lines and other cross-country routes previously operated by the 4300 class, hence the introduction of the very similar but lighter class of 7800s, otherwise known as the Manors. The quoted tractive effort at 85% was 28,875lb, giving them a D power classification, higher than a Hall, Manor or LMS 'Black Five'. They were often used for the haulage of perishable goods, such as fruit and broccoli, and for excursion trains.

In effect, a Grange was a GWR Hall with smaller wheels, and locomen said it had the edge when it came to power. Indeed they became one of the most popular engines on the GWR/WR network among footplate crews.

One visual difference between the two was that the Hall frame was straight; all the way from the smokebox to the front portion of the cab, but the Grange frame dipped behind the cylinders before carrying on to the cab.

The first Grange to be withdrawn was No. 6801 *Aylburton Grange*. Withdrawn in

ABOVE: GWR 4-6-0 No. 6841 *Marlas Grange* at Twyford on December 5, 1959. TB OWEN/6880 SOCIETY

1960 and broken up at Swindon in December of that year, the remainder of the Granges disappeared one by one until the end of WR steam in December 1965. Four survived until the end, these being Nos. 6847 *Tidmarsh Grange*, 6848 *Toddington Grange*, 6849 *Walton Grange* and 6872 *Crawley Grange*.

Nos. 6800/8/9/17/24/5/6 had all exceeded over a million miles with No. 6826 *Nannerth Grange* reaching a total of 1,072,575 miles. They were all in a pretty poor state at the end, missing name and number plates; unkempt, uncleaned, but not quite unloved. The last of the Grange class was withdrawn and scrapped in 1965.

GRANGE LIFE BEGINS AGAIN

The 6880 Betton Grange project started out just like many other 'new build' schemes; a group of likeminded people getting together with the aspiration of replicating some long-lost class of locomotive. Yet this scheme was different in many aspects.

Firstly, the Betton Grange Society was formed by a group of people who had just completed the full restoration of a former Barry wreck.

The rusting remains of GWR large prairie No. 5199 had passed 'around the houses' before a group of people got stuck in and turned it into a fully operational locomotive. This locomotive is now one of the star performers of the Llangollen Railway locomotive fleet.

Secondly, because of Churchward's GWR standardisation policy, the society had almost all of the components to build the locomotive, the main exception being the cylinders, which needed to be cast from scratch.

In 2003, the Llangollen Railway formally agreed to grant permission to the society to use the Denbighshire line as an official base and registered office. That Christmas saw the funding appeal launched, with an estimated £500,000 needed to build No. 6880.

The Vale of Glamorgan Council's decision to release its Barry 10 pool of scrap locomotives, rescued after Dai Woodham's retirement, had resounding consequences for this and other projects.

Betton Grange became an early beneficiary of the Barry 10 when the project seized the opportunity to grab the boiler from Western Region Modified Hall No. 7927 *Willington Hall*, the main frames and remaining components going to Didcot to form the basis of the scheme to build a new Hawksworth County class 4-6-0.

Outshopped from Swindon in October 1950, No. 7927 was one of the final batch of Halls to be built there. First allocated to Reading, it was also shedded at Old Oak Common, Cardiff Canton, Cardiff East Dock, Newport (Ebbw Junction) and Oxford, from where it was withdrawn in December 1965, arriving at Woodham Bros scrapyard two months later.

The society used the news of the boiler release in the railway press for maximum impact when it launched its appeal for funds.

On June 12-13, 2004, GWR large prairie No. 5199 made a triumphant return to Barry, to run on the Vale of Glamorgan

Railway during the Barry Vintage Transport Festival. No. 5199 became the first ex-Barry locomotive ever to return, in steam, to the site of Woodham Bros scrapyard.

Furthermore. No. 5199 undertook a shunting movement to bring *Willington Hall* to the front of the English, Welsh & Scottish Railway shed at Barry in which the 10 locomotives were stored. An agreement to acquire the boiler was signed on the 13th.

That year, the project received a further boost with the donation of more original parts.

ABOVE: GWR large prairie No. 5199, the modern-day history of which is inextricably linked with that of No. 6880 *Betton Grange*. It is seen at Llangollen during the Steam, Steel & Stars II gala on April 21, 2012. QUENTIN MCGUINNESS

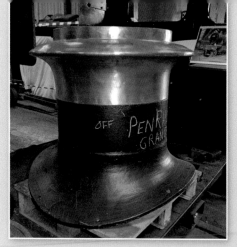

Enthusiast, Alan Marshall, owner of an original Grange nameplate, donated a pair of GWR whistles, worth in the region of £300, complete with elbows. Later, the chimney from No. 6868 *Penrhos Grange* was donated, although a new copper cap had to be made.

However, one of the first major priorities was to organise the raising of funds, and the society decided to recruit members willing to commit to £10 per month.

To maximise publicity, it was agreed to build the locomotive's cab first and take this around various shows to act as the backdrop to the society's fundraising stand. The cab was completed just in time for the Crewe Works open weekend in 2005.

The need for funds was pressing and although new Express Membership was now available at £68.80 per month, and the number of £10 per month memberships had grown significantly, a more substantial sum of money was needed to give a much-needed cash injection. And so the concept of the 'super gala' was born.

LEFT: The chimney from GWR 4-6-0 No. 6868 *Penrhos Grange* will become part of *Betton Grange*. QUENTIN MCGUINNESS

STEEL, STEAM & STARS

New-build projects big and small never come cheap, even if you are recycling secondhand parts. The *Betton Grange* team knew that large amounts of money had to be raised if the project was to maintain pace and credibility. The informed public is quick to spot a stalled project, and may be reticent about giving money if they see it going into what they perceive to be a long dark tunnel with no end in sight.

Looking at a fundraising event capable of raising large amounts of money, the team came up with the idea of a 'new' type of steam gala.

The traditional format for gala events on

heritage lines is to hire one or two affordable guest locomotives, hopefully star names, to headline the bill at which every available member of the home fleet will take part in an intensive timetable.

The *Betton Grange* team effectively dispensed with the word 'affordable' here, engaged a 'speculate to accumulate' principle

and booked a whole raft of locomotives, the idea being that the bigger the steam extravaganza was, the more enthusiasts would turn up and ride.

Branded Steel, Steam & Stars, the group's 'super gala concept' worked from day one.

Steel, Steam & Stars II in 2007 was a three-day event over April 20-22.

ABOVE: The newly cut frames for *Betton Grange* displayed at the Steel, Steam & Stars II gala in 2007. ROBIN JONES

ABOVE: New-build helping new-build: one of the star guests at the Steam, Steel & Stars III gala was A1 Peppercorn Pacific No. 60163 *Tornado*, pictured at Llangollen station on April 22, 2012. QUENTIN MCGUINNESS

ABOVE: The cab of *Betton Grange* on the frames in the Llangollen workshops. NEIL TILEY

LEFT: This LNWR duo, 0-6-2 Coal Tank No. 58926 and G2 'Super D' No. 49395 starred in the Steel, Steam & Stars III gala and are pictured waiting to depart from Llangollen on April 22, 2012. QUENTIN MCGUINNESS

With an imaginative timetable and star-studded line-up of locomotives, the SSS event was a resounding success and achieved its objective of raising a substantial sum of money to complete the main frames.

Steel, Steam & Stars II in 2009 expanded to cover nine days (April 18-26), with a stellar line-up of locomotives, including both the surviving operational GWR double framers, No. 3440 *City of Truro* from the National Railway Museum, and 'Dukedog' No. 9017 *Earl of Berkeley* from the Bluebell Railway, along with LMS No. 6100 *Royal Scot*. Every B&B for a 20-mile radius was full to sofa beds.

Sufficient money was raised to order the steel for the extension frames, which were cut, machined, drilled and delivered by the start of April 2011.

The Steel, Steam & Stars III gala of April 21-29, 2012 aimed to raise up to £60,000 to get those cylinders cast and machined, with no less than *Tornado* and BR Standard 4-6-2 No. 70000 *Britannia* topping the bill, and in 2015, Steel, Steam & Stars IV was held over

ABOVE: The Furness Railway Trust's 1925-built GWR 0-6-2T No. 5643 in action during the Steel, Steam & Stars II gala on April 19, 2009. ROBIN JONES

two long weekends from March 6-8 and 13-15, all at the Llangollen Railway.

Each event brought a mini-boom to both the railway and its hometown, with the 2015 gala seeing trains running over the new extension to Corwen for the first time.

MISSING DRAWINGS REDISCOVERED

In 2008, a set of Grange cylinder drawings had been rediscovered at the National Railway Museum in its collection of uncatalogued drawings at York.

The 6880 Betton Grange project team had been hunting for sets of drawings for one of the key missing components of the projects for several years without success.

The museum made its Swindon Drawing collection available to the team in exchange for expertise to help setting up its £4 million Search Engine research facility.

Accordingly, a working weekend with mutually beneficial aims was duly organised.

An initial inspection revealed the enormity of the task; more than 600 boxes with an estimated 6000-plus drawings.

The *Betton Grange* project team joined forces with new-build

colleagues from the Great Western Society at Didcot looking for drawings for No. 1014 *County of Glamorgan* and No. 2999 *Lady of Legend*, and set to work on November 29.

On the second day of the search, the vital documents for *Betton Grange* appeared in a roll of drawings around Castles and Kings in excellent condition as drawing number 106875 DEC 1935.

Among the more unusual finds during the research session were drawings for a fire bucket, a display stand at the 1924 British Empire Exhibition, the Swindon test plant, a wheel for the broad gauge *Lord of the Isles*, an outline drawing for Churchward's proposed standard locomotives (in which the Grange specification was set out years before the class was built) and the boiler for unique GWR Pacific No. 111 *The Great Bear*.

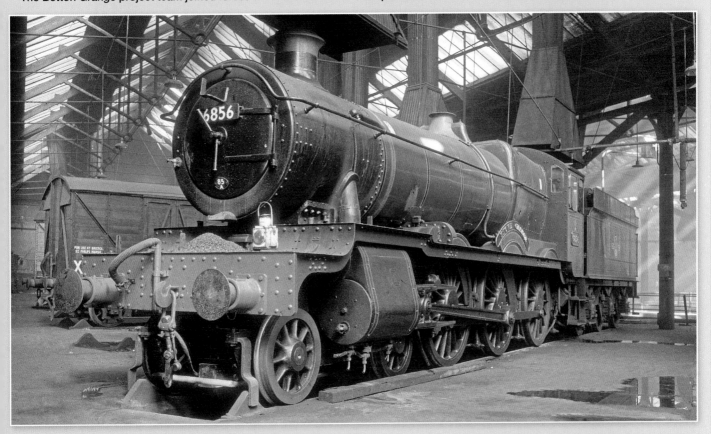

ABOVE: GWR 4-6-0 No. 6856 *Stowe Grange* at Old Oak Common, date unknown. 6880 SOCIETY

ENTER *COGAN HALL*

ABOVE: The bogie from No. 5952 *Cogan Hall* before stripping down and restoration at Williton. It is now fully overhauled and underneath No. 6880. 6880 SOCIETY

ABOVE: Unrestored GWR 4-6-0 No. 5952 *Cogan Hall* being taken from its long-term base at Llynclys near Oswestry to Llangollen on April 11, 2010. 6880 SOCIETY

Around 2009, Yorkshire fish farmer, Ken Ryder, of the Oswestry-based Cambrian Railway Trust decided that he wanted to retire and offer his collection of locomotives and rolling stock for sale. His collection included unrestored Barry wreck GWR 4-6-0 No. 5952 *Cogan Hall*, a locomotive type that had much in common with its Collett cousins, the Granges.

Built at Swindon in December 1935, *Cogan Hall* spent its first five years working from West Country sheds.

Later moving to Cardiff, Bristol Bath Road, Old Oak Common and Southall, it ended its days working from Cardiff East Dock from where it was withdrawn in June 1964.

It reached Barry scrapyard in November that year, and left in September 1981, at first being moved to Peak Rail.

Ken had invited offers of around £40,000 for the locomotive and tender plus £40,000 for 140 spare parts, some of which were new. He also sold his flagship WR 4-6-0 No 7821 *Ditcheat Manor* to the West Somerset Railway and his 'second home', the station house at Llynclys Junction, to Oswestry branch revivalists operating under the banner of Cambrian Heritage Railways.

The society's directors decided to buy *Cogan Hall*, along with a large amount of spares that Ken had been quietly amassing

ready for the day that the ex-Barry scrapyard locomotive went into the 'works' for a thorough restoration to operational condition. *Cogan Hall* moved to the back siding at Llangollen on March 1, 2010 as a ready resource of parts to use in the construction of No. 6880. The society suddenly found it had two boilers; the single biggest component of a

locomotive and the acid test for any new build project, big or small.

However, *Cogan Hall* was never intended to be a permanent donor locomotive. The society fully intends to restore No. 5952 *Cogan Hall* in its own right, once work on *Betton Grange* is completed. Parts will be borrowed, or copied as required to help speed along the construction. No. 6880 will then set about earning steaming fees to help its donor engine make its own return to steam.

Early in 2011, the bogie was removed from No. 5952 and moved to Williton on the West Somerset Railway, where locally based society members stripped it down and restored it for use under No. 6880. It is now secured to the front end of the 'Grange'.

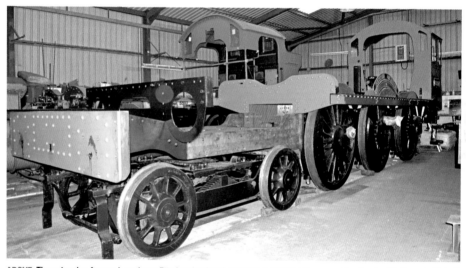

ABOVE: The extension frames have been fitted and painted, plus the locomotive is now on its wheels with the refurbished bogie underneath in the early 2014 view. 6880 SOCIETY

WHEELS FROM THE SEVERN VALLEY

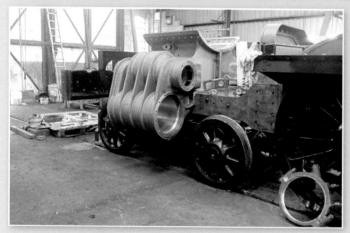

ABOVE: The newly cast cylinders test fitted in February 2015. PAUL APPLETON

Following fixing of the extension frames to the main frames the next job was to get the frames wheeled, and a set of spare wheels that had previously been used with GWR 2-6-0 No. 7325 at the Severn Valley Railway were acquired.

Back at the Llangollen Railway's workshops, the hornguides and ties, and the spring hangers, were prepared to receive the 5ft 8in driving wheels, which were removed from the Severn Valley Railway following 30 years of storage.

These were the original wheels from Collett 2-6-0 No. 7325/9303, which is on static display in the Engine House museum at Highley.

This locomotive received a replacement set that was in better condition than those it had from Barry scrapyard at the time of its original restoration on the SVR. The old ones were retained 'just in case' but had never been called upon. Agreement was reached for the loan of these with custodians the GWR (SVR) Association.

However, this set turned out to have some minor flaws that could preclude the Grange from being allowed to run on the national network, so agreement was reached to exchange them with the near-perfect set under No. 5199, as there are no aspirations to operate this on the main line.

THE CYLINDERS

The next major challenge was the cylinders, there being no suitable spares available.

The solution was to make them from scratch and so a special fund was launched. Patterns were made using new polystyrene technology, which reduced the cost considerably, and new cylinders were cast from these in 2014.

After final machining they were delivered to Llangollen in February 2015 and immediately trial fitted to the frames.

The cylinders have now been permanently fitted using optical alignment equipment. Footplating has also been completed and a set of coupling rods fitted to the wheels, visually completing the Grange bottom half, although there is still much detail work to do. This currently focuses on the brake hangers and rodding, while the piston and valve rods are being machined and connecting rod assemblies prepared.

ABOVE: Aerial view of No. 6880 with cylinders in place. The two-piece GWR-style castings also include the smokebox saddle as can clearly be seen in this view, taken in June 2015. PAUL APPLETON

ABOVE: Front end detail with overhauled buffers, draw hook and lamp brackets in place. CHRIS MOORE

THE BIG ONE

In March 2015, the society launched its '225 Boiler Club' appeal at its Steel, Steam & Stars IV gala, to raise £225,000 for the refurbishment of the boiler from *Willington Hall*. Having been manufactured in 1961, this boiler has never received a heavy general overhaul. It is therefore thought to be in very sound condition for an ex-Barry scrapyard boiler.

The boiler was retrieved from long-term storage in September 2015, and mounted on a well wagon so that work can start on cleaning and preparing it for inspection, so that interested parties can tender for its overhaul.

The work will be placed once the appeal has reached the halfway mark and this is thought will take around 18 months to complete. The fund has already passed the £60,000 mark so it is hoped to place the work early in 2016.

The target for getting No. 6880 *Betton Grange* operational is stated as being "some time in 2018", but depends solely upon the group's ability to raise the required funds.

Apart from various boiler club and society memberships each with different levels of benefits, the Betton Grange Society also has an imaginative range of other ways to support the project, including 'Adopt a Grange' and the 'On the Shelf' list of parts for sponsorship.

Full details can be found at www.6880.co.uk ●

ABOVE: Lifting the boiler of Modified Hall No. 7927 *Willington Hall* on September 17 from long-term storage. Work is now underway cleaning it before the start of its £225,000 refurbishment to main line standards for use on No. 6880 *Betton Grange*. QUENTIN MCGUINNESS

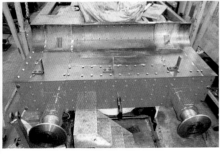

ABOVE: Front end footplating and gullwing plating in place, August 2015. CHRIS MOORE

ABOVE: The overhauled reverser and newly delivered slide bars. 6880 SOCIETY

Chapter 5

The **early** years

Massive strides have been taken in recreating the world-changing locomotives from the dawn of the steam age, which were lost largely because there were no railway enthusiasts around to preserve them!

BELOW: The replica of *Catch-Me-Who-Can* outside Bridgnorth Works on May 14, 2012, with its wooden cladding fitted. ROBIN JONES

The date: 2060. As NASA has shown scant interest in our new Tachyon 1 spacewarp vehicle, which we can show will reduce the return journey time to Mars to around 20 hours, we have decided to disassemble it, and recycle some of the best components to make its successor, Tachyon 2, which we hope will instigate interest from the private sector.

Update 2116: The company which runs daily space cruises to the moons of Titan and Enceladus has announced it is to commission working replicas of the early spacewarp vehicles Tachyon 1, 2, 3 and 4, which revolutionised space restoration and in doing so changed human society forever, but which were scrapped at the experimental stage half a century or more ago because nobody was inclined to preserve one.

Fantasy? Not so – it would be a case of history repeating itself.

It can be argued that the greatest advancement in human evolution since the wheel was the development of the self-propelled vehicle, which, in the first interest, broadly speaking, was the steam railway locomotive. Yet how many of those early locomotives were preserved for posterity?

Very, very few, is the straight answer. First, back in 1810, who would be interested in redundant machinery with an immediate scrap/recycle value? Secondly, where was the enthusiast sector if the steam railway network had yet to be invented?

Richard Trevithick, who was born on April 13, 1771, did not invent the first machine that could move itself using the power of steam. That accolade goes to Austro-Hungarian army officer Nicolas-Joseph Cugnot, who wanted to find a way of moving heavy artillery that would be more efficient than horses. What was the world's first steam tractor appeared in 1769, and a refined prototype was displayed in Paris the following year.

However, Cugnot's invention was a clumsy and overweight device that suffered from appalling steering, or lack of it, and could operate for only 20 minutes before it needed to be allowed to cool down and have fresh water added. Not an optimum choice for use in the heat of battle! His work ended when his machine overturned in a busy street.

There was no effective and comprehensive international press, let alone the internet, at this time, and it is not believed that Trevithick was aware of this machine.

Scotsman William Murdoch, experimented with steam traction while working for Boulton & Watt as its Cornish agent. In 1784, his first working model hauled a wagon around a room inside his Redruth home. Then he infamously gave an outdoor trial to a 19in-long three-wheeled steam carriage one night along the narrow lane leading to the town's church.

The machine ran off without him, at a speed of 8mph, terrifying the local rector who believed that the devil was about to attack him! Murdoch then constructed an improved model and apparently a further two carriages as well – these were seen by not only the townsfolk of Redruth but by the young Trevithick. However, Murdoch's steam carriage work ceased towards the end of the 1790s, and he is far better remembered as the man who invented gaslight, using it in his Redruth home.

While Boulton & Watt had produced giant beam engines to drain the Cornish mines using low pressure, it was high-pressure steam that formed the backbone of these early experiments with locomotives. However, technological progress was hampered until the end of the 18th century when the hated restrictive patents Boulton & Watt had jealously guarded finally ran out, and the field became an engineering free-for-all.

Watt had resisted the use of high-pressure steam, thereby halting the due process of mechanical evolution. He argued that if you needed more power, you simply built a bigger engine, as evidenced by the great 18th-century mine engine houses that are dotted across the landscape of Cornwall. By contrast, Trevithick increased steam pressure so that he could make smaller engines. He quickly saw that if a much-smaller engine could power a machine or pump, then it should also be capable of being adapted to drive itself.

This scientific principle formed the basis of a transport revolution, which within a century, would shrink the world.

In partnership with Andrew Vivian, Trevithick built a steam carriage to run on roads. It was launched on Christmas Eve 1801, and successfully ascended Camborne Hill. Several onlookers ecstatically jumped aboard.

In 1802, Trevithick obtained a patent for a purpose-designed passenger-carrying road carriage. The London Steam Carriage was built at Felton's carriage works in Leather Lane and ran from the city centre to Paddington and back via Islington, with up to eight guests on board, making it the world's first official public run of a self-powered passenger vehicle. However, as with Cugnot's contraption, steering was a major problem, and the journey ended when it crashed into house railings.

Trevithick built a second carriage for London in 1803, but at 13ft high it proved to be too big for its task and could not compete economically with a traditional horse-drawn cab.

Not to be beaten, the enterprising Cornish mining engineer tackled the problem of the roadways that could not support the weight of his carriages by switching to rail. At the time, railways and tramways were nothing new, but the sole mode of traction was the horse. They were simply little local affairs designed to move freight to transhipment points on harbours, canals and rivers.

In 1802, Trevithick began work on building a railway locomotive for use at Coalbrookdale ironworks in Shropshire, near the site of the world's first iron bridge. Surviving details of what may well have been the world's first railway engine are extremely sketchy, and it is not believed to have run in public.

In 1804, he gave a public demonstration of a railway locomotive for the first time, on the tramroad that linked Samuel Homfray's Penydarren ironworks near Merthyr Tydfil to the Glamorganshire Canal at Abercynon wharf.

The locomotive was built at Homfray's works, and proved very successful in trial runs at around 4mph. Finally, on February 21, it hauled 10 tons of iron plus 70 men along the full length of the tramway, immediately earning Trevithick the honour of being the world's first railway locomotive engineer, and Homfrey won a 500-guinea bet with the owner of the Cyfarthfa Ironworks. However, the cast-iron rails cracked under the weight of the engine in several places.

Trevithick then built a similar locomotive at Gateshead for use on the Wylam Colliery waggonway in 1805, but the mine owners decided not to buy it, probably because their railway's rails were made of wood, an even weaker material, and it was instead converted to blow the furnace as a stationary engine.

In 1808, Trevithick turned out his last steam railway locomotive, *Catch-Me-Who-Can*, which ran on a circle of track in fairground fashion for public entertainment – near the site of the future Euston station. With its carriage, it became the world's the first steam passenger train, but sadly, it also encountered problems with its track, and was withdrawn. ▶

ABOVE: A coloured version of the widely published sketch of Trevithick's first passenger train locomotive, long attributed to Thomas Rowlandson, has been said by researcher John Liffen to be a fake.

Having made no money from these experiments, Trevithick turned away from steam traction.

Christopher Blackett, who owned Wylam colliery, eventually replaced his wooden rails with iron ones – but failed to persuade Trevithick to have "one last go" at railway engines. Others, however, readily filled the gap.

William Hedley and Timothy Hackworth built a locomotive of their own around 1812 to a design believed to be similar to Trevithick's Gateshead engine.

Around this time, the need for a serious alternative to the horse arose after the loss of so many beasts in the continuing war between Britain and Napoleonic France, and colliery owners turned once more to Trevithick's Tachyon 1 concept.

George Stephenson built his first engine in 1814, and the world's first steam-powered public line, the Stockton & Darlington Railway, opened in 1825.

Trevithick sought his fortune in the mines of South America. He did not find it, and returned home in poverty, dying at the Bull Hotel in Dartford in Kent on April 22, 1833.

Needless to say, no Trevithick locomotive was preserved, despite their enormous impact.

The first locomotive to be set aside for posterity was *Invicta*, built by Robert Stephenson in Newcastle in 1829 for the Canterbury & Whitstable Railway, where it hauled the inaugural train on May 3, 1830. Retired in 1836 as the railway switched to cable haulage by stationary engines, in recent years it has been displayed in Canterbury Heritage Museum.

However, there was nothing stopping the modern heritage sector from building replicas of what went before.

CATCH-ME-WHO-CAN FOR A SECOND TIME!

A replica of the Penydarren locomotive was built in 1981 by staff at the former Welsh Industrial and Maritime Museum, Cardiff, using Trevithick's original documents.

Now displayed inside the National Waterfront Museum in Swansea, it has been abroad twice to celebrate the 150th anniversaries of both the Dutch and German state railway systems.

It also appeared in Railfest 2004, the National Railway Museum's celebration to mark the bicentenary of the original run and two centuries of railway history.

A non-working replica of Trevithick's Coalbrookdale locomotive of 1802 was built in Birmingham in 1987 by Task Undertakings Ltd, partially financed and supported by the Manpower Services Commission and the Prince's Trust, and for years was displayed at Telford Central station.

In 2012, it was moved to make way for new passenger seating areas and taken to nearby Hadley Learning Community School's engineering gallery, where it became a 'visual prompt' to discuss the local industry and how that has developed over the past two centuries.

Two years later, a fully working replica was built by apprentices at GKN Sankey in Telford in 1989, and it is now at the Ironbridge Gorge Museum.

Trevithick's last locomotive, *Catch-Me-Who-Can*, which was built at Hazeldine Foundry in Bridgnorth, Shropshire, by pioneer steam locomotive engineer John Urpeth Rastrick, has also been replicated.

For the bargain price of £50,000, a tiny fraction of the cost of building *Tornado*, a group of Bridgnorth residents formed a charity called Trevithick 200 with the aims of building a working

ABOVE: The working replica of Richard Trevithick's Penydarren locomotive of 1804 in action at the National Railway Museum during Railfest 2004. ROBIN JONES

ABOVE: Not a railway engine, but new-build all the same: in light steam at the National Railway Museum's acclaimed Railfest 2004 event at York was the Trevithick Society's replica of *Puffing Devil*, built by Trevithick and engineer Andrew Vivian, which had ascended Camborne Hill under its own power. It was the inadequacy of early 19th-centry roads to hold the weight of such machines and their inability to steer that led to Trevithick looking into railways instead. ROBIN JONES

ABOVE: Richard Trevithick, the Cornish mining engineer whose invention changed the world forever.

ABOVE: This non-working replica of the Coalbrookdale locomotive was built in Birmingham in 1987 by Task Undertakings Ltd, supported by the Manpower Services Commission and the Prince's Trust.

replica locomotive and organising events including lectures, concerts and outdoor events to celebrate the 2008 bicentenary of its historic run in London, when it became the first train in the world to collect fares from passengers.

The Trevithick 200 group also built its replica in Bridgnorth and displayed it, part completed but with a fire in its boiler, at a gala weekend at Barrow Hill Roundhouse near Chesterfield in September 2008.

Based at the Severn Valley Railway's Bridgnorth works, work on the replica has proceeded at a steady pace over subsequent years. It has since had wooden cladding, its chimney, footplating and bars fitted, so it appears just like the original.

In the summer of 2014, it was one of several early locomotives and replicas to be exhibited at the Dutch national railway museum, Het Spoorwegmuseum in Utrecht, to mark the 175th anniversary of railways in the Netherlands.

ABOVE: A fire burns inside the replica boiler at Barrow Hill. ROBIN JONES

ABOVE: Compare the Nattes' drawing with the replica's boiler as pictured in Bridgnorth works. GW (SVR) ASSOCIATION.

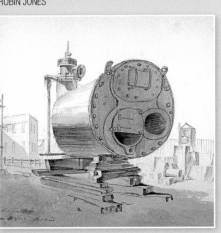

ABOVE: Revealed: the first and only surviving picture of Richard Trevithick's A, waiting for its wheels to be fitted shortly before its public demonstration on a site near present-day Euston Road in the summer of 1808, and drawn by John Claude Nattes.

ABOVE: The 1989-built 3ft gauge working replica of Trevithick's Coalbrookdale engine of 1802, built by apprentices at GKN Sankey in Telford in 1989 and based at the Ironbridge Gorge Museum. IRONBRIDGE GORGE MUSEUMS

ABOVE: The *Catch-Me-Who-Can* replica inside Barrow Hill Roundhouse in September 2008. ROBIN JONES

THE SECOND CRADLE OF EARLY STEAM

ABOVE: Beamish museum's working replicas of Locomotion No.1 (left) and *Puffing Billy* in 2008. BEAMISH MUSEUM

Beamish open-air museum in County Durham has long been recognised as both the world leader in the study of early steam railways and the building of replicas. That is apt as Durham is considered by historians to be the cradle of the steam railway, if not its birthplace.

In 1975, Beamish staff built a working replica of Locomotion No. 1, the first locomotive to run on the Stockton & Darlington Railway; the world's first public steam railway.

On September 27, 1825, the first steam-hauled public passenger train ran and carried up to 600 passengers, most of them sitting in empty coal wagons and a select few in a passenger coach called the *Experiment*.

Built in George and Robert Stephenson's works under Timothy Hackworth, the design of Locomotion No. 1 involved high-pressure steam from a centre-flue boiler driving two vertical cylinders, from which a pair of yokes transmitted the power downwards, through pairs of connecting rods, to the wheels. It was one of the first locomotives to use coupling rods rather than chains or gears to link its 0-4-0 wheel arrangement together. Incidentally, the scheduled passenger trains on the Stockton & Darlington for some years after its illustrious opening were horse-drawn affairs.

With later advances in design, Locomotion No. 1 quickly became obsolete. Withdrawn from service in 1841, it was turned into a stationary engine, but in 1857, its historic importance was acknowledged by its preservation. It is now on display at the Darlington's Head of Steam railway museum at North Road station and is part of the National Collection.

Herein lies a major impetus for new-build projects. While historic locomotives survive, to return them to running order would be all but unthinkable. The sheer amount of original material that would need to be discarded and replaced – don't even mention the need for upgrading the design to modern safety methods – would severely damage their value as artefacts. So, if you want to see them run again, build a replica!

The Beamish replica, first steamed in public 150 years after the original was unveiled, regularly runs on the museum's standard gauge Pockerley Waggonway.

THE NEW TRUNK ROUTE

In 2002, one of the most remarkable and distinctive of all new-build early locomotives was unveiled by Beamish museum.

The colossal *Steam Elephant* – as opposed to an iron horse – was an early locomotive that the world had all but completely forgotten.

All that had survived as evidence of the existence of this oversize and unwieldy beast of 1815 – very much a local and unique design by John Buddle and William Chapman for Tyneside's Wallsend Colliery – was a contemporary painting and a handful of basic sketches.

It was when a rediscovered watercolour sketch was exhibited in 1965 that it came to the attention of historians.

Its display prompted an elderly lady who had a detailed oil painting to give it to a local school, and from there it was acquired by Beamish in 1995.

A remark made by the writer Stephen Oliver in 1834 also resurfaced after nearly one and a half centuries. He had written: "The great coalfield of Newcastle appears likely to be exhausted within 200 years. Shares in railway companies will then be at an awful discount and steam elephants will inevitably perish for want of food!"

It seemed that there was far less evidence that the *Steam Elephant* existed than for arguing a case for the reality of the Arthurian legends.

Yet from a mere handful of such slight evidence, combined with exhaustive technical research, Beamish staff produced a new set of engineering drawings and set to work on replicating this mammoth from the dawn of steam.

Much of the building of the locomotive was undertaken in the north of England, with the final construction and boiler testing taking place at modern-day locomotive build Alan Keef Ltd's workshops in Ross-on-Wye.

The *Steam Elephant* now also runs on the museum's Pockerley Waggonway. Indeed, many railways would love to take it on loan for special events, if only for its novelty value, but its enormous stovepipe chimney doesn't allow it to pass under bridges.

ABOVE: The new *Steam Elephant* being prepared for a trip down Beamish museum's Pockerley Waggonway. The replica locomotives are housed and maintained in an '1825 great shed', inspired by lost buildings from Timothy Hackworth's Shildon railway works and incorporating material from Robert Stephenson & Co's Newcastle-upon-Tyne works. BEAMISH MUSEUM

ABOVE: Raising a massive amount of finance apart, one of the first tasks for any new-build project is to obtain a set of drawings. In the case of the 1815 *Steam Elephant*, this was impossible, and so a new set had to be drawn from very scant evidence such as this contemporary oil painting. BEAMISH MUSEUM

PUFFING BILLY THE SECOND

In 2006, Beamish unveiled a working locomotive of an early locomotive, which thankfully has survived, but just like the original Locomotion No. 1, is designed to remain a static museum piece.

During 1813-14, engineer William Hedley, blacksmith Timothy Hackworth and enginewright Jonathan Forster built *Puffing Billy* for Wylam Colliery near Newcastle-upon-Tyne.

Used until 1862, when its design had clearly long since passed its sell-by date, thankfully it was preserved.

The world's oldest surviving steam locomotive, it is now a star exhibit in London's Science Museum, while its sister, *Wylam Dilly*, is safe in the National Museum of Scotland in Edinburgh.

Puffing Billy's place in history is hugely important, for the success of its design encouraged more local mine owners to look seriously at steam haulage in the face of a shortage of horses because of the Napoleonic battlefields.

The replica now rubs shoulders with those of Locomotion No. 1 and the *Steam Elephant* on the Beamish running line.

RIGHT: The modern-day *Puffing Billy* outside the Beamish '1825' engine shed.
BEAMISH MUSEUM

SAMSON BACK IN THE NORTH EAST!

Beamish museum geared up for unveiling its latest completed new-build project in the spring of 2016.

Renowned for its replicas of early steam pioneers, the museum's workshops had, at the time of writing, nearly completed a full-size copy of Stephen Lewin's 0-4-0WTG *Samson*, with a steam test earmarked for January.

Lewin's Poole Foundry, one of the more obscure British locomotive builders, supplied its second railway engine in 1874 to the London Lead Company for use on the mile-long Cornish Hush Mine tramway to the south of Weardale. It is believed that the locomotive was scrapped in 1904, and the only evidence that it existed are two contemporary engravings, one photograph and a description in the engineering press of the day – almost another *Steam Elephant* scenario.

In 2012 Beamish began building a replica, based on the scant visual evidence, although the new one will be to 2ft gauge rather than the 1ft 10in of the original.

The rolling frames are complete and have been test-run, complete with the external gear drive, which engages, through a second shaft gear, with the crankshaft pinion.

The engine (cylinder, valve gear, flywheel, crankshaft) was successfully test-run on air in 2014 and is complete and ready for fitting to the locomotive once the boiler is completed.

Work in 2015 focused on the construction of the boiler, formed of a drawn tube of 2ft diameter, a pressed front tubeplate, firebox tubeplate and furnace flue plus a flat backhead. An angle ring and tubes plus two small stays complete the assembly which was prepared at the museum for riveting at the Severn Valley Railway, a large part of the work being undertaken there by Beamish staff.

Much of the design and construction was undertaken by Beamish volunteer, David Young, who previously worked on the museum's restoration of the 1871 Coffee Pot No.1 and ex-Seaham Harbour 1877-built 0-4-0ST No.18. David can trace his ancestry back to Thomas Young who was involved in locomotive building in the earliest days

of steam engine construction, on the Hetton Railway in County Durham, and the new *Samson* bears the name 'David Thomas Young – Maker' on its valve chest cover and cast on to the firehole door surround to mark his own enormous contribution to this project and the lineage of steam engineers in the North East.

Samson will operate on the narrow gauge railway at Beamish, a continually growing industrial 'network' centred on the Edwardian colliery, and in due course will reside in a new engine shed based on that used by George Stephenson's metre gauge railway at Crich, which survives today at Chadwick Nick just outside the village of Crich. ●

ABOVE: Preparing the all-new boiler for *Samson*.
BEAMISH MUSEUM

ABOVE: The only surviving photograph of the original *Samson*. BEAMISH MUSEUM

ABOVE: The rolling chassis of the replica *Samson* is track tested behind Quarry Hunslet 0-4-0ST *Edward Sholto* at Beamish. BEAMISH MUSEUM

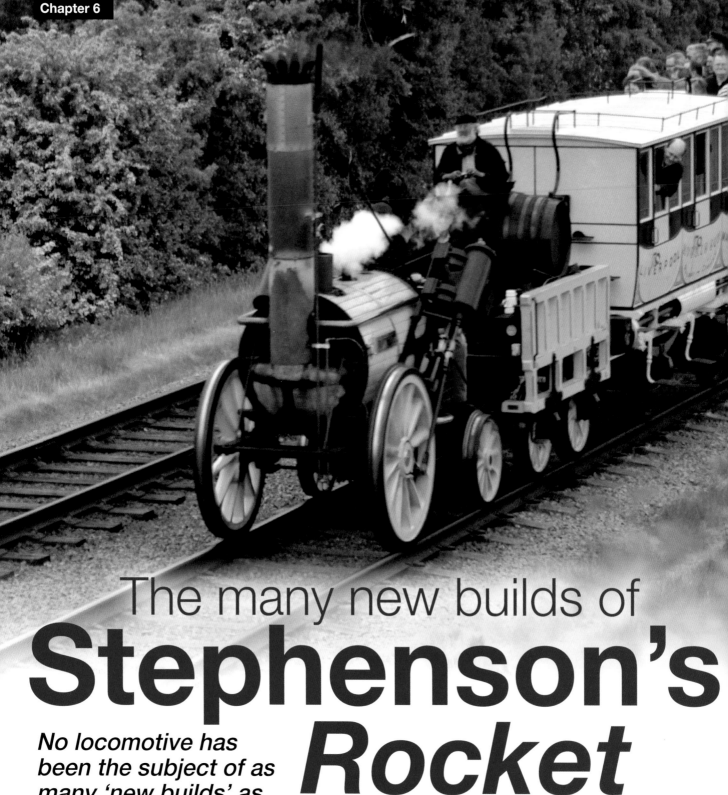

Chapter 6

The many new builds of
Stephenson's
Rocket

No locomotive has been the subject of as many 'new builds' as Stephenson's Rocket, a defining and iconic image of the early railway age. Indeed, the most recent one has been completely rebuilt, so it is unique as being 'twice a new build'!

Immediately recognisable the world over, Stephenson's *Rocket* is the defining landmark of the age of steam traction.

The locomotive transformed steam haulage by combining the technologies of blastpipes and multi-tube boilers, thereby producing a locomotive powerful enough to haul passenger trains on the world's first inter-city railway.

In doing so, it marked a watershed between the pioneer steam locomotives of the likes of Trevithick, Blenkinsop and Hackworth, and those of the Railway Age to come. Although it

was rendered obsolete within a few years, the concepts that it embodied were the blueprint for all subsequent steam locomotive design.

Stephenson's most visible decision was to use a single pair of driving wheels, with a small carrying axle behind. *Rocket* duly became the first 0-2-2 and first single driver locomotive.

However, it was built to prove a point, and to win a contest first and foremost, rather than to run in regular traffic for many years. Its main purpose was to dismiss the doubts that still lingered 25 years after Richard Trevithick

gave his first public demonstration of a steam locomotive that iron rather than equine horses were the future of travel.

The directors of the Liverpool & Manchester Railway, the building of which was arguably George Stephenson's biggest achievement, were undecided as to how their trains on the world's first inter-city line should be hauled. They divided between those who backed Stephenson and his preferred choice of steam locomotives, and those who sided with Stourbridge engineer

John Urpeth Rastrick who saw cable haulage as the best option.

Rastrick, one of the earliest steam locomotive builders, had helped Trevithick with his designs, and in partnership with James Foster, formed Foster, Rastrick & Company, which built the *Stourbridge Lion* in 1829, the first steam locomotive to run in the United States.

George received further backing from his son Robert, and when the locomotive protagonists presented a report to the directors, they decided to hold a series of open trials to find the best form of traction.

As it turned out, the Rainhill Trials of 1829 had ground-shaking consequences way beyond the Liverpool & Manchester, for it turned out to be the decisive moment in the evolution of world transport.

A £500 prize was offered to the winner of the trials, to be judged by Killingworth Colliery manager and locomotive designer, Nicholas Wood, Rastrick and Manchester cotton spinner, John Kennedy.

The engines were to be subjected to a series of tests, including 10 trips equal to a total of 35 miles, with 30 of them performed at full speed, at an average of at least 10mph. Ten were entered, but only five took part when the contest began on October 6.

The first to drop out was Thomas Shaw Brandreth's *Cycloped*, which used a horse walking on a drive belt to power it. Its participation ended when the horse burst through the floor of the engine following an accident.

Timothy Burstall's steam engine *Perseverance* was withdrawn after failing to reach 10mph, and Timothy Hackworth's *Sans Pareil* was withdrawn after developing a cracked cylinder.

The much-faster *Novelty*, built by John Ericsson and John Braithwaite, wowed the crowd when it reached a mesmerising 28mph, but was withdrawn after boiler pipe problems.

That left only one engine to complete the trials – George and Robert Stephenson's *Rocket* (it is said that the son had more to do with its construction than his father), which was the outright winner.

Combining several advances in steam locomotive technology, its features included a multi-tubular boiler; a firebox separate from the boiler and built to double thickness, with 25 copper pipes taking the heated water into the boiler. It was quickly recognised as the most advanced steam locomotive of its day.

Rocket was followed by a number of other engines of similar 0-2-2 layout with rear-mounted cylinders built for the L&MR before it opened in September 1830, culminating in the Northumbrian type of 1830, by which time the type's cylinders were horizontal.

Within a few years, *Rocket* was modified to be similar to the Northumbrian class. The cylinders were altered to a near-horizontal position, compared with the angled arrangement as new; the firebox capacity was enlarged and the shape simplified; the locomotive was also given a drum smokebox. These arrangements can be seen in the engine today. The Engineer magazine said in 1884: "It seems to us indisputable that the *Rocket* of 1829 and 1830 were totally different engines."

Stephenson followed up the 0-2-2 types with the successful 2-2-0 *Planet* of 1830, which had internal front-mounted cylinders set to the horizontal. Engines built to the *Planet* design and the subsequent 2-2-2 Patentee type of 1833 rendered the design of *Rocket* obsolete.

In 1834, *Rocket* was chosen for further (unsuccessful) modifications to test a newly developed rotary steam engine designed by Lord Dundonald.

It cylinders and driving rods were removed and two of the engines were installed directly on its driving axle with a feedwater pump in between. On October 22 that year, trials proved disappointing, with *Rocket* unable to pull a train of empty carriages.

In 1836, *Rocket* was sold for £300 and began service on the Brampton Railway, a mineral railway in Cumberland. In 1862 the Thompsons of Milton Hall, near Brampton, donated it to the Patent Office Museum in London (now the Science Museum).

Rocket is now displayed in the Science Museum in London, but in a form much modified compared with its original appearance at the Rainhill Trials.

ABOVE: The 1979-built working replica of Stephenson's *Rocket*, now in the care of the National Railway Museum, heads towards Loughborough during the Great Central Railway's 'Golden Oldies' gala on June 1, 2010. ROBIN JONES

ABOVE: The original *Rocket* in the Science Museum in London, much altered from the condition in which it won the Rainhill Trials. ROBIN JONES

ABOVE: Models of three Rainhill Trials entrants in the National Railway Museum at York. Left to right are *Rocket, Novelty* and *Sans Pareil.* ROBIN JONES

A PLETHORA OF REPLICAS

ABOVE: The 1935 cutaway replica of *Rocket* and a Liverpool & Manchester Railway facsimile coach in the Great Hall at the National Railway Museum. ROBIN JONES

A replica of *Rocket* was produced around 1904, the 75th anniversary of the Rainhill Trials, and appeared on a postcard issued by the London & North Western Railway, which by way of merger had inherited the Liverpool & Manchester.

However, little more is known about this replica, or its fate.

A working replica was built in 1923 for the Buster Keaton silent movie Our Hospitality, and also appeared in the film The Iron Mule two years later. Its fate remains obscure.

In 1929, Robert Stephenson & Hawthorns was commissioned to build two replicas for car magnate Henry Ford.

Both are now static exhibits in the USA: one is at the Henry Ford Museum in the Detroit suburb of Dearborn, while the other is at the Museum of Science and Industry in Chicago.

In 1935, an impressive cutaway static replica was built for display alongside the original in the Science Museum. It is this one that can be seen now in the Great Hall at the National Railway Museum in York, along with a pair of replica Liverpool & Manchester carriages.

Also built in 1935 was a working replica of *Der Adler*, a 2-2-2 built in 1835 by the Stephensons for the Bavarian Ludwigsbahn between Nuremberg and Fürth and scrapped in 1857. The replica is now in the Deutsche Bahn museum in Nuremberg.

In 1979, a magnificent working replica of *Rocket* was built by engineer Mike Satow and his Locomotion Enterprises for the Rocket 150 anniversary celebrations at Rainhill. First of all, however, it was displayed in Kensington Gardens, London, on the 150th anniversary of the trials.

A frequent visitor to heritage railways, it was fitted with a chimney shorter than the original in order to the clear the bridge at Rainhill: as there is now less headroom than when the line was built in the 1820s.

The 1979 *Rocket* is the one that has built new, twice. In 2009 it was completely rebuilt by Victorian locomotive restoration experts at Bill Parker's Flour Mill Colliery workshops at Bream in the Forest of Dean.

It was equipped not only with a new boiler, but also new frames, the component that gives a locomotive its identity. It returned to steam in February 2010.

In December 2015, *Rocket* appeared on the pages of the new UK passport, pictured on the Sankey Viaduct bridge in Newton-le-Willows. Known also as the Nine Arches, the bridge forms part of the Liverpool & Manchester Railway.

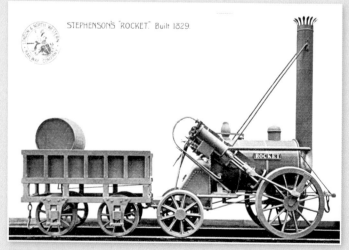

ABOVE: A LNWR postcard depicting the 1904 replica of *Rocket*. ROBIN JONES COLLECTION

ABOVE: One of the two *Rocket* replicas built for Henry Ford in 1929, steam tested outside the Robert Stephenson & Hawthorns works. DARLINGTON RAILWAY PRESERVATION SOCIETY

ABOVE: The *Rocket* replica at the Museum of Science and Industry in Chicago.

ABOVE: The replica displayed at the Henry Ford Museum in Detroit.

ABOVE: The 1935-built replica of *Der Adler*, Germany's first steam locomotive, which was also built by Stephenson & Co, inside the Deutsche Bahn museum in Nuremberg. ROBIN JONES

ABOVE: Rear view of the replica on permanent display in the National Railway Museum. ROBIN JONES

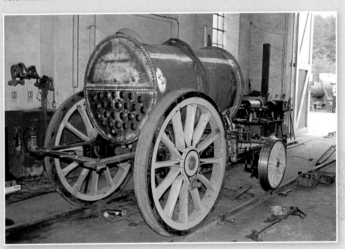

ABOVE: The 1979-built replica of *Rocket* being rebuilt at the Flour Mill workshops at Bream, in to a new version of the same locomotive! BILL PARKER

REMEMBERING RAINHILL

In 1980, the Rocket 150 event remembering the anniversary of the Rainhill Trials was held at, where else, but Rainhill.

Specially for the occasion, a working replica of one of the entrants, John Ericsson and John Braithwaite's 0-2-2 well tank *Novelty*, which has been hailed as the world's first tank engine, was built by Locomotive Enterprises at the preserved Bowes Railway in County Durham.

In 1982, it was sold to the Swedish Railway Museum in Gävle.

An earlier version of *Novelty* on static display in the Museum of Science & Industry in Manchester includes parts from the original and dates from 1929.

Also unveiled in April 1980 when it steamed for the first time was a replica of another Rainhill Trials entrant, Timothy Hackworth's *Sans Pareil*.

It had been built the year before by apprentices at British Rail Engineering Ltd's Shildon workshops and then took part in the Rocket 150.

Both the original locomotive and the replica have been on display at Locomotion: The

RIGHT: The working replica of *Novelty* at the Museum of Science and Industry in Manchester in 2005. Standing on the locomotive are Mr and Mrs Braithwaite; Mr Braithwaite being a descendant of the original locomotive builder. AH HURRELL*

National Railway Museum at Shildon since the museum opened in 2004.

In 2009, the museum's conservation workshop cosmetically restored the replica, and as a result of research by early railways expert Jim Rees, it was repainted in the livery carried by the original.

The following year, the replica visited the Nuremberg Transport Museum as part of special events to celebrate the 175th anniversary of the first steam locomotive trip in Germany.

ABOVE: This 'version' of John Ericsson and John Braithwaite's Rainhill entrant 0-2-2 *Novelty* was assembled in 1929 using many original parts, and is displayed in the Museum of Science & Industry in Manchester. MOSI

ABOVE: The working replica of *Sans Pareil* is based at the Locomotion museum in Shildon. ANTHONY COULLS

A NEW *PLANET*

In 1992, a full-size working replica of *Planet* was built by the Friends of the Museum of Science and Industry in Manchester.

Among the landmark innovations of the original was that it was the first locomotive to employ inside cylinders. Other improvements included a steam dome to prevent water reaching the cylinders, and buffers and couplings in a position setting a new standard.

Further 2-2-0s in its wake became known as Planets.

The replica is now operated by volunteers at the museum, which includes the Liverpool & Manchester's original eastern terminus, and it occasionally visits heritage lines for special events.

In 2002, the Rainhill Trials were 'replayed' at the Llangollen Railway for the BBC TV programme Timewatch – *Rocket* and its Rivals, using the working replicas.

The replica *Novelty* was brought back from Sweden just for the event, which, just like the original, was won by *Rocket*.

ABOVE: Prince Charles is shown the intricacies of the replica *Planet* during a visit to the Museum of Science and Industry in Manchester by Royal Train on February 4, 2010. ROBIN JONES

ABOVE: The twice-built 1979 replica of *Rocket* at a Tyseley Locomotive Works open day on June 25, 2001. ROBIN JONES

ABOVE: The replica *Planet* at Loughborough station on June 1, 2010. ROBIN JONES

ABOVE: The replicas of *Rocket, Sans Pareil* and *Novelty* line up for the 'Rainhill rematch' at the Llangollen Railway in 2002. PAUL APPLETON

ABOVE: The replica *Planet* in action on the Great Central Railway during a 'Golden Oldies' gala on June 1, 2010, featuring early locomotives. ROBIN JONES

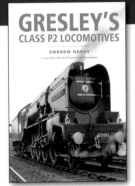

Chapter 7

The Stanier Hawksworth County

The County of Glamorgan *project is an ambitious undertaking by the Great Western Society to recreate a lost class of GWR locomotive, the Hawksworth 10XX class, no examples of which escaped the cutter's torch.*

ABOVE: The original GWR 4-6-0 No. 1014 *County of Glamorgan*, which was scrapped around the end of 1964. GWS

Thanks to Churchward's innovative policy of standard parts, in theory it is possible to dismantle GWR locomotives and build new, but different ones, from many of the components.

This principle, as we have seen, formed the basis of the new Stanier and Grange projects.

However, the Great Western Society's project to replicate one of the now-extinct 30-strong Hawksworth County 4-6-0 class goes one stage further. For in addition to reassembling secondhand GWR components, the biggest component of all, the boiler, has come from a LMS locomotive, a Stanier 8F; a move that raised a few eyebrows when it was announced but has now been accepted as an integral part of the project.

The story begins in 1941, when Frederick Hawksworth replaced Charles Collett as GWR Chief Mechanical Engineer. Three years into his tenure, he upgraded the Collett Hall to produce the Modified Hall, taking on board requirements for operating in wartime conditions.

However, Hawksworth saw that with the invasion of Nazi-occupied Europe, the end of the war was approaching, and began planning locomotives for peacetime use.

He shared the view that a further stage of development of the GWR two-cylinder 4-6-0s should involve an enlarged boiler, and so was born the 10XX County class. Ending a lineage that began with the Saints, they comprised the ultimate development of Churchward's two-cylinder 4-6-0.

Again, the design of the new Counties was influenced by deteriorating working and operating conditions during the Second World War caused primarily by a lack of skilled manpower and poor coal supplies.

The first County was outshopped by Swindon in mid-1945 as No. 1000, unnamed. Its appearance was somewhat radical because of the many new features: one-piece splashers, a double chimney and flat-sided tender and eventually a straight nameplate. They marked a return to lined green locomotives on the GWR, following wartime austerity black.

Behind the cosmetic differences from what had gone before, there were 6ft 3in diameter driving wheels, a new size for the GWR, the boiler pressure of 280lb/sq in from a new and larger boiler, together with a wider 8ft 6in cab and corresponding tender.

The biggest difference between a County and the Modified Hall was the boiler. Classified as a Standard No. 15 type OA, the new Lot 354 boiler was based on that constructed for a batch of 80 Stanier 8F 2-8-0s built at Swindon between May 1943 and July 1945 to fulfil wartime needs, but the barrel was longer than the Stanier boiler.

Swindon was one of several works totally unconnected with the LMS that built Stanier 8Fs during the Second World War. The 8F class, a goods version of the LMS Chief Mechanical Engineer's hugely successful 'Black Five' 4-6-0s, was chosen at the outbreak of war to become Britain's standard freight design, reprising the role the GCR Class 8K (later O4) had in the First World War. A total of 852 were built between 1935 and 1946, both by the LMS and other companies, which were asked to produce them for the War Department, including the GWR.

The County's GWR power classification was E, later 6MT under the BR system. They had a tractive effort of 32,580lb, greater than a Castle. From March 1946, the 10XXs were given the County class name and all were eventually named after English and Welsh counties served by the GWR.

The Counties did not find widespread favour with footplate crews, who found problems with steaming and rough riding, which caused a hammer blow on the tracks. The boiler pressure was accordingly lowered to 250lb/sq in, reducing the tractive effort to 29,050lb altering its GWR power classification to D.

Hawksworth's replacement, Sam Ell, transformed the class by installing revised double chimneys and a four-row superheater, vastly improving performance. According to OS Nock, 'their best and really brilliant work was done north of Wolverhampton where they ran very heavy trains with conspicuous success.'

THE FIRST *COUNTY OF GLAMORGAN*

No. 1014 was completed at Swindon on February 18, 1946 and named *County of Glamorgan* on March 15, 1948. Following the Ell improvements, it was fitted with a double chimney in November 1956.

Withdrawals of the class took place between September 1962 and November 1964. Withdrawn from service on April 24, 1964,

ABOVE: The locomotive before *County of Glamorgan* in numerical sequence was No. 1013 *County of Dorset*, seen at Gloucester shed on September 28, 1956. BEN BROOKSBANK*

having covered 756,762 miles, No. 1014 had the misfortune not be bought by Dai Woodham and end up at Barry scrapyard.

Instead. No. 1014 was sold to metal dealer John Cashmore Ltd of Newport, South Wales, and was scrapped between December 1964 and January 1965.

September 1964 saw the official withdrawal of the last County, and although it has been reported that No. 1011 *County of Chester* continued in traffic for a few weeks after withdrawal, it was placed in store in November 1964, and also sold to Cashmores to be cut up in March 1965.

The entire class was extinct.

A SECOND COMING

Following the success of the project to reverse engineer a Collett Hall to a Churchward Saint, Great Western Society member David Bradshaw, noted that among the last group of unrestored locomotives once stored in Barry scrapyard, there were sufficient standard 'parts' to form a basis for a Hawksworth County – with modifications and some new-build components.

Following seven years of discussion and persuasion by David with Vale of Glamorgan County Council, custodians of the Barry 10, the GW County Project was launched in December 2004, to recreate a County, at Didcot Railway Centre, utilising the frames of a Modified Hall and a Stanier 8F boiler, further demonstrating the lineage and ultimate development of the 4-6-0 two-cylinder locomotive, and again, filling a sizeable gap in locomotive history as far as the UK heritage steam fleet is concerned.

As planned, the locomotive will represent the class as they were in the mid-1950s, with a double chimney and a three-row superheater. It was also planned to build the new County to a standard whereby it would be allowed to run on the main line.

Rather than number the new locomotive 1030 and struggle to find another GWR connected county, it was decided to name No. 1014 *County of Glamorgan*, in order to reflect the links with the county council and Barry scrapyard, and to acknowledge the contribution made by the Welsh Development Agency. However, it may adopt other identities when visiting heritage lines, such as No. 1012 *County of Denbigh* while making trips on the Llangollen Railway, or No. 1026 *County of Salop* or No. 1029 *County of Worcester* when on the Severn Valley.

As the Modified Halls and Counties shared many similarities,

with almost identical bogies and similar frames, cylinders and motion, one of the Barry 10, No. 7927 *Willington Hall* – which, as we saw, donated its boiler to the Betton Grange project – gave its frames to the County project.

THE DISAPPEARING 8F
Another of the Barry 10, Stanier 8F No. 48518, has provided the boiler for the project. At the outset, it was a decision that caused controversy among some in the enthusiast fraternity.

A total of 14 Stanier 8Fs are believed to have survived. Six apart from No. 48518 have been preserved in Britain, another three have been repatriated from Turkey (one of them subsequently being sold on to a museum in Israel), two are preserved in Turkey, which used wartime examples for decades after the end of hostilities, and others are known to lie derelict in that country. At least one other survives in Baghdad, while two are also visible underwater on the wreck of the *SS Thistlegorm*, which was sunk on October 6, 1941 near Ras Muhammad in the Red Sea and is now a well-known diving site.

As with the Halls, the class is clearly well represented in preservation, and so the idea of losing one of many survivors to recreate an extinct type came into play.

Critics, however, pointed out that No. 48158 was the last survivor of the batch of 8Fs built at Doncaster.

Outshopped at the end of August 1944, No. 48518 was kept on by the LNER to run heavy freight trains to Edinburgh, Leeds and Hull and after the war ended was based at Heaton.

It was officially returned to the LMS in April 1947 and allocated to Wakefield, but was switched to Cardiff in February 1948.

ABOVE: LMS Stanier 8F No. 48518 at Watford in 1960. The locomotive is now no more, but its components have been distributed among several *Vale of Glamorgan* new-build projects, with its boiler being modified for No. 1014. MICHAEL G HARVEY/COLOUR-RAIL

ABOVE: LMS Stanier 8F No. 48474 stands alongside the original No. 1014 *Vale of Glamorgan*. The new locomotive will use a modified 8F boiler. GWS

ABOVE: Unrestored Barry hulk No. 48518 at Bute Road station in Cardiff, the original headquarters of the Vale of Glamorgan Railway where a scheme for a Welsh national railway museum never materialised as planned. JEFF MORGAN

ABOVE: The Stanier 8F boiler, which will be used to build a new GWR Hawksworth County; the two types being very similar even though not exactly the same size. GWS

From there it worked services over the Central Wales Line to Shrewsbury.

Further allocations were at Bescot, Newton Heath and Willesden, and it could occasionally be seen on empty stock duties at Euston.

In late 1964/early 1965 it spent three months 'on holiday' at Croes Newydd shed at Wrexham, working heavy freight. It was withdrawn from Willesden in July 1965 and arrived at Barry that October.

As the LNER had fared badly in terms of numbers of locomotives preserved when compared with the GWR or Southern Railway because of the absence of a Dai Woodham in the regions where its engines were sent for scrapping, there would be all the more reason to save a Doncaster-built engine.

It was also pointed out that while the 8F boiler may be similar to that of the County, it was not exactly the same size and would need to be modified.

It was still possible to repatriate 8Fs from Turkey, and so it was suggested that the frames of No. 48518 might be used to house a Turkish 8F boiler, after its own was taken for the County project. Otherwise, the remains of No. 48518 could be cosmetically restored for static display. However, neither suggestion has been taken up.

Hard decisions often have to be made, and it was generally agreed that having a new County running on the national network would be far better than another 8F rusting away until the day came when a group might be willing to start on the long laborious process of restoration.

THE PROJECT UNDERWAY

The County project was divided into four phases – modification of the frames and manufacture of three new driving wheelsets, rebuilding the 8F boiler to a No. 15 OA type with double chimney, acquisition and refurbishment of the motion, manufacture of the fittings and pipework and construction of a new flat-sided tender.

The frames of *Willington Hall* were converted to County specification at the Llangollen Railway workshops during 2005-06, and since 2007, the rest of the rebuild has been progressing at Didcot.

One major design challenge is to redesign the frame mounts for the boiler and smokebox so that the gauging is compatible with the current Network Rail parameters. This modification involves a reduction of the

boiler centreline by 1.75in and corresponding reductions at the cab shoulder and at the top of the tender side sheets to achieve a total height reduction of a whisker under 4in.

In early 2008, No. 48518 was dismantled at the Llangollen Railway to, as agreed, provide a source of components, big and small, for several new-build projects, with the boiler subsequently being taken to Didcot Railway Centre.

The boiler was moved to LNWR Crewe on July 18, 2012, for work to commence on stripping and assessing the work needed to adapt it for use in No. 1014.

Most of the work was funded by a legacy from a Great Western Society member, and involved replacing the LMS partly coned barrel to the required fully coned type of the

correct length for a County class locomotive, albeit with the same front and rear diameters. A new coned barrel in two parts together with a new front tubeplate and smokebox became part of the new Country blueprint.

Three pairs of 6ft 3in driving wheels arrived at Didcot on October 18, 2011, from Riley & Son's works in Bury aboard an Axle Haulage low loader, and DRC operations manager, Roger Orchard, oversaw the delicate operation to crane them into Network Rail's West Yard.

ABOVE: The new driving wheelsets for *County of Glamorgan* delivered to Didcot on October 18, 2011. GWS

ABOVE: Unloading the new County's driving wheels at Didcot on October 18, 2011. GWS

ABOVE: One of the coupling rods for No. 14 being forged. GWS

ABOVE: Components for the new County tender. GWS

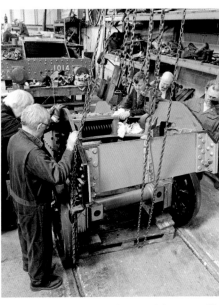

ABOVE: The bogie of *County of Glamorgan* being reassembled at Didcot on July 30, 2011. FRANK DUMBLETON/GWS

The Counties' larger-diameter driving wheels were among their unique features and, because no originals survived, the new No. 1014's had to be specially made.

The patterns are in two parts, and were made with reference to the original drawings by William Cook in Sheffield, which cast all six wheels.

The centre driving wheels have a slightly bigger centre boss than the other four – to take account of the extra stresses induced by the connecting rod – so the pattern was convertible to allow casting of all six wheels from the same pattern.

The axles and tyres came from South Africa and Rileys mated them with the axles. They then went to the South Devon Railway's Buckfastleigh works for the tyres to be shrunk on and turned, and then back to Rileys for fitting of the crankpins, eccentrics and balancing.

Other work on No. 1014 focused on modifying the frames, fitting new splashers and running plates, refurbishing the brake gear, positioning the reverser and reach rod, plus the construction of a new tender.

In the spring of 2014, the frames of No. 1014 were moved to Tyseley Locomotive Works for the hornguides to be machined and the six driving wheel axleboxes to be fitted and aligned under contract.

Meanwhile, many components were sourced from the society's own spares collection, including pistons, firehole doors and operating mechanisms, a four-cone ejector, and castings for an exhaust steam injector.

ABOVE: The frames of No. 1014 unloaded at Didcot on August 20, 2015. ADRIAN KNOWLES

NEARING THE HOME STRAIGHT

By spring 2015, the firebox was almost complete at Crewe, and work to estimate the cost of a new boiler barrel and smokebox was completed in late August before negotiations with potential contractors for a fixed-price contract. The estimates placed the cost at around £132,000. It was hoped to complete the conversion of the boiler from the LMS type to the GWR one in 2016.

The project took a major step forward on August 29, 2015, with the return of the frames from Tyseley into Didcot West Yard, paving the way for a rolling chassis for the first time, hopefully early in 2016. Meanwhile, work on the tender was making steady progress.

No sizeable new-build project can be held to an exact date for completion, but the project team was aiming to have No. 1014 *Vale of Glamorgan* ready "for the early 2020s".

■ Help bring the Hawksworth County completion date closer. For details of how to help boost the project, contact Richard Croucher at chairman@didcotrailwaycentre.org.uk or visit www.didcotrailwaycentre.org.uk

Alternatively, send donations to Richard Croucher, Appeal Co-ordinator (County 1014 Project), Great Western Society Limited, Didcot Railway Centre, Didcot, Oxfordshire, OX11 7NJ ●

RIGHT: The frames of the new County at Didcot on October 10, 2015. FRANK DUMBLETON

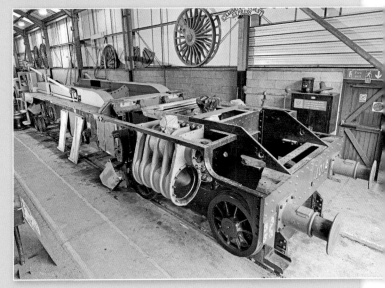

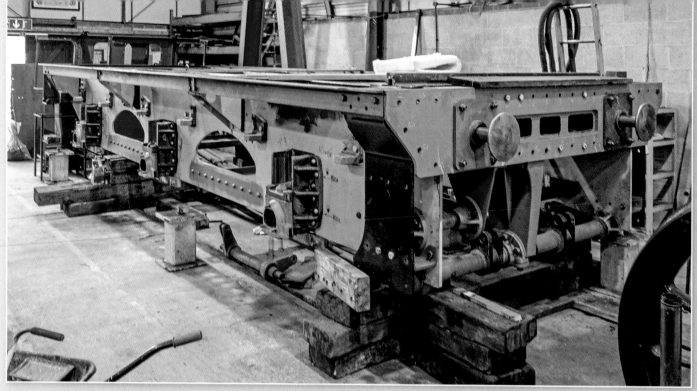

ABOVE: The frame of the new tender for No. 1014 on October 17, 2015. ADRIAN KNOWLES

ABOVE: The new exhaust injector casting and pattern on July 10, 2015. ADRIAN KNOWLES

ABOVE: One of the bearings for the new County. FRANK DUMBLETON

RIGHT AND ABOVE RIGHT: An unprecedented gathering of 21 Counties – or rather memorabilia from them – took place on July 27, 2013 at the Didcot Railway Centre during a mostly sunny County Day. The focus of the fundraising event was a display of nameplates – straight ones from the Hawksworth 1000 series locomotives and curved ones from the earlier Churchward 3800s – along with cabside and smokebox door numberplates. While some plates came from the museum at Didcot, most were loaned and personally delivered by private owners, a gesture much appreciated by the Great Western Society and the County project team. The name and numberplates – some very shiny and some unrestored – attracted a stream of visitors throughout the day, many of whom took the opportunity to quiz the County of Glamorgan team about No. 1014 and the project's progress with some placing cash in the collecting chimney or writing cheques. FRANK DUMBLETON

BELOW: Patriot 4-6-0 No. 45519 passes Dore & Totley in June 1960. PJ HUGHES/COLOUR-RAIL

The National Memorial Engine

Not only will the project to build a new Patriot 4-6-0 fill a major gap in today's heritage main line fleet, but it will be different from any other similar project – because it will become a national memorial honouring Britain's servicemen and women.

ABOVE: Another milestone in the assembly of new-build Patriot *The Unknown Warrior* was when the bogie was fitted beneath the frames for the first time at Tyseley Locomotive Works in Birmingham on February 3 – making it a 4-6-0 for the first time. The bogie has been made from all new material apart from one wheelset which was reused from ex-Barry LMS Stanier 8F 2-8-0 No. 48518. ANDY COLLINSON/LMS-PATRIOT PROJECT

A major spin-off from the Great Western Society's 'mix and match' new-builds is the replication of an extinct type from rival company the LMS, in the form of a Fowler Patriot 4-6-0.

It was the society's David Bradshaw – who grew up in Midland territory, and saw that the LMS was, in comparison with the Southern and GWR, poorly represented in Barry scrapyard – in 2006 came up with the idea of recreating the class. There was no LMS equivalent of Dai Woodham's legendary scrapyard, and so many magnificent classes went to the cutter's torch before anyone had chance to save them.

Also, David, who has played a significant part in Didcot's new-build *County of Glamorgan* project recognised a big gap in the market, for there was no LMS new-build project in existence, and the building of a new example of a once-popular locomotive could attract widespread support from followers of the company's heritage who felt they had been left out in the cold.

However, this Patriot will be different from the rest – because it will be literally a patriot, just what it says on the tin.

ABOVE: Patriot No. 45517 on Whitmore Troughs picking up water with an Up train on August 3, 1957.
DICK BLENKINSOP/LMS-PATRIOT PROJECT

ABOVE: Patriot No. 45518 heads 'The Mancunian' past Castlethorpe Troughs in August 1958. TB OWEN/COLOUR-RAIL

ABOVE: The Patriot class had much in common with the Royal Scots. Here, No. 6100 *Royal Scot* is seen running on the Severn Valley Railway on June 15, 2015, following the completion of a long-running overhaul. The completion of a new Patriot will fill a significant gap in today's LMS big engine fleet. BRIAN SHARPE

For not only will it fill a void in the heritage steam fleet but it will also become the National Memorial Engine, a steam 'version' of the Cenotaph.

Endorsed by the Royal British Legion, the locomotive, to be numbered 45551 (the last in the original class) and named *The Unknown Warrior*, will honour those servicemen and women who gave their lives in both world wars and subsequent conflicts.

The three-cylinder LMS Patriot class was introduced towards the end of Sir Henry Fowler's reign as Chief Mechanical Engineer from 1925-32.

The class was presented as a rebuild of Bowen-Cook's large-boilered Claughton 4-6-0s; indeed, the first two were produced from the remains of two Claughtons that had been badly damaged in accidents, retaining the original driving wheels with their large bosses, the 'double radial' bogie truck and various other parts.

The subsequent 50 locomotives of the Class 40 were nominal rebuilds of Claughtons, being in fact new-builds classified as rebuilt engines so that they could be charged to revenue accounts, rather than capital. The last 10 were classified as new-builds.

The Patriots, as they were known after 1937, had more in common with the Royal Scot, having a very similar chassis combined with the smaller G91/2S boiler as used on the rebuilt large Claughtons. They were known as 'Baby Scots' as a result.

A total of 57 were planned, but the last five were built with taper boilers and became the first of the Jubilee class.

After the First World War, three railway companies named locomotives to honour the railway employees who had fought and died during the conflict. These were *Valour, Remembrance* and *Patriot*.

The London & North Western Railway's memorial engine, a Claughton, was named *Patriot*. This name was later transferred to the new 4-6-0 locomotive No. 5500, which became the new Patriot memorial engine for the LMS and after which the class took its name.

Naming of the class was somewhat erratic. Some retained old Claughton names, while others continued the military associations of the names Patriot and St Dunstans, and 13 carried names of holiday resorts served by the LMS. Seven remained unnamed, although they had been allocated names in 1943.

Between 1946 and 1948, 18 Patriots were rebuilt with Stanier 2A boilers, cabs and tenders. From 1948, these were fitted with Royal Scot pattern deflectors. The two original members of the class, and the first 10 of the nominal rebuilds, were not owing to their non-standard parts.

All the Patriots were painted out in LMS crimson lake livery with pale yellow and black lining when first built, but after 1946 most were painted out in LMS lined black with straw and maroon lining. All of them were later reliveried in British Railways standard Brunswick green with orange and black.

Highly successful, the Patriots covered around 1.3 million miles each. They were all withdrawn in 1960-65 and scrapped; the standard gauge preservation movement having yet to become sufficiently empowered to save one. The last two to be withdrawn were Nos. 45543 and 45550.

THE FIRST GREEN SHOOTS

In July 2007, the scheme to build a new Patriot was floated by David.

The following January, the project received a major boost when 'Barry 10' LMS Stanier 8F 2-8-0 No. 48518 was taken out of storage at Barry and moved to the Llangollen Railway for its boiler to be lifted off, for use on the *County of Glamorgan* at Didcot. The frames of the 8F, however, remained for use in the Patriot project, which is seeing the new locomotive built in the Llangollen Railway's workshop.

An appropriate spare Fowler tender had also been identified among the Barry collection, and would be rebuilt for the Patriot.

The project was formally launched at the Llangollen Railway gala on April 18-20, 2008. The event was duly named the Patriot Gala.

A presentation was made to Kevin Finnerly, a resident of Giggleswick, a village near Settle, who came up with the name *The Unknown Warrior* for what will be numbered 45551, the next in the class. Rather fittingly, one of the Patriots, No. 5538, was named after Giggleswick. The name is in keeping with the abovementioned tradition of war memorial engines.

The nameplates and smokebox numberplate for the new locomotive were on display at the gala. The LMS-Patriot Project, the official title, has received the endorsement of the Royal

British Legion, and No. 45551 will carry a Legion crest above *The Unknown Warrior* nameplate, in recognition of this.

David said: "Our partnership with the Legion will enable us to spread our message to a larger audience who will support the creation of the new Patriot.

"The project will also work with the Legion to promote the educational aspects of the project and the important role the railways played in the war effort."

In its first few months, the project raised pledges of more than £100,000 towards the estimated total cost of £1.5 million, reflecting the popularity of the type more than 40 years after the last one ran on the national network. The cost breakdown for the new Patriot was estimated at £48,000 for the frames, £54,000 for the cylinders, £150,000 for the driving wheelsets, £70,000 for cab fittings and pipework, £30,000 for the tender refurbishment, and the biggest component of all, the boiler, was costed at £500,000.

David said: "We have now gone from amber to green, and are convinced that the project is a goer."

Another boost for the Patriot came with the availability of patterns for the driving wheels, which as far as the last 10 members of the class were concerned are the same as those on a Jubilee.

Tyseley Locomotive Works chief engineer, Bob Meanley, offered to loan the set of patterns used to make new driving wheels for Jubilee No. 45699 *Galatea*, which was rebuilt by the West Coast Railway Company at Carnforth and is now a regular performer on the main line. The kits of parts that was *Galatea* – which was in Barry scrapyard from 1960-80 and was bought originally to provide

ABOVE: Bought from Barry scrapyard as a donor locomotive, Jubilee No. 45699 *Galatea*, seen passing Birkitt on May 3, 2015, is now a regular main line performer in its own right. The planned final batch of 10 Patriots became the first Jubilees, and the patterns for the new wheels for *Galatea* were used to cast those for *The Unknown Warrior*. BRIAN SHARPE

a spare boiler for preserved sister engine No. 45690 *Leander* had been based at Tyseley for several years, and Birmingham Railway Museum retained ownership of the patterns, although they were subsequently used by West Coast.

ASSEMBLY BEGINS AT LLANGOLLEN

Masterminded by Dave Owen, Chief Mechanical Engineer at the Llangollen workshops, the assembly of *The Unknown Warrior* began in 2009.

Corus Steel at Cradley Heath in the West Midlands cut the frame plates for the new Patriot that March. The plates were taken to

The Boro' Foundry in nearby Lye for drilling and machining, before being delivered to Llangollen that summer.

After the abovementioned Fowler tender was acquired from the Vale of Glamorgan Council, the restoration of its chassis began at Cambrian Transport's Barry Railway

Centre in November 2010, with an all-new tender body to be built.

It was clear at this early stage that minor adaptations to the original design would have to be made. Running on the national network – which has always been the intention of the project team – would require the locomotive to be built to a height of 13ft – 2½in less than the LMS design. The design of the chimney and cab would be affected by the reduced height requirements and additional items that are required for mainline running including Train Protection & Warning System and On-Train Monitoring & Recording apparatus as well as the consideration of air braking. The LMS-Patriot Project is working closely with a Vehicle Acceptance Body representative to allow *The Unknown Warrior* to be main line certified.

In January 2011, a set of genuine LMS buffers of the type fitted to Patriots was acquired from a rail-mounted crane that was being scrapped at the Great Central Railway (Nottingham). At least three of the buffers are stamped LMS, with 1930s dates. The diesel-electric crane was built at Derby Works in 1947 and fitted with a set of buffers from an LMS locomotive that had been scrapped there.

ABOVE: The first casting for *The Unknown Warrior*, the bogie bolster, which supports the front pony truck, is seen after casting and shot blasting at The Boro' Foundry on June 26, 2010. BOB SWEET/LMS-PATRIOT PROJECT

ABOVE: The North Wales branch of the Royal British Legion unveiled the new Patriot's nameplate design and dedicated the locomotive to the memory of British servicemen.

ABOVE: The frames for the new Patriot are cut. LMS-PATRIOT PROJECT

ABOVE: The nameplate of *The Unknown Warrior* with the Royal British Legion crest on top. ROBIN JONES

PATRIOT UNVEILING

The North Wales branch of the Royal British Legion unveiled the new Patriot's nameplate design and dedicated the locomotive to the memory of British servicemen.

The ceremony was held at the Llangollen Railway's locomotive works on November 2, 2009, nine days before Remembrance Day.

Following a dedication speech by Legion representatives delivered in both English and Welsh, a bugler sounded the last post before poppy petals rained down on to the frames of No. 45551 and its union-flag draped nameplate.

As the Legion standards were dipped, the flag was removed in order to reveal the magnificent new nameplate.

In keeping with engineering tradition a bottle was then broken against the frames to confirm the launch of the Patriot Project.

HERITAGE RAILWAY READERS PAID FOR THE WHEELS!

The £60,000 needed for the six driving wheels was raised by readers of *Heritage Railway* magazine through an appeal launched on the front cover of issue 131.

The first driving wheel for *The Unknown Warrior* was cast at The Boro' Foundry on September 14, 2010.

At 6ft 9in, it was believed to be the biggest standard gauge locomotive wheel cast in the heritage era, beating the 6ft 8½in wheels for GWR Saint No. 2999 *Lady of Legend* by just half an inch.

The pouring of the molten steel for the first wheel took only 90 seconds. After cooling for two days the new casting was revealed and was later shotblasted and machined, reducing the weight of the finished wheel.

All six driving wheels were cast by January 2011. The fitting of the tyres, crank axle, plain axles and crank pins was contracted to the South Devon Railway, which assembled the six new wheelsets in January 2013.

The completed driving wheelsets for new LMS Patriot No. 45551 *The Unknown Warrior* were delivered to Tyseley Locomotive Works at the beginning of July 2013.

At Tyseley they were balanced with lead weights, turned, and had the axleboxes fitted before being taken to the Llangollen Railway Works to be fitted to the frames of *The Unknown Warrior* to enable the rolling chassis (minus the front bogie), to be completed.

The running plates, cab steps and front steps have been fitted to No. 45551 as the 'kit of parts' rapidly became a locomotive, enabling the rolling chassis with smokebox and cab to be displayed at the Warley Model Railway Exhibition on November 23-24 that year.

ABOVE: Author Robin Jones with one of the newly cast wheels at The Boro' Foundry on September 15, 2010. Readers of *Heritage Railway* magazine, which he edits, paid for the wheels through a national appeal. ROBIN JONES COLLECTION

ABOVE: The dragbox was completed during December 2010 at the Llangollen workshops where coded welder, Ian Massey, welded the pre-cut sections together. ANDREW LAWS/LMS-PATRIOT PROJECT

ABOVE: The wheelsets for *The Unknown Warrior* are loaded at South Devon Railway Engineering on July 2. RICHARD ELLIOTT

ABOVE: Pouring the metal for the new wheels at The Boro' Foundry in Lye. ROBIN JONES

ABOVE: One of the machined Patriot driving wheels at The Boro' Foundry. LMS-PATRIOT PROJECT

ABOVE: A further boost to the project came in June 2011 with the offer of this appropriate bogie wheelset from the Churchill 8F Locomotive Group, which overhauled repatriated former Turkish Stanier 8F No. 45160 at the Gloucestershire Warwickshire Railway. The Patriot team already had the bogie wheelset from 8F No. 48518. LMS-PATRIOT PROJECT

ABOVE: The pattern for the driving wheels being delivered to The Boro' Foundry. LMS-PATRIOT PROJECT

ABOVE: A newly cast driving wheel is lifted from its mould. ROBIN JONES

ABOVE: Steve Blackburn, LMS-Patriot Project quality and engineering director, Kevin West, project draughtsman; South Devon Railway workshop manager, Rob Le Chevalier, and project chairman, David Bradshaw, are pictured with the fourth driving wheel after it was cast at The Boro' Foundry in December 2010. LMS-PATRIOT PROJECT

ABOVE: Artist Colin Wright paints *The Unknown Warrior* on shed at Llangollen. A limited-edition print was produced to raise funds for No. 45551. A signed print was presented to Stuart Gendall, director of corporate communications at the Royal British Legion on September, 2010 in recognition that *The Unknown Warrior* had been endorsed as the new National Memorial Engine. JOHN HASTINGS-THOMSON/LMS-PATRIOT PROJECT

BOILER APPEAL LAUNCHED BY PETE WATERMAN

ABOVE: Pete Waterman, supporters and officials of the new-build Patriot project at the launch of the boiler appeal at Crewe on May 19, 2012. ROBIN JONES

ABOVE: This is how the front of the new-build LMS Patriot 4-6-0 No. 45551 *The Unknown Warrior* will look. Supporters of the project were shown the assembled front end at a preview in the Llangollen Railway workshops on July 31, 2013. LMS-PATRIOT PROJECT

On November 19, 2010, the project announced that Pete Waterman's LNWR Heritage Ltd at Crewe had been chosen as the preferred builder of the boiler.

The all-new boiler is being built in the traditional way, with a copper firebox, riveted seams and screwed stays.

LNWR Heritage Ltd had already built new copper fireboxes at Crewe, including the one for LNER B1 4-6-0 No. 61264 owned by the Thompson B1 Locomotive Trust, and the spare A4 boiler for LNER Pacific No. 60019 *Bittern*.

When completed, the new Patriot boiler will be the first traditional, large steam boiler to be built in the UK for a standard gauge main line steam locomotive since 1960.

Steve Blackburn, engineering and quality director for the LMS-Patriot Project said: "Crewe is the obvious choice for building the boiler for *The Unknown Warrior*. With

LNWR's technical capabilities and the historical links going back to the original Patriots at Crewe, we are delighted that the new boiler will be constructed in the railway town that was synonymous with the LMS and world-renowned railway engineering."

A national fundraising campaign for the new boiler was launched on May 19, 2012.

The boiler barrel sections for LMS Patriot 4-6-0 No. 45551 *The Unknown Warrior* were completed at Deepdale Engineering in Dudley during the beginning of March 2015.

The front section, 5ft 3¹¹/₁₆in diameter, and the rear section, 5ft 5¹/₈in diameter, will be

riveted together to form the 14ft long barrel of the locomotive.

The sections were rolled from steel plate and then welded along the joint before being subjected to the necessary testing processes.

David Bradshaw said: "The completion of the boiler barrels is another step towards completing the new boiler for *The Unknown Warrior*.

The boiler barrel sections were taken to LNWR Heritage at Crewe, where the all-new boiler for *The Unknown Warrior* is being constructed.

The new boiler is expected to be steamed during 2017 before being fitted to the frames.

ABOVE: Sections of the boiler barrel. LMS-PATRIOT PROJECT

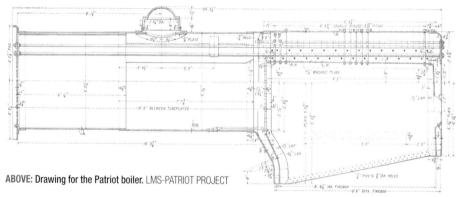

ABOVE: Drawing for the Patriot boiler. LMS-PATRIOT PROJECT

ABOVE: The smoke deflectors were sponsored by Patriot project member David Collins and were fabricated by John Whiteman Engineering of Long Eaton under the supervision of project supporter Neil Kinsey who has overseen their construction. LMS-PATRIOT PROJECT

ABOVE LEFT: The steel former for the backplate for the new copper inner firebox, made at the workshops of LNWR Heritage in Crewe, is seen on June 3, 2014. It enabled the copper sheet to be formed to create the first large section of the inner firebox of the G9 ½in S Fowler design parallel boiler, the first all-British built new mainline boiler to be built since 1960. LMS-PATRIOT PROJECT ABOVE RIGHT: Pete Waterman discusses tubeplate manufacture and coppersmithing skills with Crewe Borough mayor Roy Cartlidge. ROBIN JONES

A NEW WAY TO CAST CYLINDERS

The first outside cylinder for *The Unknown Warrior* was cast at the Coupe Foundry in Preston, on April 16, 2014, from a polystyrene pattern, manufactured by Premier Patterns of Smethwick using the same pioneering technique used to manufacture the middle cylinder the previous year. After casting, the cylinder was left to cool for a week before being knocked out of the mould and shot blasted to reveal the first new Patriot outside cylinder for more than 60 years. The use of polystyrene patterns has significantly reduced the costs of producing the three cylinders for *The Unknown Warrior*, with the patterns costing around £1700 for the outside cylinders, casting £2400 and machining approximately £3000 each. The technique has blazed a new-build trail, significantly reducing costs.

However, the inside cylinder block was recast after problems arose with the first one. There was no problem with the polystyrene pattern method, but during cooling, the block shrank more than had been predicted, leading to problems with final machining.

It was decided that rather than rectify the fault, it was cheaper to use the polystyrene method to cast a new one at Coupe Foundry, with greater machining tolerances, and it was duly knocked out of the mould on October 7, 2013.

ABOVE: Metal poured into the polystyrene mould for the first outside cylinder. LMS-PATRIOT PROJECT

ABOVE: The left-hand cylinder being fitted to the motion bracket in January 2015. LMS-PATRIOT PROJECT

ABOVE: The first of the new Patriot's outer cylinders. LMS-PATRIOT PROJECT

ABOVE: One of the new outside cylinders being machined at Harco Engineering in the West Midlands on October 1, 2015. OAKWOOD VISUALS

ABOVE: Both cylinders in place on the frames. LMS-PATRIOT PROJECT

ABOVE: Checking the alignment of the right-hand cylinder to the setting wire in January 2015. LMS-PATRIOT PROJECT

A SECOND TENDER

The first tender acquired by the LMS-Patriot Project was formally handed over to Cambrian Transport on May 4, 2010 in a ceremony involving the Vale of Glamorgan Council, Cambrian Transport and directors of the LMS-Patriot Project.

This tender was completely dismantled in December 2010; the driving wheels have been turned and the journals polished at Tyseley Locomotive Works, with the springs refurbished by Owen Springs in Rotherham. Two of the axleboxes were removed for refurbishment, but the other four had been damaged and were not useable. Sadly, the frames were found to be beyond economic repair as they were badly corroded.

The opportunity to acquire a second Fowler tender came in July 2012 when the East Lancashire Railway agreed to sell a spare Fowler tender to the project.

This tender had been acquired for spares for the Bury-based LMS 'Crab' No. 13065/42765, which at the time was being overhauled at Bury.

Also in ex-Barry scrapyard condition, this tender was found to be in better condition, with less corroded frame plates. The frames from this tender are likely to be restored for use with *The Unknown Warrior* along with a further two axle boxes. Two other axle boxes will need to be obtained or cast.

New tender drawings have been produced to enable a new tender tank to be manufactured. The new tank will be made slightly wider with a slightly reduced coal space to increase water capacity to around 3900 gallons.

In September 2014, the project team announced that it had entered into an agreement with Rowlescourt Engineering Ltd of Alfreton, Derbyshire, which will be refurbishing the tender frames and building the new tank. The distinctive feature of the Fowler tender, being narrower than the 7ft 10½in Patriot cab, will be retained.

The extremely generous terms of this agreement will require the project to pay only for the materials, estimated at around £10,000,

while Rowlescourt Engineering, which has spent more than 30 years in the design and supply of safety-critical parts to Network Rail and its major subcontractors will provide all the labour required for the construction of the tender, for which most parts, including refurbished wheelsets and springs, already exist.

This sponsorship will save the project around £40,000 and will speed up construction of *The Unknown Warrior* significantly as it will allow three work streams to operate simultaneously – the boiler at L&NWR Heritage at Crewe, the locomotive frames at Llangollen and the tender at Alfreton. The target completion date of the tender is August 2016.

ABOVE: The stripped-down frames of the tender acquired from the East Lancashire Railway. ANDREW LAWS/LMS-PATRIOT PROJECT

ABOVE: Progress on the tender frames as seen at Rowlescourt Engineering at the end of August 2015. ANDREW LAWS/LMS-PATRIOT PROJECT

HONOURING OUR SERVICEMEN AT THE NATIONAL MEMORIAL ARBORETUM

The National Memorial Arboretum is a site of remembrance at Alrewas near Lichfield, which honours the fallen, recognises military service and sacrifice, and fosters pride in Britain.

A world-renowned centre for remembrance, it was officially opened on May 16, 2001.

A registered charity, it is part of the Royal British Legion family of charities.

On November 21, 2013, *The Unknown Warrior* was taken there for a service of dedication, at which members of the Army, Navy and RAF were present. It was the

locomotive's first public appearance away from its Llangollen construction base.

Two days earlier, over the November 9-10 Remembrance weekend, the partially completed locomotive was decorated with poppies in the Llangollen workshops.

After the ceremony in the arboretum, No. 45551 was taken for display at the 2013 Warley National Model Railway Exhibition, which had a Great War theme that year. Around 17,400 people attended the show at the National Exhibition Centre near Birmingham over its two days.

Once the show was over, *The Unknown Warrior* was taken to Tyseley Locomotive Works for the next phase of its construction.

ABOVE: The new Patriot takes centre stage at the Warley Model Railway Show. PAUL BICKERDYKE

ABOVE: In late 2013, Colin Wright produced another oil painting of new-build LMS Patriot 4-6-0 No. 45551 *The Unknown Warrior* to mark its first public appearances away from its Llangollen construction base, and to raise more funds for its completion. It depicts No. 45551 in pre-1936 LMS crimson lake livery outside Crewe North Shed with the original LNWR Memorial Engine: Claughton Patriot No. 5964, in May 1934, when the original No. 5551 had just been outshopped. The Claughton Patriot lasted only another two months before withdrawal in July 1934. The trio of locomotives outside the shed is completed by the last 'Large Jumbo' No. 25001 *Snowdon*. In the background lurks George the Fifth 4-4-0 No. 5401 *Windermere*. LMS-PATRIOT PROJECT

PATRIOT FIREBOX BUILDING STARTS

The building of the Patriot's inner copper firebox began in the LNWR Heritage workshops at Crewe in late 2013, after £130,000 was raised through the boiler loan scheme launched that October. With the copper sheet for the firebox already obtained, thanks to a sizeable loan from a project member, and with the boiler drawings available, construction was started.

The smokebox, the first part of the boiler, had already been fitted to *The Unknown Warrior*. Now the heart of the boiler – the firebox – which is being made to the original design, began to take shape at the workshops, a short distance from Crewe Locomotive Works where the enlarged G9 ½in Claughton boilers were built, these were later fitted to the Patriot class locomotives from new.

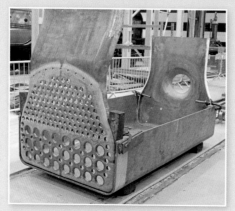

ABOVE: The firebox inside LNWR Heritage Ltd's new premises (the former Crewe Diesel depot) on May 9, 2015. ZOE ELIZABETH HUNTER/LMS-PATRIOT PROJECT

ABOVE: The new Patriot firebox copper door plate taken on January 20 at Crewe. GAVIN SHELL/LMS-PATRIOT PROJECT

FIRST MILLION RAISED

Crowds of visitors to the Great Dorset Steam Fair over August 27-31, 2014, saw *The Unknown Warrior* exhibited as part of the 100th anniversary commemoration of the start of the First World War.

A display of special vehicles including tanks, traction engines, ambulances and even a petrol-driven Simplex narrow gauge locomotive that would have seen action a century ago, were displayed in a special area of the steam fair, next to a specially recreated area of trenches that showed the harsh conditions of trench warfare. Donations, sales, raffle and new memberships saw the project raise around £9000.

A major milestone was passed, appropriately on November 11 – Armistice Day – that year. For the fundraising reached the £1 million mark, a remarkable achievement in the six years since the project was launched.

ABOVE: The assembly of the bogie making good progress at Tyseley Locomotive Works in August 2015, with the frame assembly almost complete and the equalising spring beams fitted; as the locomotive was about to become a 4-6-0 for the first time. The tyres for the new wheelset arrived in the UK from South Africa on August 21 and were delivered to South Devon Railway Engineering the following week for machining and assembly on to the wheel centres. LMS-PATRIOT PROJECT

ABOVE: No. 45551 on display at the Great Dorset Steam Fair in 2014. COLIN TYSON

THE PATRIOT BECOMES A 4-6-0 AT LAST!

The Unknown Warrior was 'reunited' with three nameplates from class members when it appeared at the Barrow Hill LMS Ticket To Ride gala on September 25-27, 2015.

Loaned for the occasion were plates from No. 45509 *The Derbyshire Yeomanry*, No. 45536 *Private W Wood V.C.* and No. 45537 *Private E. Sykes V.C.*

Looking more like a locomotive with every public appearance that it makes, and now fitted with its front bogie and one wheelset, around £200,000 was still needed to complete the £480,000 boiler and fill in the 'gap'.

The Barrow Hill 65 gala marked the 50th anniversary of the closure of the Staveley Midland roundhouse to steam.

No. 45551 became the first member of its class to visit the roundhouse since the Sixties. At Barrow Hill, it was in excellent company, for the event marked one of the biggest gatherings of LMS locomotives in the heritage era, with Princess Coronation Pacific No. 46233 *Duchess of Sutherland* making its first-ever visit to the roundhouse.

On February 3, 2016, the bogie was fitted beneath the frames for the first time at Tyseley. At last, the new Patriot had become a 4-6-0.

The Unknown Warrior was also at Tyseley to have the cylinder liners and valve liners fitted. Issues had been encountered during the casting process resulting in porous castings which only became apparent when the cylinder and valve liners were being machined. That resulted in delays while further castings were made.

Once the remaining valve and cylinder liners were fitted, assembly was scheduled to be back on track at Llangollen.

The LMS-Patriot Project has set a target date of 2018 for the completion of No. 45551, to coincide with the 100th anniversary of the signing of the Armistice, which brought about an end to the Great War, but again, funds from supporters and well-wishers are paramount. The project is raising funds through public donations and regular contributions (with Gift Aid where applicable), mixed-interest loans, legacies, commercial sponsorship and grant applications. ●

■ If you would like to support this doubly patriotic project, donations can be sent with cheques made payable to: The LMS-Patriot Co Ltd, and sent to: The LMS-Patriot Co Ltd, PO Box 3118, Hixon, Stafford, ST16 9JL

Donation and membership forms can be downloaded from the website www.lms-patriot.org.uk

ABOVE: Nameplates of long-scrapped Patriots displayed on *The Unknown Warrior* at Barrow Hill. ANDREW LAWS/ LMS-PATRIOT PROJECT

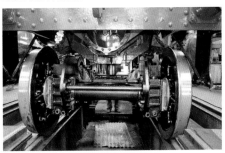

ABOVE: The front bogie fitted for the first time, at Tyseley Locomotive Works on February 3, 2016. ANDY COLLINSON/ LMS-PATRIOT PROJECT

RIGHT: A minute's silence was held at Tyseley Locomotive Works at 11am on November 11 to mark Remembrance Day and to remember all of the railway employees who lost their lives fighting in the Great War and subsequent conflicts. LMS PATRIOT PROJECT

ABOVE: All it needs is the boiler: *The Unknown Warrior* proudly displayed inside Barrow Hill Roundhouse on September 26, 2015. ROBIN JONES

Chapter 9

Tornado
from dream to steam

The jewel in the crown of the new-build movement has to be the construction from start to finish of an all-new A1 Peppercorn Pacific and its successful operation on the national network. Graham Nicholas, quality and certification director for The A1 Steam Locomotive Trust outlines the remarkable story of this pinnacle of the heritage movement.

Peppercorn class A1 Pacific No. 60163 *Tornado* has rightly become the standard bearer for 21st century new-build steam, creating headlines all round the world and making minor celebrities of the enterprising team that brought this most British of projects to successful fruition – The A1 Steam Locomotive Trust.

So how did an idea that has its origins in an, "is anyone interested in…?" letter in a railway journal turn into such a success story when other similar ideas have either disappeared without trace or become lost in the wilderness of good intentions?

At the time, rebuilds of Barry scrapyard wrecks were becoming more and more technically challenging – yet the movement was rising to each challenge, with more and more new components requiring to be made. The rebuild of unique BR Standard 8P Pacific No. 71000 *Duke of Gloucester* was a particular case in point, requiring complete new manufacture of its complex cylinders and poppet valve gear.

Surely a complete new build was the next logical step?

It was North East businessman David Champion (destined to become the project's driving force through much of the 1990s) who first realised, however, that this could not be just

BELOW: *Tornado* crosses the Royal Border Bridge with 'The Auld Reekie Express' on February 28, 2009. GEOFF GRIFFITHS/A1SLT

ABOVE: The public launch of The A1 Steam Locomotive Trust at the Railway Institute in York on November 17, 1990. A1SLT

another preservation scheme, relying solely on good will and begging bowls. This needed to be a business-led project, with a mission statement and business plan, run on sound business principles.

The mission statement sounds simple enough – blindingly obvious maybe: "To build and operate a Peppercorn Class A1 Pacific for mainline and preserved railway use."

Yet it has remained unwavering throughout the project's history, serving as a rallying call for the project team and supporters alike.

AN A1 FOR THE PRICE OF A PINT!

Four business principles were agreed: experienced people applying best business practices, a simple funding method, a focus on the mission statement and recognition based on effort.

The first of these is a straightforward enough maxim but fundamental to the project's success. When a bank manager stepped forward to offer to help, he wasn't given a wire brush and a welding set – he was asked to manage the trust's finances. Using this principle, a diverse team was formed, able not only to offer engineering expertise but also marketing, administration, project management and legal matters. The trust was even fortunate to have an expert on taxation for much of the time that *Tornado* was being built, able to make the most of favourable financial benefits available to charitable organisations.

But it was the evolution of the business plan that was perhaps the single biggest step forward.

Faced with an early cost estimate of "around a million pounds" (a figure that was subsequently proven overly optimistic, even at 1990s prices) David Champion sat down one evening with a glass of wine and began doodling on the back of an envelope.

By breaking such a daunting figure down into manageable chunks, he calculated that, if 1000 people could be persuaded to donate £1.25 a week (or £5 a month), it would take 'only' 10 years to raise that amount of money (allowing for charity gift aid). 'This will work!' wrote David, triumphantly – and the concept of the covenantor was born.

The key to the success of the A1 covenantor scheme was to make a simple, attractive offer so that supporters of all ages and means could actively buy into a dream. The figure of £1.25 happened to be the average price of a pint of beer in the North East of England in the 1990s hence: "An A1 for the price of a pint!" What simpler funding method could there be?

THE *TORNADO* TIMELINE

1990, November 11
The A1 Steam Locomotive Trust formally launched

◆

1994
First and last components ceremonially presented (a bogie swivel pin and a regulator nut)

◆

1994, April 22
Construction starts, with the frame plates rolled at Scunthorpe

◆

1995, January
Nameplates presented at the frame-laying ceremony

◆

1995
First wheel cast

◆

1996, May 25
Three cylinder castings unveiled at Tyseley Locomotive Works

◆

1997, March
Frame displayed at the Great Hall at the National Railway Museum

◆

1997
Tornado unveiled at Darlington Locomotive Works

◆

1999
Smokebox door complete

◆

2000, summer
Construction more than 50% complete

THE CHOICE OF LOCOMOTIVE

Coupled with this was the inspiration behind that message. The project had clearly chosen well with the idea to recreate the lost Peppercorn class A1 Pacific.

Essentially a product of the postwar LNER design team, yet actually built under BR auspices, the type proved to be the worthy successor of the Gresley class A3 and A4 designs, being a highly capable and reliable machine, perfectly suited to the challenging postwar conditions it found itself born into.

A total of 49 Peppercorn A1s were built. They were designed to cope with the heaviest passenger trains in the postwar period on the East Coast Main Line between King's Cross, Edinburgh and Aberdeen, which consisted normally of trains with up to 15 coaches and weighing up to 550 tons. They were able to haul such trains on the flat at a speed of 60-70 mph.

Like previous LNER Pacifics, the class had a three-cylinder arrangement. The five examples of the class that were fitted with Timken roller bearings turned in some of the highest reliability and mileage between overhauls of any of BR's steam express passenger fleet (a technical detail that was not lost on the nascent project team).

With such a pedigree and sound service record, the Peppercorn class A1 was arguably the most significant locomotive type of the postwar era not to be represented in preservation.

In the indecent haste with which steam traction was eliminated, railway enthusiast and businessman, Geoff Drury, had to make a choice between saving the last operational class A1 No. 60145 *Saint Mungo* (which had a working life of just 17 years) or A2 Pacific No. 60532 *Blue Peter*. He chose the latter.

Had he chosen the A1 instead, would there have been such strong support for the recreation of a Peppercorn class A2? One of modern preservation's unanswerable questions. By summer of 1966 all 49 class members had gone for scrap.

ABOVE: Pictured in late June 1962, Peppercorn A1 Pacific No. 60120 *Kittiwake* drifts into Grantham with a northbound train that is signalled to stop. This locomotive was based at Copley Hill (56C) motive power depot in Leeds. CECIL VOGEL/A1SLT

MAKING A START

With a sound business plan in place and funds starting to flow from the contributions of early covenantors, the A1 team could make a start on building the 50th Peppercorn A1. As any self-respecting engineer knows, you can't build anything without drawings.

It was known that a large collection of former LNER drawings from Doncaster survived, uncatalogued in the vaults of the National Railway Museum and so began the painstaking process of sorting and cataloguing the vital information required to support manufacture, a process led by another key figure in the *Tornado* story – project engineer David Elliott.

An early decision, of the type that has come to characterise the team's approach, was to embrace modern technology and digitally scan the drawings, rather than just take paper copies.

Although the technology was in its relative infancy, the digital files thus created were invaluable, being created in a format that lasted throughout the build programme and can still be accessed today.

Suitably cleaned up and sorted, David Elliott was able to use these, together with his own drawings derived from them, to specify the manufacturing requirements for the first components.

Ably assisted by the still sprightly widow of the designer of the original locomotives, Dorothy Mather (who was to become honorary president of the trust), the button was pressed on BSD's state-of-the-art plasma cutting machine at the firm's Leeds plant to create the mainframes of the locomotive. *Tornado* now officially existed.

ABOVE: The frames for the new A1 being cut at the BSD plant in Leeds in 1994. The cutting machine was started by Dorothy Mather, widow of designer Arthur H Peppercorn. A1SLT

ABOVE: The name *Tornado* was chosen in honour of the RAF Tornado air crews in the Gulf War and was chosen by an early sponsor of the project. In January 1995, RAF officers presented a pair of nameplates to the trust during the frame-laying ceremony at Tyseley Locomotive Works. AISLT

MAIN SPONSOR COMES ON BOARD

ABOVE: *Tornado's* 6ft 8in driving wheels being turned at the Severn Valley Railway's Bridgnorth workshops. DAVID ELLIOTT/A1SLT

It was at this point, with the project starting to gain momentum and an air of believability, that the trust received another welcome boost.

Andrew Cook, chairman of Sheffield-based steel manufacturer William Cook Cast Products, was sufficiently inspired by the project to take on the not inconsiderable task of casting the main driving wheels for the locomotive on extremely generous terms.

All involved were quick to realise that not only was this a wonderful offer of support but also that the publicity potential was significant.

Accordingly, a staged photograph of one of the wheels being fettled was produced, capturing the drama of the moment. That picture introduced a wider world to the vision and burgeoning endeavour of the A1 project team.

Further covenants and offers of support duly followed. Success was starting to breed success.

As the first components began to be created, Bob Meanley at Tyseley Locomotive Works oversaw the start of assembly. Meanwhile, the trust team members sought a place of their own and initially courted the local council at Doncaster in the search for a highly appropriate construction location.

ABOVE: In June 2007, the completed boiler for *Tornado* was lifted on to the rolling chassis at Darlington Locomotive Works. DAVID ELLIOTT/A1SLT

A BASE AT DARLINGTON

It was to be the alternative spiritual home of the Peppercorn A1 – Darlington – that was to ultimately provide a construction location and a permanent home, which has since become known as Darlington Locomotive Works. Based on what is itself an historic building, the original carriage works of the Stockton & Darlington Railway no less, a mutually beneficial arrangement was agreed that endures to this day.

The partially completed frames were delivered there in 1997 (transferred from Tyseley by rail, via a temporary exhibition at the NRM) and the trust had a sound basis to complete the locomotive.

The Darlington Borough Council of today is rightly proud of its association with a project that has given worldwide positive publicity to the town; but in 1997 this was a bold step and great credit is due to the council in putting such faith in a project that still had so much to prove.

THE BIG ONE

As the Millennium approached and with frames and wheels well-progressed there was one aspect of the project that was occupying the minds of the project team above all else – the boiler.

Whereas all other aspects of the locomotive were considered to be examples of components or assemblies that the preservation world had already tackled, it was more than 40 years since a boiler of comparative size had been constructed for a British mainline steam locomotive. Once again, it was a challenge that was tackled in typical forward-thinking fashion.

While the search for a suitable manufacturer was underway, the realisation dawned that this was one aspect of the project that could not be funded by the now established covenantor scheme. To go down that road would have put a virtual halt to all other work on the locomotive while funds were built up for the single largest item. That in turn would have turned off the tap to the regular stream of project updates and milestones that had already been proven to be the money-generating virtuous circle.

Instead, the trust made the bold decision to the launch a bearer bond scheme to fund the boiler, in effect a 'friendly loan', banking on there being sufficient people, already suitably inspired with the progress so far, to be willing to make funds available for the construction of the boiler on the understanding that the loans would subsequently be repaid (where claimed) once the locomotive was in service.

It proved to be spectacularly successful, with more than £100,000 (20% of the total) raised within four weeks of the launch and all bonds subsequently taken up in time to support full payment of the boiler.

Meanwhile, the trust's search had taken it some 500 miles eastwards, deep in the heart of Germany's Thuringian forest, to the delightful anachronism that is Meiningen locomotive works.

Now part of German state railway's engineering capability, the workshops at Meiningen date from 1914 and have been continually involved in the manufacture of steam locomotives ever since.

And, thanks to the idiosyncrasies of former Eastern Europe and the impact of reunification, Meiningen finds itself involved with the overhaul/manufacture of steam locomotives and components in the present day. In particular, it has a continuing order book for replacement steam locomotive boilers and the design capacity to support it. Although unorthodox, it was to prove the ideal solution to the challenge of sourcing *Tornado's* beating heart.

Once again prepared to meet a challenge head on, the concept of redesigning the boiler around an all-steel, welded manufacture was readily embraced. Crucially, Meiningen had nearly 50 years' experience of this technology; all-welded boilers being adopted as part of the postwar rebuilding programme for the nation's railways.

Remarkably, the boiler under construction at the time that the trust visited to discuss the design details, was for a German three-cylinder Class 01 Pacific. This was being built as a direct replacement for its postwar steel, welded boiler – using a drawing dating from 1955. If anyone knew about the technology then it was Meiningen.

With a thoroughly efficient and business-like design and build schedule that fitted perfectly with the overall project plan, the boiler was duly delivered on time to Darlington Locomotive Works in the summer of 2006. It was the defining moment when the completion of *Tornado* became a matter of 'when', not 'if'.

2000, autumn
Wheelset added

2004
The book value of Tornado's components reaches £1 million

2004, August 25
First synchronous smooth wheel motion

2007, June
Boiler/firebox assembly fitted to frame

2008, January 9
First static steaming

2008, February
Tender completed

2008, August 1
Tornado publicly launched at Darlington Locomotive Works

2008, August 7
Tornado entered into the TOPS (Total Operations Processing System)

2008, September 21
First passenger train hauled, Great Central Railway, Loughborough

2008, November 4
Main line testing begins, National Railway Museum, York

2008, November 18
Third and final main line test run completed, York. Tornado driven at 90mph, in excess of speed limit.

THE LAST STRETCH

ABOVE: Rays of sunshine penetrate the smoky interior of Darlington Locomotive Works on January 9, 2009, after the first fire was lit inside *Tornado's* boiler. ROBIN JONES

RIGHT: Dorothy Mather warms her hands after lighting the first fire in the boiler of *Tornado*, the first new main line steam locomotive built for the British main line since *Evening Star* in 1960, on January 9, 2008, a seminal moment in the history of the heritage sector. ROBIN JONES

With the finishing line in sight, there was one more final hurdle to surmount. It might be considered that, with all the major components in place and a sound funding strategy, the final assembly would be straightforward but if anything this was the most challenging part of all.

Items such as pipework and bracketry that had been tiny minutiae on the project plan for so long suddenly became significant bottlenecks as all workstreams converged into one single area, increasingly exercising the minds of David Elliott and his construction team at Darlington Locomotive Works.

More significantly, these tiny details consumed a seemingly disproportionate amount of time and resources and the trust soon found itself looking at a funding gap with success an agonising touching distance away.

Once again, an innovative solution was found. While conventional funding institutions would not entertain lending against what was effectively a pile of metal parts, an approach to Venturesome (part of the Charities Aid Foundation) and some generous supporters was more forthcoming and these bridging loans provided the trust with the necessary funds to maintain its momentum.

THE BOILER IS LIT

On a cold, dank January 2008 day in Darlington, a match was lit and, almost 18 years after the project was launched, a still incomplete *Tornado* had fire in its belly at last. After a careful few days of staged testing, the safety valves lifted successfully in front of the boiler inspector and the project had the first significant piece of approval paperwork under its belt.

The completion clock suddenly started ticking a whole lot louder. Any further delays here on in would reduce the operational life of the locomotive under that boiler certificate and so Darlington Locomotive Works frequently saw up to 12 people working on the locomotive simultaneously on some days, recreating scenes reminiscent of the great locomotive erecting shops of the past. Fitters and painters, electricians and coppersmiths alike worked around each other in a crescendo of activity to install and link up the final parts to create an operational locomotive.

Meanwhile, the trust's latter-day chairman, Mark Allatt, a marketing professional specialising in brand management, found himself with the prospect of launching a brand like no other. A carefully orchestrated plan to maximise the publicity potential was executed to perfection. The story was adopted by the BBC 24-hour news channel which recognised a quirky good news item when it saw one, celebrating that perennial old favourite – British endeavour to conquer seemingly impossible odds.

FIRST MOVEMENT

The morning of Friday, August 1, 2008 dawned bright and clear and a hitherto quiet corner of Darlington became the focus of a media scrum as the outside broadcast vans and journalists from all the major newspapers gathered round the brand new, 50th example of Arthur Peppercorn's A1 Pacific, looking surprisingly fetching in her coat of plain 'works' grey. The A1 Trust's website address – www.a1steam.

com – emblazoned on the tender sides, was an unashamedly modern twist.

At 11am, Darlington's mayor blew the whistle and waved the green flag and, live to a worldwide audience, *Tornado* moved gracefully along the short length of running line outside the works, Dorothy Mather proudly taking her place on the footplate. At that instant, one of the UK preservation

movement's greatest achievements also became a worldwide phenomenon.

The story since then is well known. *Tornado* worked from day one 'out of the box' and has gone on to wow both railway enthusiasts and the general public alike. While highlights are too many to mention, the royal naming on February 19, 2009, at York station by Prince Charles and the Duchess of Cornwall and

ABOVE: Still in works grey primer, *Tornado* arrives at Quorn & Woodhouse on the Great Central Railway on September 2008, its first day in passenger service. ROBIN JONES

RIGHT: *Tornado* lets off steam as it moves up the short running line outside Darlington Locomotive works in full view of the world's press on August 1, 2008. A1SLT

ABOVE: Apple green at last: *Tornado* in the National Railway Museum's workshops at York on December 10, 2012, after being painted. ROBIN JONES

RIGHT: Hero's welcome! King's Cross station was packed on February 7, 2009, for the first arrival of *Tornado*. ROBIN JONES

ABOVE: *Tornado* waits to depart Newcastle-upon-Tyne with the 'Peppercorn Pioneer' maiden trip on January 31, 2009. ROBIN JONES

ABOVE: Watched by A1 Trust chairman, Mark Allatt, and the Duchess of Cornwall, the Prince of Wales delivers his speech to formally launch *Tornado* into traffic at York station on February 19, 2009. ROBIN JONES

ABOVE: *Tornado* operations manager, Graeme Bunker, signs autographs after *Tornado's* faultless first passenger-carrying main line run on January 31, 2009. ROBIN JONES

ABOVE: On the footplate, the Prince of Wales is shown the intricacies of the newest locomotive to pull the Royal Train on February 19, 2009. ROBIN JONES

ABOVE: Passing Hadley Wood, *Tornado* heads 'The Talisman' southwards for its triumphant first entry into King's Cross on February 7, 2009. ROBIN JONES

participation in the BBC Top Gear 'Race to the North' feature highly in the annals of the locomotive's history to date, as does its participation in the Winton evacuation 70th anniversary special, a poignant and proud moment when the locomotive was not, for once, the centre of attention.

Central to this success has been the careful attention that continues to be paid to the loyal

band of *Tornado* covenantors. Such support is integral to the trust continuing to deliver on the "and operate" part of its mission statement. As well as regular news updates and mailshots, there is always at least one special event each year, based around the annual convention.

At such events, the covenators typically get special and exclusive access to 'their' locomotive, allowing the unique bond between

2008, December 13
First full livery unveiled (minus nameplates), LNER apple green, York

2009, January 13
'The Peppercorn Pioneer', the first main line passenger journey

2009, January 7
First run into King's Cross, with 'The Talisman'

2009, February 19
Tornado *officially named by the Prince of Wales and the Duchess of Cornwall at York station before hauling the Royal Train*

2009, March 23
East Midlands trains names Class 222 Meridian trains vehicle No. 60163 (part of set No. 222003) after No. 60163 Tornado *in a ceremony at Sheffield station alongside the A1.*

2009, April 18
Tornado's *first run out of King's Cross, with the 'Yorkshire Pullman'.*

2009, April 25
BBC Top Gear's race from London to Edinburgh filmed

2009, April 27
Tornado *moves to North Yorkshire Moors Railway to take part in a 10-day gala during which it hauled a rake of Gresley teak coaches for the first time*

2009, May 23
Institution of Mechanical Engineers presents Tornado *with Engineering Heritage Award at York*

ABOVE: With the Prince of Wales' motif on the smokebox, *Tornado* prepares to depart from York with the Royal Train on February 19, 2009. ROBIN JONES

ABOVE: On February 4, 2010, *Tornado* again hauled the Royal Train, this time taking Prince Charles to the Museum of Science & Industry in Manchester. There, the A1 met up with another new-build project, the replica Liverpool & Manchester Railway *Planet* 2-2-0. The original Liverpool & Manchester terminus is in the background. Very sadly, such trips will no longer possible once Network Rail's Ordsall Chord has cut off the route of the original line into the historic station and museum. ROBIN JONES

ABOVE: *Tornado* back at Waterloo after its December 21, 2009, circular tour of Kent, in which it picked up stranded commuters on the outward journey after wintry weather brought suburban electric services to a standstill. ROBIN JONES

ABOVE: *Tornado* heads the 'Yorkshire Pullman' through Doncaster on April 18, 2009. GEOFF GRIFFITHS/ A1SLT

people and machine to be continually reinforced. Early such events saw many visibly moved as they perhaps saw the completed locomotive for the first time in all its magnificence.

With the locomotive finally earning money rather than consuming vast quantities of it, combined with the continued, unwavering support of the loyal covenantors, the Venturesome and other loans were repaid – early – and the boiler bearer bond repayments have since been honoured.

The business plan and the mould-breaking approach to management of the project have well and truly been vindicated. At the trust's 25th anniversary annual convention in September 2015, in front of a packed room of covenantors, now vice-president David Champion symbolically made a presentation of that famous, wine-stained envelope to Mark Allatt, to live in perpetuity in the trust's archive. 'This will work!' It certainly did.

BELOW: East Coast Main Line superpower extraordinaire: lining up at Barrow Hill Roundhouse during the venue's 'Fab Four' gala on April 13, 2012 were, left to right, A4 No. 4464 *Bittern*, *Tornado*, A4 No. 4468 *Mallard*, A2 No. 60532 *Blue Peter* and V2 No. 4771 *Green Arrow*. ROBIN JONES

ABOVE: Newly reliveried in British Railways Brunswick green, *Tornado* passes through York station with its support coach on a test run to Scarborough on May 18, 2011. DAVE RODGERS

ABOVE: Blue-liveried *Tornado* entertains a throng of lineside cameramen as it powers past Strickland on February 27, 2014, with a rake of red-and-cream carriages appropriate to its period livery. BRIAN SHARPE

ABOVE: During a visit to the Nene Valley Railway, *Tornado* heads past Longueville on May 8, 2014. BRIAN SHARPE

2009, July 5
Tornado *clocks up 10,000 miles while hauling the 'Torbay Express'*

2009, September
Tornado *hauls the final leg from Harwich to Liverpool Street, of a special 'Winton Train' from Prague, marking the 70th anniversary of the intended last Kindertransport train organised by humanitarian Sir Nicholas Winton to take Jewish children out of Nazi Europe.*

2009, December 21
Rescues stranded commuters with 'The White Cliffs' tour after Kent's railways shut down after heavy snowfall, with EMUs unable to cope and the Eurostar trains frozen inside the Channel Tunnel.

2010, May 31
First main line failure, on 'The Canterbury Tornado*' tour*

2010, June 24
Beats previous record for fastest steam hauled railtour over Shap summit by 19 seconds

2010, June 16
Runs to Swanage for the first time, with UK Railtours' 'Purbeck Tornado*' from Waterloo.*

2010, November 20
Failed at Rugby on 'The Christmas Coronation' with low steam pressure after several problems en route, mainly owing to poor-quality Russian coal

2010, December
Returns to National Railway Museum for maintenance and to be repainted into lined Brunswick green

TORNADO: FIRST FOR FUNDRAISING!

Tornado is not only the market leader in the new-build sector in terms of widespread public appeal and main line operation.

For it to happen, it had to go where no other similar scheme had gone before – and raise vast amounts of money, persuading donors to believe in a scheme effectively drawn up on the back of an envelope.

Not only did The A1 Steam Locomotive Trust confound the critics and get the engine built, but it raised the £3 million needed to do it.

It wrote the fundraising textbook – and is still doing so.

The trust is permanently appealing for funds, to ensure that *Tornado* – which to many people is to the 21st century what *Flying Scotsman* was to the 20th – will stay running on the national network for generations to come.

REGULAR DONATIONS

A monthly payment made by standing order in units of £5 – "the price of a pint of beer a week" in 1990! In recognition of contributors' support, they will receive:

- A print showing *Tornado* hauling the south-bound 'Tyne Tornado' at sunset
- Access to view *Tornado* at all reasonable times
- The trust's newsletters on a regular basis
- The opportunity to attend the trust's annual convention
- The opportunity to attend days out at heritage railways
- Priority travel on trust-organised trains hauled by *Tornado*
- Their name inscribed on the Roll of Honour at Darlington Locomotive Works

ABOVE: By The A1 Steam Locomotive Trust's annual convention at Darlington Locomotive Works in October 2002, *Tornado* was sufficiently advanced to move on its wheels for the first time, and attention turned to the boiler, the item that's so often the biggest hurdle for new-build projects. Supporters were invited to raise £350,000 to fill the gap between the cab and the smokebox. The A1 Trust's fundraising acumen has blazed a trail for other projects to follow. A1SLT

Of course, single donations for any amount are most welcome at any time.

Steam fans are also invited to consider legacy donations. Anyone who would like to support No. 60163 *Tornado* through a legacy is invited to email legacy.coordinator@a1steam.com or telephone 01325 460163.

SILVER JUBILEE APPEAL - THE 163 PACIFICS CLUB

Since 2008 The A1 Steam Locomotive Trust has worked hard to repay the £1 million debt incurred during No. 60163 *Tornado's* construction.

The final step is to purchase its tender, which is currently on a 15-year lease from William Cook Cast Products Ltd.

In 2006 Andrew Cook, chairman of WCCP, offered to pay for the construction of *Tornado's* tender. The trust now needs to raise £200,000 to purchase the tender from WCCP when the lease expires in 2021 – thereby making the trust debt free and finally completing the project that it embarked upon in 1990.

Although *Tornado* carries the number '60163' – the next in the Peppercorn class A1 series following No. 60162 *Saint Johnstoun* – its pre-nationalisation LNER number would have been '163'. If 163 people were to donate £10 per month over the eight years until the trust needs to purchase the tender (or alternatively make a one-off donation of £960) with the addition of Gift Aid (£2.50 per month or £240 one-off), this would raise £195,600.

Those who take part will receive:

- A numbered certificate (1-163) recording the details of the donation and the number/name of their favourite ex-LNER express passenger Pacific from the Gresley class A3s/A4s, Thompson class A1/1 and Peppercorn class A1s.
- Their name inscribed on the official Roll of Honour in Darlington Locomotive Works detailing the Pacific sponsored.
- Entry into a draw for a main line footplate ride on *Tornado*.

There are many other ways in which support can help towards the operation of *Tornado*.

Enjoy meeting people? The trust has established a successful team, which travels on trains and attends events to promote *Tornado* and sell the trust's merchandise. More people are always needed to help with this, wherever they live.

The trust is always on the lookout for volunteers to help with engineering. Experience is useful but many jobs on the locomotive require the services of a fitter's mate so qualifications are not essential.

For further information on any aspect of supporting No. 60163 *Tornado* visit www.a1steam.com, email enquiries@a1steam.com, call 01325 460163 or write to Darlington Locomotive Works, FREEPOST RTJS-XECR-XARL, The A1 Steam Locomotive Trust, Hopetown Lane, Darlington DL3 6RQ.

The trust's online store can be found at www.a1steam.com

RIP DOROTHY MATHER: FIRST AND LAST LADY OF STEAM

The steam world was in mourning following the death of A1 Steam Locomotive Trust president, Dorothy Mather – arguably the last direct link with the age of the Big Four locomotive engineers.

The widow of LNER Chief Mechanical Engineer, Arthur H Peppercorn, designer of the A1 and A2 Pacifics, who had lit the first fire in new-build *Tornado*, died on Tuesday, November 10, 2015 at the age of 99. She had been ill for two years.

Born Dorothy Patricia Louch in 1916, she grew up in a railway family near Doncaster and, following a stint of voluntary work during the Second World War and working for the regional coal board, she ended up in the Doncaster Works drawing office. It was there that she met Arthur Peppercorn, who had become CME in 1946, and despite their 26-year age gap, they married in 1948.

It was during this period that his A2s and the A1s entered traffic. Leaving BR Eastern Region in good shape, Arthur retired at the

end of 1949, much loved and admired, only to die prematurely in 1951 at the age of 62.

A few years later, Dorothy met Col William Mather, OBE, TD and an ex-LNER employee. In due course they married, bought a country house near Stokesley in North Yorkshire and settled down.

As Bill's health failed, they moved to a more modern house and Dorothy nursed him until his death. A widow once again, albeit one with an ever-wider circle of friends and Bill's many nephews and nieces.

In August 1993, Dorothy was approached by the trust about the A1 Project. She was sufficiently impressed to join informally at first, and from there her involvement grew.

She attended BSD Leeds on July 13, 1994 to start the CNC machine that cut *Tornado's* frameplates, the trust's first convention that September, and at Tyseley Locomotive Works in December for the ceremony marking erection of the frameplates.

Trust chairman, Mark Allatt, said: "She attended many A1 Trust occasions since then, always immaculately dressed, always interested and courteous to everyone she met. In September 1995 she became joint vice-president, later president.

"Not just a figurehead, she did a tremendous job for the trust in countless interviews with press and television. She proved quite as vital as our ISO 9000 quality standard because, if *Tornado* was good enough for her, it would be good enough for Arthur Peppercorn.

"Those of us who knew her will miss her quiet dignity, kindness and valued contributions to any conversation about the work of her first husband. She has provided enormous encouragement and support to trust members, particularly council members

"Because of the age difference between her and Arthur Peppercorn, she mixed in social circles with people such as Sir Nigel Gresley, Sir William Stanier and Edward Thompson."

ABOVE: *Tornado* at Scarborough on November 4, 2008, midway through a test run. A1SLT

THE DAY WHEN *TORNADO* HIT 90MPH TWICE

Tornado has twice reached speeds of 90mph on the main line, one of its former drivers publicly revealed.

Speaking at a public session on Saturday, October 26, 2013 the first day of the National Railway Museum's award-winning Mallard 75 Autumn Great Gathering of all six surviving LNER Gresley A4 Pacifics, Dave Court said that he took No. 60163 to 90mph twice on its third test run, over the East Coast Main Line between Newcastle and York on November 18, 2008.

Dave, who drove A3 Pacific No. 4472 *Flying Scotsman* through 17 states on its ill-fated tour of the USA in the Sixties, which left owner Alan Pegler bankrupt, told the audience that *Tornado* reached 90mph before Darlington and again south of the town while approaching Croft during the run.

The test train was being handled by Train Operating Company DB Schenker, with no input from the locomotive's builder and owner, The A1 Steam Locomotive Trust, on the day.

No prior dispensation had been obtained by DB Schenker, the body solely responsible for the test runs, for the A1 to run above the maximum permitted speed of 75mph.

"The design speed is 90mph and I took it up to 90mph with 14 coaches on," Dave told an audience of around 150 at the museum, as part of a five-member panel of former drivers and firemen who had handled A4s under British Railways.

"I got suspended on the last run for speeding," he told the meeting, which was open to members of the public.

Rumours that *Tornado* had reached 90mph had long been circulating among the enthusiast fraternity, but no official confirmation had ever been given.

The late-night test run, which ended early the following day, would have seen *Tornado* run in grey primer, before its first livery was applied at the museum. A1 Trust chairman, Mark Allatt, declined to comment.

The trust has been talking for several years about applying to have *Tornado* registered to run at 90mph, but no date for any official test run to this end has been set.

Dave Court, who drove *Tornado* on all of its three inaugural test trips, also revealed at the seminar that one A4, No. 60009 *Union of South Africa*, had run at an average speed of 80mph on June 15, 2004, while hauling a Steamy Affairs' trip from Newcastle to York with 13 coaches on, in conjunction with the museum's Railfest 2004 event.

On June 29, 2013, A4 No. 4464 *Bittern* set a new preservation-era steam locomotive speed record with a maximum speed of 92.8mph near Arlesey in Bedfordshire on the first of three authorised high-speed runs to mark the 75th anniversary of *Mallard's* 126mph world steam speed record in 1938. Earlier, on May 29, *Bittern* set a new official record by reaching 90mph during late-night tests on the Great Western Main Line, but with prior dispensation. •

On Wednesday, January 9, 2008, she lit the first fire in *Tornado's* boiler at the trust's Darlington Locomotive Works, and on August 1 that year, she rode on its footplate in the works yard with the locomotive making its inaugural run for the media still in grey primer, stating: "My husband would be proud".

On December 13, 2008, Dorothy, who lived in Hutton Rudby in North Yorkshire, unveiled *Tornado* in its apple green livery at the National Railway Museum.

She also attended the official naming of *Tornado* at York station by Prince Charles and the Duchess of Cornwall on February 19, 2009, and met the royal couple on the platform before *Tornado* had the honour of hauling the Royal Train to Leeds.

Dorothy's funeral took place at Faceby parish church in North Yorkshire at 11.30am on November 18, 2015, after which she was buried next to her mother and her second husband.

RIGHT: Immaculately presented as always, Dorothy beams with delight as the smoke from *Tornado's* boiler fills the interior of Darlington Locomotive Works for the first time. ROBIN JONES

2011, September 21
Power output of 3000idhp produced while climbing Beattock bank on with the 'The Caledonian Tornado'

2012, April 13-15
Tornado lines up alongside LNER greats including Bittern, Mallard, Blue Peter, The Great Marquess *and* Green Arrow *at Barrow Hill Roundhouse, for the 'Fab Four' gala sponsored by The Railway Magazine*

2012, November 24
Tornado appears in British Railways' express passenger blue livery for the first time, hauling the 'Cathedrals Express' from Paddington to Shrewsbury

2012, November 25
Runs to Didcot Railway Centre for the official presentation of the new livery by A1 Trust chairman, Mark Allatt

2014, October 4
After withdrawal for an intermediate overhaul, Tornado's boiler is lifted at Barrow Hill and returned to DB Meiningen

2015, June 17
Tornado returns – repainted in apple green livery – after its overhaul, with a test run from Darlington to Millerhill depot

2015, September 13
Tornado runs from Edinburgh to Tweedbank, the terminus of the new Borders Railway, the rebuilt northern section of the legendary Waverley Route, for the first time.

Chapter 10

Resteaming the
Lynton & Barnstaple

Rebuilding a complete 19-mile narrow gauge railway piece by piece is in itself an awesome project, but one of its trademark locomotive designs has run again over its first section.

The Ffestiniog Railway's Boston Lodge Works has not only built new steam locomotives to fulfil the need for motive power and plug the missing gaps in its own heritage. It has done the same for the legendary narrow gauge line, the Lynton & Barnstaple Railway.

Running between the two North Devon towns for 19 miles, the 1ft 11½in gauge line opened on May 11, 1898 with public service commencing five days later. Intended to link the popular resorts of Lynton and Lynmouth to the national network, the line twisted and turned through hill pastures and Exmoor scenery, serving sparsely populated villages; for much of its existence running at a loss.

Taken over by the Southern Railway in 1923, it succumbed to competition from cars and lorries, and was one of a swathe of closures of classic British narrow gauge lines in the mid-Thirties. The last train ran on September 29, 1935.

Famously, the next day a wreath of bronze chrysanthemums was laid on the Barnstaple Town station stop block. Sent by Woody Bay resident paymaster Captain Thomas Alfred Woolf, RN (retired) it bore a black-edged, hand-written card on which was written: "To Barnstaple & Lynton Railway, with regret and sorrow from a constant user and admirer. Perchance it is not dead but sleepeth".

It became the dream of many a railway enthusiast to wake the L&B from that sleep and the Lynton & Barnstaple Railway Association was formed in 1979 with that aim. Not only did it seek – and still does – the complete reinstatement of the railway throughout, but an early aim was to recreate it exactly as it was, with rebuilt original carriages and replica locomotives.

Woody Bay station, at 964ft above sea level the highest in Southern England, was purchased by the Lynton and Barnstaple

Railway Company in 1995 and, after much effort, a short section of railway reopened to passengers in 2004. This was extended in 2006, with steam- and diesel-hauled trains running between Woody Bay and a new, temporary terminus at Killington Lane a mile to the west. Revivalists also bought two stations, Chelfham next to the line's landmark viaduct, and Snapper Halt.

In October 2007, the railway announced plans for reinstating enough trackbed to reopen nine miles of the route, linking Woody Bay to both Lynton (at a new terminus on an extension to the original, closer to the town) and a new station at Wistlandpound Reservoir. As a first phase, the line would be extended to Blackmoor, where a new engine shed and workshop would be built.

Yet what about motive power for a restored line, if the aim was to replicate the original?

Sadly, four of the L&B's locomotives, Manning Wardle of Leeds 2-6-2Ts *Exe*, *Taw*

BELOW: Carrying Southern Railway Maunsell green livery as No. 190, and making its third visit to the Lynton & Barnstaple Railway, Manning Wardle replica 2-6-2T *Lyd* climbs the 1-in-50 approach to Woody Bay on October 4 during the line's 2014 autumn gala, with the award-winning rake of original coaches. A fourth rebuilt coach was delivered in April 2015. TONY NICHOLSON

and *Yeo*, and Baldwin 2-42 *Lyn*, were sold for scrap after closure. A fifth locomotive, Manning Wardle *Lew*, effectively disappeared without trace and into the mists of myth and legend.

Britain's top narrow gauge lines such as the Ffestiniog, Talyllyn, Welshpool & Llanfair and Vale of Rheidol railways today are fortunate enough to have retained original locomotives.

Lew was used by the contractors dismantling its railway before being sold for use in South America. In September 1936, *Lew* was loaded on to the *SS Sabor* destined for Recife (then Pernambuco) in Brazil.

Nothing has been heard of *Lew* again, leading to multiple theories about its fate. With shipping records destroyed in the Second World War, nobody knows exactly where it ended up, whether it was dumped overboard as a means of lightening the ship in a storm as often postulated, whether it was scrapped in 1957, as once reported, or simply left to rust away in the jungle.

There is nothing like an absence of facts to engender a legend of colossal proportions. Take King Arthur for instance. There are only a handful of pieces of evidence to indicate (not prove) that he even existed, but the legend of the Romano-British leader has inspired countless books, poetry, works of art and films for centuries. Compare and contrast him with King Alfred, who similarly fought off invaders, this time the Vikings,

ABOVE: Southern Railway No. 188 *Lew*, then just a year old, and sister Manning Wardle 2-6-2T *Taw* doublehead a service from Barnstaple in 1926. LBR

and who covered basically the same ground as Arthur, and of whom we have numerous written records. He has had by comparison with Arthur scant interest from writers, artists or the silver screen.

Lew has become the Holy Grail of railway preservation, with attempts made by both British and US enthusiasts either to locate it in South America, or discover its true fate, but all so far in vain.

If *Lew* was ever rediscovered and repatriated, current thinking is that because of its historical importance, it would be more likely to end up on display at the National Railway Museum in York than rebuilt for use on the revived L&B. In any case, it would almost certainly be more cost effective to build a replica from scratch.

And here unfolds a somewhat complex story of new-build projects.

WOODY BAY'S FIRST NEW-BUILD

The first steam locomotive to run at Woody Bay was *Emmet*, a freelance 0-4-0T built by Jim Haylock, owner of the Moors Valley Railway near Ringwood in Dorset.

This locomotive was not a total new-build by any means.

It started off as Orenstein & Koppel type RL3 four-wheeled diesel No. 21159, which was used in Germany during the Second World War and was later imported via George W Bungey Ltd at Hayes Middlesex and sold to the ECC ball clay mines at Norden near Swanage.

In November 1972, it was purchased by Hampshire Light Railway Society & Museum in Durley, Hampshire. Later acquired by Jim, in 2003 it was converted into a steam locomotive and named after a cat who lived on the moors Valley Railway.

Emmet, which weighed 6½ tons and was just 12ft long, visited the L&B throughout 2003-04, but it was not possible to use it on the first heritage-era passenger trains because it was not fitted with air brakes during its loan period.

Public passenger trains over the first reopened section of the L&B commenced on Saturday, July 17. However, maroon-liveried *Emmet* could only haul demonstration works trains. It was left to borrowed Hunslet four-wheel diesel hydraulic No. 6348 of 1975 which came to Woody Bay on a two-year loan from Wansbeck District Council, and was renamed *Exmoor Ranger* in commemoration of the 50th anniversary of Exmoor National Park, to haul the first modern-day L&B passenger trains. A former NCB mining locomotive, it normally runs on the Woodhorn Colliery Museum's QEII Country Park Railway near Ashington in Northumberland.

Emmet returned to its owner at the end of the 2005 season. It has since visited other heritage lines, and in September 2013, ran on the short length of track relaid at the award-winning Purbeck Mineral & Mining Museum at Norden... on the route of the ball clay tramway where it had operated as a diesel – surely a first for new-build steam! Indeed, it was the first steam in action on the Isle of Purbeck's ball clay lines since 1953.

RIGHT: The first steam locomotive to run on the revived Lynton & Barnstaple railway was Jim Haylock's freelance 0-4-0T *Emmet*, pictured at Woody Bay in May 2004. ROBIN JONES

THE FIRST NEW L&B LOCOMOTIVE

The first new-build locomotive to be based on a L&B design, that of the four Manning Wardles, was never intended for use in Britain.

A full-size 2ft gauge Manning Wardle-style 2-6-2T, named *Green Breeze*, was built by Winson Engineering of Daventry in 1998 for the Usui Pass Museum near Tokyo and exported in the same year. Works number 19, was described as combination of the original design with later modifications, and is still running there today.

Whether or not there will be a future attempt to bring it back to Britain remains to be seen.

Winson Engineering built and rebuilt narrow gauge and miniature steam locomotives and rolling stock during the 1990s.

The firm was founded in the mid-1980s, although it was not incorporated until March 21, 1990. The engineering works were initially at the harbour in Porthmadog, a stone's throw from the Ffestiniog terminus. In 1988, the company moved to nearby Penrhyndeudraeth, and again, to Daventry, in 1995.

In June 2001 the company went into receivership and subsequently closed. During its existence, it had built five locomotives for the 15in gauge Bure Valley Railway in Norfolk (including the rebuild of a diesel to steam) and one for the revived Corris Railway.

ABOVE: *Green Breeze*, a Lynton & Barnstaple-style Manning Wardle replica 2-6-2Y built by the now-defunct Winson engineering, is in regular service at a museum line in Japan. USUI PASS MUSEUM

ENTER THE FFESTINIOG

While L&B revivalists rebuilt original carriages, which had been retrieved from private use in back gardens, as a short gap measure a series of carriages from the railway at Thorpe Park theme park in Surrey were pressed into service, repainted into original L&B livery.

However, no original and therefore authentic steam locomotives were available, so if the modern L&B wanted a Manning Wardle, it would have to build its own from scratch.

Back in 1996 it was thought appropriate that because *Yeo* had been the first of three engines delivered by Manning Wardle in 1897 it should be the first replica to be built for the new L&B. A project to construct the locomotive was launched, even though the revivalists had only just bought Woody Bay station the previous year and did not have an inch of track on which to run it.

Following initial fundraising, a set of frames for a *Yeo* replica were built by Winson Engineering around 2000.

However, the *Yeo* project quickly lost impetus, because also in 1996, a project to build a new L&B Manning Wardle was launched by the Ffestiniog Railway at Boston Lodge Works. It was to be closely based on *Lew*, the locomotive supplied to the line by the Southern Railway in 1925.

This locomotive, to be named *Lyd* after the L&B tradition of choosing names of Devon rivers with three letters, first moved under its own steam at Boston Lodge at 1.46pm on August 5, 2010 as the culmination of a project which was undertaken in fits and starts as money and resources became available.

Later the same day, *Lyd* made its first trip across the Cob to Porthmadog Harbour station where it shunted five carriages without difficulty.

Tts first scheduled appearance of the £300,000 locomotive came at sister line the Welsh Highland Railway's 'Superpower' event on September 11-12.

After that, it appeared at the Launceston Steam Railway, whose owner Nigel Bowman had supported the project throughout.

However, the climax to its debut month was undoubtedly its visit to the autumn gala at Woody Bay on September 25-26, when for the first time in the 75 years since the line closed, a L&B Manning Wardle locomotive was heard climbing the 1-in-50 gradient to Woody Bay.

Thousands packed the little line's autumn gala to see the 'new Lew' haul former L&B coach No. 15

RIGHT: *Lyd* has never been passed off as a direct replica of *Lew*, although the pair are very similar. However, the Boston Lodge Works maker's plate arranged the names of the engineers involved in the *Lyd* project to read Lewin, Yates, Evans & Whalley, which strategically aligned give the game away! ROBIN JONES

BELOW: New-build Manning Wardle-style 2-6-2T *Lyd*, closely based on the Lynton & Barnstaple Railway's missing *Lew*, made its debut on the North Devon line at the autumn gala in 2010. It is seen ascending the grade to Woody Bay with two coaches also loaned by the Ffestiniog Railway, which have L&B links. It is carrying a replica of the wreath laid at Barnstaple Town station the day after the original line closed in 1935, with a note that read: "Perchance it is not dead... but sleepeth." ROBIN JONES

ABOVE: *Lyd* slows on the final approach to Woody Bay station during its Lynton & Barnstaple Railway debut on September 24, 2010. ROBIN JONES

ABOVE: *Lyd* crosses Britannia Bridge at Porthmadog on a Lynton & Barnstaple charter train running over the Welsh Highland Railway on May 22, 2011. The note on the wreath reads: "Perchance it is awake". ANDREW THOMAS

and Ffestiniog Railway observation car No. 102, which had been based on an L&B design. Both had been loaned for the occasion by Ffestiniog general manager, Paul Lewin, to run behind *Lyd* for the big occasion.

Although clearly externally similar to *Lew*, *Lyd* utilises several modern design and construction techniques to improve overall efficiency. A FR spokesman said: "The outshopping of Lyd means that Boston Lodge – the oldest operational railway works in the world – now holds the unique accolade of having built new steam locomotives in the 19th, 20th and 21st centuries, starting in 1879 with Double Fairlie *Merddin Emrys*, which is still in regular use today."

Lyd appeared in plain black livery until final adjustments

were completed. In December 2010, *Lyd* was painted in early 1950s British Railways lined black livery with the number 30190, showing what might have been had the line not closed in 1935, and had, like the Vale of Rheidol, Welshpool & Llanfair and Corris railways, passed into public ownership after Nationalisation in 1948.

In August 2011, it was taken into the paint shop at Boston Lodge to be turned out in the livery everyone wanted to see; Southern Railway lined Maunsell green, as carried by *Lew* on the L&B, and numbered 190.

Lyd returned to Woody Bay for the May 2013 especially to haul No.7 and No.17; the first two original L&B carriages to be restored by volunteers.

ABOVE: What could have happened had the Lynton & Barnstaple Railway survived until nationalisation: *Lyd* in mock BR mixed-traffic livery with the fictitious BR number 30190! It is pictured on the Ffestiniog Railway on December 30, 2010. GLENN WILLIAMS

ABOVE: Newly repainted *Lyd* at Harbour station, Porthmadog, on December 14, 2011. FR

ABOVE: *Lyd* back at Boston Lodge on September 6, 2011, being repainted into the livery that all Lynton & Barnstaple enthusiasts had so long waited for. ANDREW THOMAS

ABOVE: Just as if it were 1935 again: *Lyn* resplendent in Southern Railway livery stands in Woody Bay station with two original carriages. PHIL WATERFIELD

A YANKEE BORN IN HEREFORDSHIRE!

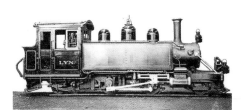

ABOVE: Baldwin's official manufacturer's photograph of the original *Lyn*. 762 CLUB

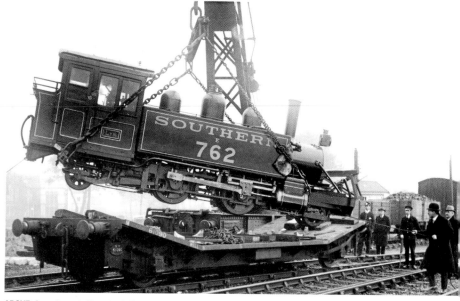

ABOVE: *Lyn* returns to Barnstaple Town station from the Southern Railway's Eastleigh Works following overhaul in 1929. 762 CLUB

Visitors to Woody Bay during the 2010 autumn gala would have also seen the cab of another new-build locomotive taking shape, that of a replica of the Baldwin *Lyn*.

The original *Lyn* was a 2-4-2T built in Philadelphia in 1898. Between July 1897 and January 1898, employees of many British engineering companies were striking in an attempt to win the right to an eight-hour working day, leaving UK locomotive builders with large backlogs of unfulfilled orders.

Needing an extra locomotive, the L&B looked to the far side of the Atlantic.

Baldwin effectively 'flatpacked' *Lyn*, which was shipped as a kit of parts, and for assembly at the L&B's Pilton works near Barnstaple.

Like all the locomotives on the L&B, *Lyn* was named after a local river with a three-letter name. Its distinctive American outliner, meant that *Lyn* was commonly referred to by the staff as 'The Yankee'.

Despite a few teething problems, *Lyn* was a popular and distinctive engine that was also the most powerful on the line – on occasion pulling five-coach trains, one more than normally allowed.

After the L&B became part of the Southern Railway, *Lyn* was given a number: E (for Eastleigh – the Southern shed Pilton was

attached to) 762. *Lyn* was taken to Eastleigh Works for a major overhaul in 1928, returning the following year in Southern green livery and carrying the number E762 on the side tanks, as well as the original nameplates on the cab sides.

After the auction following the closure of the line in 1935, *Lyn* was reduced to scrap very quickly with only the nameplates surviving.

In 2008, L&B revivalists formed the 762 Club, taking its name from the original *Lyn*'s Southern Railway number. The idea was that 350 supporters would each buy a share for £762 and raise the £266,700 needed to build the locomotive.

Sufficient numbers took up the share offer for a serious start to be made. A contract for a new all-welded boiler was awarded to Bennett Boilers of Highbridge in Somerset, and although based on the original dimensions will feature many improvements in detail.

The contract for the erection of the finished locomotive was awarded by the 762 Club – a registered charity – to Alan Keef Ltd in Ross-on-Wye, and on April 14, 2011, the first two of eight wheels were cast at the Trefoil Steel Company plant in Tinsley, Sheffield, and later machined.

By 2013, *Lyn*'s wooden cab had been built, along with the boiler and most fittings, wheels, cylinders and many other components. Like

ABOVE: Local artist, Eric Leslie, is renowned for his beautiful watercolours of the Lynton & Barnstaple Railway. Scenes past, present and future regularly appear in the L&B Association's quarterly magazine. This one depicts the new *Lyn* heading a rake of original coaches on the revived railway. 762 CLUB

ABOVE AND BELOW: The first wheels for *Lyn* being cast in Sheffield on April 14, 2011. TREFOIL

ABOVE: Lynton & Barnstaple Railway Trust chairman, Peter Miles, explaining to a reporter from the North Devon Journal how the 16ft boiler of the new *Lyn* works, when it was displayed at Woody Bay during the autumn gala in 2013. TONY NICHOLSON

ABOVE: The wooden cab of new L&B Baldwin 2-4-2T *Lyn* built by AWH Joinery of Luton on display at Woody Bay in 2010, along with a pattern for one of the driving wheels. ROBIN JONES

the original, the cab was constructed out of American ash.

CAD and modern engineering techniques are being employed to ensure that, while the finished locomotive remains true to the original in appearance, it will perform much more efficiently and be easier to maintain and operate.

The project's technical director Peter Best said: "*Lyn* is the most suitable of the original locomotives for the line in the short to medium term, being efficient, flexible and comfortable – very necessary given the exposed location of the railway.

"We are building a new locomotive that will have all the appearance of the original – in the condition that it returned from a rebuild at Eastleigh works in 1929. However, we are intending to provide an efficient, easy-to-maintain and powerful engine that is fit for very many years of service in the 21st century.

ABOVE: The frames of the new *Lyn* at Alan Keef's Ross-on-Wye works in 2015. 762 CLUB

ABOVE: The newly delivered connecting rods for the new *Lyn*. 762 CLUB

So, for example, there will be roller bearings for the wheels, coupling and connecting rods, higher-boiler pressure, welded tanks and various other improvements."

Lyn – which was 96% complete in October 2015 with just the brake assembly, ashpan

and manifold to build, may steam in 2016. It will be finished in the colours and configuration of the original as it returned from overhaul in 1929.

The latest information can be found at www.762club.com

AND WHAT ABOUT *YEO*?

In 2007, with the railway running and relying on hired steam locomotives, L&B trustees decided that in view of the *Lyd* project proceeding rapidly, and it being unlikely that there would ever be sufficient funds to support the simultaneous construction of two Manning Wardle replicas, that efforts should be diverted from *Yeo* towards the restoration of Kerr Stuart Joffre 0-6-0T No. 2451 of 1915, which the line had by then owned for more than two decades. This locomotive was restored to running order and named *Axe*, in line with the three-letter river name tradition.

However, the new L&B had strengthened its tie with the Ffestiniog over the completion of *Lyd* and its debut on 'home' territory.

Lessons from the construction and operation of *Lyd* will be incorporated into the design of the new *Yeo*, which latest estimates indicate will cost in the region of £500,000.

Following the demise of Winson engineering, *Yeo's* frames were stored for several years at the Gartell Light Railway in Somerset before being brought to Woody Bay for display.

The L&B revival has always been at a colossal disadvantage when compared with its Welsh counterparts. Most of their revival schemes had access to a near-complete line: on the L&B, the track had gone in 1935 and all 19 miles and station buildings sold off piecemeal. Before any railway can run over the whole length again, parcels of land big and small have to be bought.

That will in itself involve a marathon fundraising effort, but it is do-able. What it will mean, however, that there is no capacity left for raising cash for new-build projects.

However, even for a line extended to five miles in length, more reliable motive power will be needed – most likely in the shape of a 2-6-2T, but clearly a considerable fundraising initiative will be required before the *Yeo* project can recommence.

The plan is to have it constructed entirely under contract, with the timescale for completion, as always, dependent on the availability of funds. ●

ABOVE: *Yeo* runs again at Woody Bay! This superb one-third scale 7¼in gauge model of 2-6-2T *Yeo*, the first locomotive delivered to the L&B by Manning Wardle in 1897, was bought by the railway's Chief Mechanical Engineer Stuart Wells. It was built by Milner in 1979 and has seen service on the South Devon Railway's miniature line at Buckfastleigh, on the Gorse Blossom Railway near Newton Abbot, at Powderham Castle near Exeter and at Bolebroke Castle in East Sussex. It is pictured in operation during the L&B's September 2010 gala. ROBIN JONES

ABOVE: In 2013, Jim Haylock's freelance new-build *Emmet* returned to the Isle of Purbeck, where it had it its original incarnation as a diesel and worked on the 2ft gauge ball clay tramways. It is pictured on the Purbeck Mineral & Mining Museum line at Norden on September 3. ANREW PM WRIGHT

ABOVE: The frames of the new *Yeo* on display at Woody Bay. Tradition has it that the fames of a locomotive comprise its identity, so technically another new Manning Wardle exists! L&B

Chapter 11

Bringing back Brunel's
broad gauge

Rendered extinct by the march of 'progress', nobody in Britain had seen a GWR broad gauge locomotive run for nearly a century, until the National Railway Museum built a 'new' one. Now we have two, both now based at Didcot Railway Centre.

ABOVE: The replica *Fire Fly* and *Iron Duke* 2-2-2s line up at Didcot Railway Centre on April 19, 2014. FRANK DUMBLETON

The march of progress has not always bestowed humanity with the best products that science can deliver.

Discovery, invention and innovation are all well and good, but their success so often depends on marketing. The better product often loses out because it misses the bandwagon. It has been argued that such was the case with rail transport.

Most railways in Britain, Europe and the United States are built to a standard Stephenson gauge of 4ft 8½in, which was a figure broadly derived from the space between the wheels of horse-drawn coal carts in the North East. Yet what if the world's railways had been built to a wider gauge, one that could carry bigger payloads?

When Isambard Kingdom Brunel was appointed as engineer to the Great Western Railway at the age of 27, he insisted that

he would not build a railway on the cheap. He wanted to be given the scope to build the best railway of them all, or else he was not interested in the post.

He had been unimpressed by the Liverpool & Manchester, which had been built to standard gauge by its main early protagonist, George Stephenson.

Brunel showed his disdain for the often uncomfortable motion of the four-wheel carriages on the Liverpool & Manchester. His railway would be taking in the well-to-do to places such as Bath, and he wanted accommodation that would suit them accordingly. So, he sought a wider gauge, which would allow bigger rolling stock and locomotives with wheels placed outside of their frames, so as to allow for bigger boilers and greater speed. The lower centre of gravity would allow trains to run more steadily and safely.

He wanted to reduce the rolling resistance of carriage and wagon stock. A wider gauge would allow larger wheel diameters, lessening the effect of friction while facilitating the ability to build wide carriages with bodies mounted as low as possible, minimising air resistance. In short, the bigger they are, the more they will carry and the faster they will go.

In the defeated Great Western Railway Bill of 1834, the gauge for the proposed new railway had been restricted to standard. By the time the next Bill was lodged, Brunel wanted a gauge of 7ft and so asked Lord Shaftesbury, who was drafting the Bill, to leave out the gauge limitation.

When questioned by a member of Shaftesbury's staff about the problem of the break of gauge, and the fact that his trains would not be interchangeable with standard gauge lines, Brunel said he did not consider the problem to be significant. In this respect, the legendary engineer lacked foresight and displayed tunnel vision.

He was clearly aware of the potential problems with break of gauge, and knew that building broad gauge would be more expensive because of the larger tunnels, cuttings and embankments that would be needed, but did he foresee the extent to which the problem would literally divide Britain for the rest of that century?

By and large, Brunel took the parochial view that his railway would serve only the region through which it was built, and did not need to take account of the gauge of other railways.

When debating the Bill, and hearing all sorts of absurd objections to steam railways, MPs failed to pick up on the omission of a gauge clause – leaving the door open for Brunel to choose his gauge.

On September 15, 1835, he proposed a broad gauge of between 6ft 10in and 7ft to the GWR board, producing mathematical and scientific reasons as to why it was superior to Stephenson's system, rather than developing 4ft 8½in gauge to suit his needs, and on October 29, 1835, the directors approved his gauge of 7ft 0¼in.

Using the benefits of his broad gauge, Brunel's GWR Locomotive Superintendent, Daniel Gooch, produced designs of locomotive, which in their day, were the fastest in the world.

The GWR and associated companies' broad gauge eventually stretched to Penzance and west Wales, and northwards as far as Wolverhampton. However, where broad gauge met standard gauge lines serving the rest of the country, passengers and goods had to be inconveniently taken off one train and on to the other.

As the national rail network took shape, Parliament set up a Gauge Commission to decide which gauge was the best. Its findings conceded that broad gauge locomotives had superior performance, but ruled in favour of standard gauge, which was more widespread, and ordered no more broad gauge lines to be built – a ruling ignored by Brunel.

ABOVE: The 21st-century *Fire Fly* is seen coupled to a full-size replica covered broad gauge coach on Didcot Railway Centre's broad gauge demonstration line on April 4, 2010. FRANK DUMBLETON
LEFT: Replica GWR broad gauge signal at Didcot. ROBIN JONES

ABOVE: Broad and mixed gauge track on the Didcot Railway Centre's demonstration line. ROBIN JONES

THE LOCOMOTIVE ENGINEERING WIZARD

While Brunel was one of the greatest engineers of the Victorian age and is renowned for his ground-breaking, bridges, tunnels and cuttings, when it came to choosing steam locomotives for his broad gauge railway, he was way out of his depth.

Out of a total of 19 locomotives that he ordered, most of them were barely fit for purpose.

Most successful of all was *North Star*, built by Robert Stephenson & Co and delivered by barge to Maidenhead Bridge on November 28, 1937. On May 31 the following year, it hauled the inaugural train for the GWR's directors.

However, help came with Brunel's appointment of his first locomotive engineer, Daniel Gooch, who was then just 21 years old. Sharing Brunel's enthusiasm for broad gauge, he improved *North Star's* performance, and soon went on to design his own locomotives.

A total of 62 examples of Gooch's Firefly class 2-2-2s were built by seven different outside manufacturers over two years.

The first, named *Fire Fly*, was built by Jones, Turner & Evans of Newton-le-Willows. Delivered on March 12, 1840, it made its debut 13 days later, hauling two carriages with 40 passengers on board and a truck from Paddington to Reading. It reportedly covered the 30¾ miles from Twyford to Paddington in 37 minutes, an average speed of 50mph. Back in 1840, such speeds were unheard of.

This was the era of huge copper domes, stovepipe chimneys, boilers shielded with wooden planks, a lack of cab roofs or weatherboarding to offer protection to drivers and firemen, and gigantic central driving wheels: the bigger they were, the faster the locomotive ran.

During the abovementioned Gauge Commission trials, Firefly *Ixion* exceeded 60mph and ran from London to Didcot with a 71-ton load at nearly 55mph , far superior to what standard gauge rivals could offer.

Fireflys were used on the postal trains between Paddington and Bristol introduced from February 1, 1855.

Eventually, Gooch saw that the way ahead for the expanding broad gauge network was to build its own engines, rather than buy them in, and to cut a long story short, a site in the market town of Swindon was chosen for the GWR workshops.

The first all-Swindon locomotive was appropriately named *Great Western*.

A 2-2-2, it looked like a Firefly, but was an improvement on the design. At a time when the GWR was under intense political pressure to justify its use of broad gauge, it told Gooch to produce a "colossal locomotive working with all speed" to prove a point.

Outshopped in April 1846 after just three months, it was a world beater from the outset. Its 8ft driving wheels saw it reach

ABOVE: The original *Fire Fly* emerges from Box Tunnel's classic western portal. This coloured sketch, based on a contemporary work by JC Bourne, remains one of the distinctive images of Brunel's broad gauge system.

ABOVE: A watercolour by Sean Bolan depicts one of Daniel Gooch's Iron Duke locomotives at Chippenham station around 1850. NRM

speeds that few dared dream about a few years earlier. It covered the 194 miles from Paddington to Exeter in just three hours 28 minutes, at an average speed of 57mph, with Brunel and GWR chairman Charles Russell on board. It took just three minutes longer for the return journey. Such speeds were then astonishing.

Gooch pulled off a masterstroke with the his 29-strong class of Iron Duke 2-2-2s, all with 8ft driving wheels.

The class was so named because the trial run of the first example took place on April 29, 1847, the Duke of Wellington's birthday. That first locomotive was duly called *Iron Duke* and it gave its name to the type.

They too were world beaters of their day: *Great Britain* ran between Paddington and Didcot at 67mph in 1848, and the class permitted regular 60mph trains to be timetabled.

Many of the Iron Dukes were later rebuilt to 4-2-2s.

THE GENIUS WHO SCRAPPED A MASTERPIECE

Most 7ft 0¼in gauge lines were gradually converted to dual or standard gauge from 1864 onwards, as the Swindon empire accepted slowly but surely that standard gauge had won the day.

The last of Brunel's broad gauge lines were converted over a single weekend in May 1892, with the remaining fleet of locomotives, carriages and wagons rendered totally redundant overnight, with nowhere to run.

They were stored on specially laid stock sidings at Swindon where they awaited scrapping.

However, the historical importance of the concept had been recognised, and kept by the GWR were pioneer *North Star*, preserved after withdrawal in 1871, and celebrity Iron Duke class 4-2-2 *Lord of the Isles*, the GWR exhibit at the Great Exhibition of 1851, which was also exhibited in Chicago in 1893 and Earls Court in 1897.

With space at Swindon Works at a premium, and no museum willing to offer either of the pair a home when Chief Mechanical Engineer, George Jackson Churchward, went away on holiday leaving William Stanier – the future designer of the world-beating streamlined LMS Princess Coronation Pacifics – in charge, the latter decided to scrap both.

Churchward was aghast at this destruction of historical artefacts when he returned, and salvaged many of the parts of *North Star*, but could save only the driving wheels from *Lord of the Isles*.

Stanier had no regrets, and when he later took over as Chief Mechanical Engineer at the LMS, he scrapped four historic locomotives that had also been set aside for posterity.

When the GWR was invited to take part in the 1925 Stockton & Darlington Railway centenary celebrations, it had no locomotive from its formative years. So, the surviving parts of *North Star* were tracked down and used to build a non-working replica at Swindon. It is this locomotive that is today exhibited inside STEAM – Museum of the Great Western Railway at Swindon. It can hardly be called a new-build as it largely comprised original components.

ABOVE: The last broad gauge train from Paddington to Penzance was 'The Cornishman' which departed at 10.15am on May 20, 1892. ROBIN JONES COLLECTION

ABOVE: GWR pioneer *North Star*, as reassembled for static display in 1925, is a popular exhibit inside STEAM – Museum of the Great Western Railway at Swindon. ROBIN JONES

THE WAY BACK

Broad gauge was never forgotten, and in the Eighties, retired Royal Navy Commander, John Mosse, was working as consultant architect to British Rail on the restoration of Brunel's Temple Meads Old Station in 1981, when he came up with the idea of building the 63rd member of Gooch's Firefly class.

Building a working locomotive with no railway on which to run may have seemed a ludicrous idea, but Cmdr Mosse's enthusiasm was shared by many others, including Leslie Lloyd, general manager of the Western Region, and his chief mechanical and electrical engineer, John Butt.

A major boost came when Gooch's original drawings for the class were rediscovered at Paddington. By 1982 The Firefly Trust was established and fundraising began.

It was always intended that the new *Fire Fly* would run, and eventually a broad gauge line for the purpose would be built. Yet as with many new-builds, it became obvious that much of the original specification needed to be modified to fulfil health and safety regulations. Such adaptations would include the braking, which on the original was not on the engine but on one side of the tender only, and the boiler, that Gooch had designed to be the main longitudinal strength member while additionally taking all the horizontal drag loads. Nor was there provision for boiler expansion in the original design.

The frame was redesigned to act as a support to the boiler rather than the other way round, with boiler expansion being permitted by the introduction of a dummy firebox, which would also take the drag loading. The frame, although considerably stronger than that of Gooch's, would still be true to the appearance of the original.

By 1987, sufficient money had been raised to allow building to start; as a Manpower Services Community project backed by Bristol City Council, but within a year, the council funding was lost and the group was forced to leave its riverside workshop when it was declared unsafe.

Help was at hand in the form of the Great Western Society, which offered space in its new locomotive workshop at Didcot Railway Centre.

IRON DUKE REBORN!

At the same time, the National Railway Museum commissioned a working replica of Gooch's first Iron Duke 2-2-2 for the Great Western 150 celebrations in 1985, together with a matching open carriage.

Unlike Cmdr Mosse's *Fire Fly*, which was built from scratch, the new *Iron Duke* was constructed using parts from two standard gauge Austerity 0-6-0 saddle tanks.

It was a case of losing two locomotives to make one new one, but Austerity saddle tanks were hardly rare. Out of a total of 484 built, nearly 100 have been preserved.

The new *Iron Duke* was built using modern materials and methods to exactly resemble Gooch's 1847 drawings, complete with exposed wooden lagging.

A short demonstration broad gauge line was laid at the York museum on which it could run.

Meanwhile at Didcot, a broad gauge track was laid complete with a mixed-gauge section and the transhipment shed from Burlescombe, where in the days of the break of gauge, passengers and goods were switched from one train to another.

Following the untimely death of Cmdr Mosse, retired airline pilot, Sam Bee, took over as chairman of The Firefly Trust in November 1998.

A boiler was built by Israel Newton & Sons of Bradford and the

ABOVE: The National Railway Museum's *Iron Duke* replica on display at Toddington station during a visit to the Gloucestershire Warwickshire Railway in 2010. ROBIN JONES

ABOVE: A musket salute to the Iron Duke, the Duke of Wellington in front of *Iron Duke* the locomotive at Didcot Railway Centre to commemorate the 200th anniversary of the Battle of Waterloo on June 18, 2015. FRANK DUMBLETON

£200,000 replica, named *Fire Fly* after the original, ran under its own steam for the first time at Didcot on March 2, 2005.

It was the first new main line steam locomotive to be built in Britain for use in the country since BR Standard 9F 2-10-0 No. 92220 *Evening Star* had been outshopped from Swindon Works 45 years before, and the first express passenger locomotive since *Duke of Gloucester* in 1954.

On April 30, 2005, the new *Fire Fly* was unveiled to an appreciative public launched into traffic by 72-year-old veteran of film, TV and stage, Anton Rodgers.

Sadly, it will never be able to show just what the class was capable of doing, for apart from the two short demonstration lines, there are no other 7ft 0¼in gauge railways in Britain, let alone a main line.

The new *Fire Fly* and *Iron Duke* brought back to life a huge slice of Britain's forgotten railway heritage, for at its greatest extent, Brunel's system amounted to a quarter of the country's national rail network.

If history had taken a different turn, and broad gauge had somehow managed to steal a march on its great rival system, who knows which way global transport technology would have taken us?

As far as railway heritage is concerned, history has repeated itself. Just as we scrapped broad gauge stock in 1892 because there was no longer anywhere for it to run, so many classes of redundant electric locomotives and multiple units are today rendered extinct because there is no heritage electric line.

ABOVE: *Fire Fly*, and *Iron Duke* now represent a lost railway system that in its day led the world in transport technology. FRANK DUMBLETON

ABOVE: *Fire Fly*, the 63rd member of the Firefly class in action at Didcot Railway Centre. FRANK DUMBLETON

Chapter 12

The Night Owl:
A tale of three jigsaw engines

Two of the final three rusting hulks at Barry scrapyard donated major components to build an example of a GWR classic that has not been seen for half a century – a Churchyard 4700 'Night Owl' heavy freight 2-8-0.

B ack in the Thirties, the GWR's publicity department often appeared more switched on than those of its Big Four counterparts, and thoroughly appreciated the value of merchandise, especially for younger passengers and fans.

The department commissioned Birmingham toy firm, Chad Valley, to produce some attractive wooden jigsaws depicting its trains.

One of the most popular of them all was The Freight Train, which depicted June 1918-built Churchward 28XX No. 2861.

First allocated to Pontypool Road, it was later transferred to Chester, Wolverhampton, Stourbridge and Tyseley. However, after its move to Aberdare in 1928, it was singled out for fame and fortune as the subject of a jigsaw.

No. 2861 later served at Pontypool Road again, Severn Tunnel Junction (three times), Neath, Oxford and Newport (Ebbw Junction).

Withdrawn from Severn Tunnel Junction in March 1963, it arrived at Barry in November of that year, and was one of the last to leave the scrapyard, being initially earmarked for the aforementioned Welsh national railway museum scheme in Cardiff that never materialised. It was taken back to Barry, as one of the 'Barry 10' locomotives in the custody of the Vale of Glamorgan Council, and there it was to become part of a big jigsaw itself.

No. 2861, a member of a class already well represented in preservation, with six others of the 84-strong class saved, along with nine of Collett's derived 2884 class, of which 83 were built, was dismantled to provide parts

for several new-build projects. Again, it was the GWR policy of using standardised parts interchangeable between several classes, which as we have already seen, has facilitated Great Western Society's new-build projects to 'jigsaw' parts from redundant locomotives to build new ones.

The cylinder and saddle block from No. 2861, along with several other components, is being used in the construction of a new Churchward 47XX 2-8-0 'Night Owl' No. 4709.

CHURCHWARD'S 4700 CLASS
At the end of the First World War, the running department of the GWR identified the need for a larger version of the successful GWR 43XX 2-6-0 incorporating the Swindon No. 1 boiler,

BELOW: No. 4704, an example of a class that represented George Jackson Churchward's final locomotive design. GWS

for express goods trains. Churchward opted for a 2-8-0 design.

The prototype, No. 4700, emerged from Swindon in May 1919 and represented the last design by Churchward.

The No.1 boiler proved to be inadequate for such a large engine and so in May 1921 it was rebuilt as a newly designed and larger Swindon No. 7 version.

Eight more class members with No. 7 boilers and detail differences were ordered by Churchward in 1921 and were numbered 4701 to 4708. Mechanically successful, their large size severely restricted their route availability and so no more were built. The design was superseded somewhat by Collett's Halls.

The 47XXs were primarily used on fast overnight freight services on the London, Exeter and Plymouth, London-Bristol and London, Birmingham and Wolverhampton routes. Such nocturnal duties earned the locomotives the nickname 'Night Owls' and during daylight hours they could often be found simmering in the larger sheds, awaiting their next overnight outings.

In later years they were often used on heavy relief passenger services to the west of England during the summer months.

Withdrawal of the class began in June 1962 with No. 4702, while the last were taken out of service in May 1964. None was preserved.

ABOVE: No. 4700, the doyen of Churchward's 47XX mixed traffic 2-8-0 class of nine locomotives, in British Railways' passenger service. GWS

THE STIRRING OF BRUNSWICK GREEN SHOOTS

Already inspired by the new Saint Lady of Legend project, Great Western Society members began looking around to see what other extinct locomotives could be recreated using second-hand parts.

In spring 2000, issue 15 of *Heritage Railway* exclusively reported that the redundant cylinder block from Saint donor locomotive No. 4942 *Maindy Hall* might be used to build a new 47XX.

Other discarded parts were offered to the Betton Grange team.

At the time, then Didcot Railway Centre general manager, Michael Dean, said it was "just wishful thinking," but planning continued behind the scenes.

Ten years later, on May 2010, in the immediate aftermath of the release of the 'Barry 10' hulks for restoration purposes as opposed for rebuilding in their own right, the society formally launched its 47XX project, which initially was on condition of sufficient interest from the enthusiast fraternity accompanied by pledges of donations to get it off the ground.

In addition to No. 2861, the society had already secured an option to acquire prairie tank No. 4115 as a parts donor. The prairie was to provide three of the four necessary 5ft 8in driving wheelsets and the extension frame assembly, while No. 2861 was to donate the outside steampipe cylinder block, to be modified to suit the 47XX, as well as the pony truck.

Many components below the running plate of a third 'Barry 10' engine, GWR 2-8-0T No. 5227, are also common with the 47XX class, in particular the axleboxes.

'Team 47' already had the 4000-gallon tender that came with *Maindy Hall*.

Society chairman, Richard Croucher, said: "We know that it is technically feasible to build a 47XX 2-8-0.

"While the GWS would be happy to coordinate such a project, as well as contributing the experience gained on other new builds and the extensive research and preparatory work already carried out for a 47XX, the society does not currently have the capacity or resources to undertake another major locomotive project. For this reason we propose creating an entirely new team to tackle this project as a stand-alone entity outside of the GWS, which may be incorporated as a charitable trust."

In order to run on the main line – the locomotive must comply with RSSB mandatory regulations through a Vehicle Acceptance Body. The original drawings form the basis of Grandfather Rights where industrial practices have moved on and new techniques have been adopted. The drawings will also ensure that the locomotive is built as close to the Swindon prototype as the modern railway world will accept.

The GWS specified that the engine was to run on the main line and appear in its final form as remembered in the Sixties. However, the design had to be reviewed in the light of the requirements of the Twenties compared with those for an engine running on the modern network.

An example of this is the current Network Rail Structure Gauge, which requires the locomotive to conform to a different dynamic profile. The 47XX class is fortunate in that its scantlings allow for very subtle changes to the chimney, safety valve bonnet and cab, allowing the team to meet these requirements without visual impairment. Other new-build schemes have not been so lucky.

The 'final form' requirement means that the project involves the building of a brand new No.7 boiler. This is the single most expensive component and one requiring both manufacturing expertise and heavy pressing plant.

While the team located many drawings, it found that there were still some important gaps. Here, Computer Aided Design (CAD) allows the production of components and the carrying out of trial assemblies with interfacing components to ensure that there are no issues or clashes.

Even better, once confident that the drawing is correct, it can be sent electronically to anywhere around the country and loaded directly into a CNC machine where it can be accurately replicated. This process eliminates the common sources of error that come from misreading the drawing.

The 4709 Project Plan sub-divided the project into 15 modules to allow flexibility in sequencing of the work at several work centres as follows: dismantle donor engines, mainframes, horns, wheels, suspension, pony truck, cylinders, motion, brake gear, boiler, smokebox, tender, ancillary pipework, platework and cab.

The base for the project is Didcot, but specialist aspects of the work will be contracted out to workshops where the necessary high standards and expertise can be met, such as the Llangollen Railway workshops.

ABOVE: The frame plates machined at TM Engineering in the Black Country. GWS

ABOVE: A final farewell to prairie tank No. 4115, seen here arriving at Llangollen for dismantling. Much of it will be 'reborn' as the new 47XX. DON ASHTON/GWS

ABOVE: The main frames and cylinders of No. 4115 lifted off the wheels at Llangollen. DON ASHTON/GWS

ABOVE: The extension frames on prairie No. 4115. DON ASHTON/GWS

BECOMING A REALITY

In 2011, the society gave the final green light for work on building its new 47XX to begin, after pledges of more than £50,000 towards the project had been received.

The first major job was the careful dismantling at the Llangollen Railway's workshops of 1936-built No. 4115, again a member of a class well represented in preservation.

A large number of common GWR parts were retrieved not only for No. 4709, the identity of the new locomotive, but also for future projects. Wherever possible parts have been unbolted, and where rivets are involved these have been carefully torched through the centres to minimise damage.

The tanks, cab and bunker were set aside for further use, while the boiler – which did not form part of the items donated to the GWS – was sent to LNWR at Crewe for use elsewhere.

The pony truck assembly and its associated components were removed, allowing the wheelsets to be dropped out. The extension frames and cylinder sub-assembly from the main frames were taken out.

Despite rusting in the salty air of the Severn Estuary for so long, a large percentage of the structure common to the 47XX was found to be in much better condition than expected.

The three existing 5ft 8in driving wheelsets from No. 4115 were to be refurbished, with a new fourth driving wheelset made.

A few weeks later, the pattern for the two missing driving wheels, largely made from a hardwood called jelutong, was built by Caddick & Moss pattern makers of Bristol to extremely high standards. It came with a removable boss, which enables leading/trailing driving wheels to be cast, as well as the 'centre' drivers that have a larger boss to accommodate loads from the connecting rods.

Tony Caddick and Tim Moss were given the Swindon Works' drawing for the 5ft 8in driving wheel, and produced 3D CAD drawings to generate all the complex curves and then wrote programs to drive their 3D milling machine.

The original compensated springing of the 47XXs proved expensive in cost and maintenance, and although all other classes had this mechanism removed after a short life, the 47s went to the scrapyard unaltered. The reason is obscure, as it appears that any gain over normal independent spring gear was minimal, and therefore, as a cost-saving measure, the new 47xx will not have compensated springing.

In 2012, a search was made for a suitable Swindon alternative and it discovered that Swindon spring No.147 (as used on the 47XX) and its accompanying fittings are common to the Collett Grange 4-6-0s. New spring hangers that will be stronger and of a later pattern than the original parts can therefore be made, although the unique axle 4 needs special attention.

OFFICIALLY A LOCOMOTIVE

According to the tradition that says the identity of a locomotive rests with the main frames rather than frequently changed items such as the boiler, No. 4709 became a locomotive in its own right, when its massive 31ft 1in main frames were plasma-cut to profile in March, 2012 by Tata Steel at Cradley Heath.

The frame plates were machined and drilled at nearby TM Engineering, which carried out similar work for the A1 *Tornado* project.

Visitors to the 6880 Betton Grange Society's Steel Steam & Stars III gala at the Llangollen Railway that April saw the newly manufactured main frames married to the front extension unit from No. 4115 ready for the all-important alignment process.

Don Ashton from the 47XX project team said: "The sheer physical size of the main frames came as quite a surprise, even to those close to the project. It's a real tribute to the engineering expertise and skill that still exists in the Black Country that local companies were able to carry out the work so efficiently.

"Tata Steel has been very supportive of the 47XX project, as well as being most helpful with the technical issues, while TM Engineering applied a most enthusiastic and professional approach to the machining and drilling of more than 200 holes."

MORE PIECES FOR AND FROM THE JIGSAW

Both new driving wheels for No. 4709 were cast at Micron Alloy Castings in Dudley in April 2013, followed by non-destructive testing and machining.

Once assembled on to a new axle and fitted with tyres, crankpins and balance weights, the two new wheels were to form the rear set of driving wheels, complementing the three driving wheel sets already recovered from No. 4115.

Before the chassis of No. 4709 can be wheeled, all the wheelsets will have their tyres turned, with the axle journals and crank pins being machined and polished.

At Llangollen, No. 4709's frames were erected and the new stretchers tack welded into position in preparation for final drilling and riveting up. The motion plate frame stretcher angles from No. 4115 were cleaned up and fitted to the new motion plate stretcher.

On May 6, 2013, the second donor 'Barry 10' locomotive, No. 2861, was moved from Barry to Llangollen where the donor cylinder block and smokebox saddle were removed.

Indeed, No. 2861 staked its claim to becoming the last ex-Barry scrapyard locomotive to leave the Barry area. One of the 'Barry 10' remained at what is now titled the Barry Tourist Railway, as the former Vale of Glamorgan Railway had been rebranded.

ABOVE: The popular GWR jigsaw of the Thirties, The Freight Train, made by Chad Valley in Birmingham, featured No. 2861. Just like a jigsaw, it has been taken apart and its components used to build another locomotive. ROBIN JONES COLLECTION

ABOVE: The final journey of one-time celebrity 28XX No. 2861. It left Barry on May 6, 2013, for Llangollen, where it was to be dismembered permanently. GWS

BR Standard 9F 2-10-0 No. 92245, which had earlier been linked with a move to the Somerset & Dorset revival base at Midsomer Norton, has been taken apart to become a sectioned exhibit highlighting the importance of the scrapyard to the heritage sector. It will, however, still be available for restoration in its own right if the right offer came along.

Although the radius of the 28XX saddle is wrong for the larger diameter smokebox of No. 4709 a method of using a separate plate inside the 47XX smokebox curved to suit the 28XX radius has been devised, allowing the 28XX saddle to be used unaltered, and at the same time lowering the pitch of the boiler by 2in to meet Network Rail loading gauge requirements. The modification will be invisible on the outside.

As we saw earlier, the boiler of No. 2861 was shipped to Didcot to allow it to be used as a template for fitting the pipework runs on new-build Saint 4-6-0 No. 2999 *Lady of Legend*.

The boiler was found to be in relatively sound condition, so when its current use is finished it will be stored as a spare for whichever locomotive needs it.

No. 2861 also yielded the majority of the parts for the braking system and the vacuum cylinder. Other parts may be used to restore another ex-Barry locomotive, sister No. 2859, at Llangollen.

By that stage, with the exception of the new axle, two tyres, two crank pins, a complete set of springs and the axlebox underkeeps, the GWS now has the majority of components ready to complete the rolling chassis.

February 2014 saw the final assembly of the main frames at Llangollen, with the new dragbox and five stretchers aligned and bolted up and two of the stretchers riveted into place.

The society took out a short term-loan that enabled the frames to be aligned properly.

In a unique partnering arrangement with the Llangollen Railway and the 6880 Betton Grange group, the society jointly funded an apprentice at Llangollen to divide his time equally working on Nos. 4709 and 6880, as well as Llangollen projects and attending college one day a week.

ABOVE: A model of No. 4709 displayed above the drawings. GWS

ABOVE: A donor horn guide bolted in position. GWS

ABOVE: Rivets on the main frames aligned at Llangollen. GWS

Sadly, the frames of No. 2861 were subsequently scrapped, wiping out its identity as a locomotive.

Society director David Bradshaw said: "While it's always sad to see a locomotive permanently dismantled in this age of preservation, No. 2861 would have been prohibitively expensive to restore to working order.

"There are other examples of the 2800 and later 2884 classes that have yet to steam, all of which are in far better condition – after all, there is a reason that No. 2861 spent more than four decades at Barry without finding a buyer.

"Thanks to the input of the Great Western Society, 10 of the last 11 locomotives remaining at the former Woodham Brothers scrapyard site have been recovered, with half of these expected to steam again and the remainder providing parts to build new locomotives and restore other examples of their class."

And 4709 Project engineering manager, Paul Carpenter, added: "Using parts of old locomotives to build new ones is nothing new – this practice has been used by the GWR on many occasions in the past to produce fine classes such as the Dukedogs, while other companies used the same methods; who could forget the Patriots and Thompson's rebuild of *Great Northern?*

"Through adopting a similar process we're able to build new examples of a number of long-lost locomotive classes, with the 4700 class 'Night Owls' being at the top of many people's 'wish list' because of their strong association with summer holiday excursions to the seaside.

"By salvaging parts from Nos. 2861, 4115 and 5227, we can not only ensure that we will see a new 'Night Owl' running again within a much shorter timescale and at lower cost than if we had to build all the components from scratch, but we're also providing a wealth of parts to a number of restoration projects that would otherwise be faced with large bills for patterns, casting and machining to reproduce them from scratch."

A LONG ROAD AHEAD

Steady progress was made over the following 18 months in assembling the frames at Llangollen, including all new platework.

During early autumn 2015, further work was completed as the project team advanced within striking distance of completing the chassis. The bufferbeam assembly had been completed and the extension frames were then offered up to the main frames, fitted and bolted up. Once the frames were laid, by convention, the locomotive came into existence as the latest in the class.

Since the launch of the project, the team had by then spent just less than £200,000, much of it from regular monthly income from supporters' banker's orders, plus a number of major donations. A similar sum had been pledged over the following five years.

It is estimated that the project needs another £100,000 to complete the rolling chassis, and to help boost progress, a 4709 Supporters Club has been established to increase regular income. For more details visit www.4709.org.uk or email Richard Croucher at chairman@didcotrailwaycentre.org.uk ●

ABOVE: The cabside and smokebox number plates for No. 4709, the next in sequence to the original class. GWS

RIGHT: In late autumn 2015, the opportunity has also been taken to lift the 28XX cylinder block for No. 4709 and place it on the extension frames. Before bolting the cylinder block to the frames permanently it is intended to carry out a hydraulic test on it. GWS

BELOW: A CAD drawing for the rolling chassis of No. 4709. GWS

Chapter 13

Rare gauge
replicas

What happens if you want to run steam, but your railway is of an unusual gauge, and there are no ready-to-run locomotives to buy or hire that will fit it, let alone ones waiting to be restored? Answer – build your own!

S o far we have seen the main impetus for building examples of extinct locomotives is to plug gaps in the heritage fleet.

However, in central Wales, the Corris Railway has added a modern replica of one of its original locomotives to its fleet, and is well on the way to building another.

Yet both locomotives are 'copies' – albeit with tweaking to the original design to suit present-day standards – and have been running for several decades a few miles away.

For the pair that served the Corris for many, many years went on to give sterling services on the neighbouring Talyllyn Railway after the line closed.

As we know, in 1951, the Talyllyn Railway became the world's first volunteer-run railway, planting the seed which grew into the might oak that is today's preservation movement. Yet at the time of its revival, nobody thought that the Corris, which became one of the earliest British Railway closures in August 1948, well before Beeching, could also be saved.

The two remaining Corris locomotives, Hughes 0-4-2ST No. 3 and Kerr Stuart Tattoo class 0-4-2ST No. 4, both in need of major overhauls, were locked in their shed at Machynlleth station after the line closed.

There would be no buyer for them outside central Wales, because both were built to the extremely rare 2ft 3in gauge. Machynlleth stationmaster Campbell Thomas hoped they would find their way to the Talyllyn rather than the scrapman, and in its first year of operating the line, the Talyllyn Railway Preservation Society bought the pair for £50. On the Talyllyn, they retained their fleet numbers, No 3. being named *Sir Haydn* and No. 4 *Edward Thomas*.

LEFT: No. 4 Sir *Haydn* back on Corris Railway metals in 2003, hauling the Tayllyn Railway's Corris heritage train. The Corris Railway is now building a replica so that it can have a Hughes 0-4-2ST of its own once again, even though the original is far from extinct. TR

If not for the Talyllyn, there would have been nowhere else for them to run.

The vast majority of narrow gauge lines on the British mainland are built to 2ft gauge or a fraction of an inch less: 2ft 3in gauge is very rare, with the best-known surviving examples being the Talyllyn and the Corris.

Research indicates that 2ft 3in gauge was widely used in the North Wales slate quarries around the 1820s. A sleeper from an ancient 2ft 3in gauge tramroad was recently discovered in Lord Quarry at Ffestiniog. It appears that the gauge was imported from North Wales to the quarries that the Corris would later serve, possibly by Joseph Tyson in the early 19th century.

The nearby Plynlimon and Hafan Tramway at Talybont, a short-lived seven-mile line serving the lead mines around Hafan between 1897-99, was also 2ft 3in gauge.

Outside Wales, one of the better-known 2ft 3in gauge lines was Scotland's Campbeltown & Machrihanish Railway, which opened in 1877 and closed in 1932.

At the Quarry Close China Stone Works at Nanpean in Cornwall, a network of 2ft 3in lines connected several quarries to the line from Drinnick Mill between 1863 and 1973. The nearby Hendra China Stone quarry, which operated from the 1860s to the late Sixties, had a 2ft 3in gauge internal quarry tramway system with cable-hauled inclines.

Between 1915 and 1959, the York Gasworks Company had a 400ft long 2ft 3in gauge electrified railway, operated by a Dick Kerr diesel, at its York plant.

The National Coal Mining Museum at Wakefield has a demonstration 2000yd 2ft 3in gauge funicular railway.

Accrington's Huncoat Colliery's mine railway, which closed in 1968, was built to 2ft 3in gauge. One diesel was sold to the Talyllyn Railway, and runs as No. 9 *Alf*. Where else could it go?

Britain's heritage lines big and small hold regular gala events, bringing in guest locomotives to delight enthusiasts. Not so the Talyllyn and Corris: apart from exchanging engines with each other, their gauge renders this impossible.

CORRIS REVIVAL AND HOMECOMINGS

The Talyllyn revival placed the railway on the map, but there were those enthusiasts who bucked the trend and despite the headline-grabbing success of its revitalised neighbour, did not forget the dodo that was the Corris.

In December 1966 a group of enthusiasts, led by Alan Meaden, founded the Corris Railway Society with the intention of preserving what was left of the line, opening a museum, and relaying part of the route as a short demonstration horse-drawn tramway. Five years later, the group obtained use of the railway stables adjacent to the demolished Corris station and laid a short length of track in 1971.

In 1981, the original locomotive shed at Maespoeth was acquired and track was laid over the three quarters of a mile between there and Corris. April 20, 1985 saw Corris Railway No. 5, a Simplex Motor Rail four-wheeled diesel named *Alan Meaden* in honour of the group's founder, hauling a rake of wagons forming the official 'first train' back to Corris run, which was watched with pride by Corris Railway workers.

The autumn of 1996 saw No. 4 make a brief loan from the Talyllyn to celebrate its 75th anniversary.

Public passenger trains on the Corris finally ran again, after a 72-year gap, at 11am on June 1, 2002. And when the Corris celebrated the 150th anniversary of its enabling Act of Parliament in 2003, the Talyllyn loaned its complete heritage Corris train, comprising No. 3 *Sir Haydn*, appropriately repainted into Corris Indian red livery, coach No. 17 and original Corris brake van No. 6.

In 1958, Talyllyn volunteers had retrieved the remains of a Corris bogie carriage, which had been used as a summerhouse in Gobowen, rebuilt it and returned it to service, allowing the genuine Corris train to be formed by adding the surviving brake van.

A STEAM ENGINE OF OUR OWN

Corris revivalists realised that there was no chance of buying one of the two surviving original locomotives back from the Talyllyn, and so decided to build their own.

They chose a replica Kerr Stuart Tattoo class locomotive as a substitute for the original No. 4.

An appeal for funds to build the new engine, to become No. 7 in the Corris fleet, was launched in 1994, and agreement was reached with now-defunct locomotive builder Winson Engineering of Daventry. It was to become the first new 2ft 3in gauge steam engine to be built for service in the UK since No. 4 in 1921, and would be named *Tattoo*, in honour of the name of the Kerr Stuart design of the original.

However, the new Corris No. 7 would not be an exact replica of No. 4, but a modern interpretation, including improvements made to the prototype by the Talyllyn. This principle is largely followed by all of the new-build replicas, from the biggest such as *Tornado* downwards: had the original survived, it is likely that modifications would need to be made to conform to modern requirements, such as running on the national network.

ABOVE: No. 7 *Tattoo* hauls its replica Corris train through the Spinney north of Maespoeth. PETER GREENHOUGH/CORRIS RAILWAY SOCIETY
RIGHT: The first official service train hauled by new Kerr Stuart Tattoo class 0-4-2ST No. 7 *Tattoo* leaves Corris on August 20, 2005. RICHARD GREENHOUGH/ CORRIS RAILWAY SOCIETY

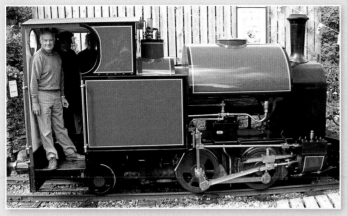

ABOVE: Selwyn Humphries, whose late father Humphrey drove the last Corris Railway train on August 20, 1948, stands proudly on the footplate of the new No. 7 at Corris station 57 years later. RICHARD GREENHOUGH CORRIS RAILWAY SOCIETY

ABOVE: Pictured in February 2010, Talyllyn Railway No. 4 *Edward Thomas* is the locomotive that the modern-day Corris Railway effectively replicated as No. 7 *Tattoo*. ROBIN JONES

Society members undertook fabrication separately of the sheet metal parts for No. 7, the cab, bunkers and saddle tank, and the completed parts were delivered to Daventry. No. 7 had its first official steaming in Daventry, and on May 17, it arrived at its new home at Corris. The project had cost £120,000.

On May 27, it hauled a train that carried the Welsh Assembly's

First Minister Rhodri Morgan over the railway. When No. 7 hauled a public passenger train for the first time, the 11am from Corris on August 20 that year, it was 57 years to the day since the last goods train ran on the original line. Among those present was Selwyn Humphries, whose late father Humphrey drove that last train in 1948.

AND ANOTHER...

In 2006 discussion centred on the idea of having a second new locomotive to take the pressure off *Tattoo* when maintenance and repair work became necessary. So, after a vote by members early the following year, the railway launched an appeal to build a second replica original locomotive, based on Hughes Locomotive & Tramway Engine Works of Loughborough, Falcon class 0-4-2T No. 3 with modern improvements to the design. The locomotive is to become No. 10 in the fleet and will be named *Falcon*, again after its maker's design.

The drawings for the original no longer existed, so the original No. 3 at Tywyn had to be measured up so new ones could be produced.

The project was undertaken by the Corris' boiler inspector, Graham Morris, and his colleague, David Potter, and cost £26,000.

The drawings were in September 2009 the drawings were complete at a cost of £26,000.

The first components for the new £250,000 engine were delivered to Maespoeth on January 29, 2011. They included the chimney and dome cover, and the boiler was completed by Israel Newton Ltd at a cost of £31,250 and arrived at Maespoeth in late summer 2012.

The next job was the cutting of the main frame plates for the locomotive, which was

done using the water jet method to produce the outside profiles and also all holes needed for bolts and rivets. The frame plates were taken to the workshops of Alan Keef Ltd where they have now been riveted.

At the time of writing, the next phase of construction will be the hornguides followed by the axleboxes and wheels. The driving wheels of the Corris Falcons as built in 1878 are unusual for a small narrow gauge tank engine because they are larger than the norm at 30in diameter and are solid with spokes cast on.

The day when a new Falcon 0-4-2ST can be heard again in Cwm Dulas is fast approaching.

ABOVE: The frames for the new Corris Falcon, a modern replica of the original Corris No. 3, now *Sir Haydyn* on the Talyllyn Railway. CORRIS RAILWAY SOCIETY

ABOVE: The original Corris Railway No. 4 crossing the Dyfi Bridge with a goods train in the late 1940s. CORRIS RAILWAY SOCIETY

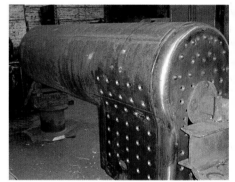

ABOVE: The completed boiler for the new Falcon. PETER GUEST/CORRIS RAILWAY SOCIETY

NEW LOCOMOTIVE BUILT BEFORE ITS RAILWAY!

Another rare gauge was 3ft, commonplace in Ireland and the Isle of Man, but one that didn't take off in on the British mainland. As we saw earlier, the original Ravenglass & Eskdale Railway was built to this gauge, and so was the legendary Southwold Railway in Suffolk.

Had history taken a different twist, the Southwold Railway might have become Britain's and the world's first heritage line, not the Talyllyn.

After the line closed on April 11, 1929, two local attempts to revive it floundered. The first involved relaying the 3ft gauge track and extending it to meet the Mid-Suffolk Light Railway.

The second would have retained the gauge while introducing special wagons on which standard gauge wagons could be carried, increasing freight revenue, while bringing in petrol railcars.

Sadly, the line was lifted in 1941 as scrap for the war effort, and the locomotives, along with virtually all of the stock, was scrapped.

In 1994, the Southwold Railway Society was formed with the aim of preserving the heritage of the railway, which was often lampooned during its existence. Eight years later, it began planning a revival of the entire 8¾-mile original railway using a new route west of Blyth, following the northern bank of the river estuary rather than the south.

However, ever since it has met with opposition from local residents, even though it has tried to allay their fears.

Suffolk Coastal and Waveney District councils rejected the society's planning application for the new line on a fresh alignment in 2007.

Switching tack, in February 2009, the Southwold Railway Trust won permission to build a steam theme park with a 2ft gauge demonstration railway on the site of a car spares outlet and waste disposal site in the town's Blyth Road.

However, before that could get off the ground, members focused on a fresh scheme to relay 1¼ miles of the original line at Wenhaston station.

A core plank of that scheme, which is intended to highlight the history and heritage of the line, is to build a replica of one of the original Sharp Stewart 2-4-0Ts of 1879, No. 3 *Blyth*, to head a complete replica mixed train as ran on the railway at its opening in 1879.

The Southwold Railway Trust has completed the design work necessary to create a replica that can run in the 21st century as well as a certificated, insured boiler and firebox design.

In early 2010, the frames of the £120,000 replica, made by Aldeburgh metalworkers Sam and Dennis Pegg, were unveiled at

the launch of a share scheme to raise the rest of the necessary finance. Inside a shed owned by local builder Duncan & Son, two 15ft lengths of original 30lb rail on sleepers were installed to support the construction.

The society has launched the 2-4-0 Club to generate funds by seeking sponsorship.

It is planned to use volunteer labour to assemble the new *Blyth* and involve local schools and colleges in its construction.

The trust has already built the main frames, bufferbeams and frame stretchers, footplating, footplate brackets, cab floor, motion brackets, chimney, and smokebox door.

The Wenhaston scheme, however, has also been dogged by local resistance, despite the trust's extensive modifications to its original plans, and at the time of writing, was still awaiting a breakthrough in its aim to win planning permission either for that site or somewhere else where *Blyth* will one day run.

ABOVE: The original Southwold Railway No. 3 *Blyth*. SOUTHWOLD RAILWAY TRUST

ABOVE: The frames for the new Sharp Stewart 2-4-0T. SOUTHWOLD RAILWAY TRUST

LEFT: The chimney of the new *Blyth*. SOUTHWOLD RAILWAY TRUST

AFTER 85 YEARS: THE REAL THING AT LAST

Miniature railways are typically regarded as those with an 18in gauge or less.

However, two pleasure lines in England were built to the much rarer 20in gauge: the Great Woburn Railway, which runs through Woburn Safari Park in Bedfordshire, and the older North Bay Railway at Scarborough.

The North Bay Railway was built in 1931 and runs for approximately ⅞ mile (between Peasholm Park and Scalby Mills in the resort.

Up to recent times, it has relied on four steam outline diesel locomotives built by Hudswell Clarke, two for the line's opening, and another pair that were supplied new to the Golden Acre Park in Leeds, and later were used at Woburn Safari Park. Indeed, the three oldest diesel hydraulic locomotives in the world are based at the railway.

However, after 80 years of running steam outline diesel hydraulic engines, in 2011 the North Bay Railway decided to build a pair of new 'genuine' steam locomotives, based on a Bagnall Sipat class 0-4-0ST, one at a 20in gauge to run at Scarborough and a duplicate at 2ft gauge to run elsewhere.

Built in the railway's own workshops, the Scarborough engine is to be called *Georgina* and the second one *Wendy*. Apart from the gauge, they will be identical. *Georgina* will be used for special occasions and for driver experience only. It is not envisaged that it will run on service trains on a regular basis.

Georgina's frames and boiler were united for the first time on June 11, 2014, following the riveting of the frames. The cylinders, recycled from 1998-built 0-4-2T *Annie* on the Isle of Man's Groudle Glen Railway, are on site ready to be bolted on.

On October 30, 2015, *Georgina* ran for the first time, but powered on air, not steam, for a demonstration run.

Georgina is funded by North Bay Railway owner, David Humphreys, but the construction is being used to train Lottery funded Heritage Skills Initiative apprentices by retired professional engineers who want to pass on their skills before they are lost.

With trials in the early part of the year, the locomotive is expected to steam in the spring

of 2016, after which work on *Wendy*, built to 2ft gauge, will start.

Following the launch of the project, a new business, NBR Engineering Services Limited, was formed. Hunter Engineering of Scarborough was bought to provide a workshop base for this part of the railway's business.

It is envisaged that services will be provided, not only to heritage railways that require steam engineering, but also others, such as boats and traction engines.

ABOVE: A Bagnall Sipat class 0-4-0ST; the basis for the new North Bay Railway locomotives. DAVID HUMPHREYS

ABOVE: The motion of *Georgina* in place in October 2015. DAVID HUMPHREYS

ABOVE: *Georgina* taking shape rapidly at the North Bay Railway workshops in October 2015. DAVID HUMPHREYS

Chapter 14

New build of a great locomotive works!

What can eclipse the feat of building a new steam locomotive from scratch? Maybe the reincarnation of one of Britain's lost steam engine builders to restart production?

Despite a commonplace belief, the last steam locomotive built in Britain during the steam age was not British Railways Standard 9F 2-10-0 No. 92220 *Evening Star*, which emerged from Swindon in 1960.

That may have been the last one built for the British main line network, but the country's locomotive builders still turned out steam engines for export and industrial use for several years afterwards.

History records that the last steam locomotive of all built in Britain for industrial use was Hunslet 0-4-2ST No. 3902, which was supplied in 1971 to a Javanese sugar mill system where it became Trangkil No. 4.

This locomotive was in recent times repatriated to the private Statfold Barn Railway near Tamworth… where businessman owner, Graham Lee, had acquired the rights to the name of its illustrious manufacturer.

Not only that, but he began to produce new steam locomotives under the Hunslet banner.

The Hunslet firm was founded in 1864 at Jack Lane in the Leeds suburb of Hunslet by John Towlerton Leather.

Its first engine was *Linden*, a standard gauge 0-6-0ST built in 1865 for engineering contractor Brassey & Ballard. Hunslet thereafter specialised for many years in shunting and short-haul locomotives, ideal for colliery railways.

ABOVE: The locomotive that brought the curtain down on the British steam age first time round: Hunslet 0-4-0ST No. 3902 *Trangkil No. 4* was built at the firm's Jack Lane plant in Leeds in 1971, three years after British Railways stopped using steam on its services and 167 years after Richard Trevithick's first public demonstration of a railway engine. Of paramount historical significance, *Trangkil No. 4* was repatriated by Graham Lee and restored to run on his Statfold Barn Railway. ROBIN JONES

ABOVE: All hands on deck: *Jack Lane* visited Woody Bay for the Lynton & Barnstaple Railway's autumn gala in September 2007. TONY NICHOLSON

ABOVE: New Quarry Hunslet 0-4-0ST *Jack Lane* heads a passenger train along the Statfold Barn Railway on September 13, 2014. ROBIN JONES

In 1870, Hunslet constructed its first narrow gauge engine, *Dinorwic*, an 0-4-0ST for the Dinorwic Slate Quarry in Snowdonia. Another 19 followed, and established the company's reputation as a builder of engines for use in quarries. The term Quarry Hunslet became used to describe several different types of 0-4-0STs, mainly used in the Snowdonia slate workings, and numerous examples of the 50 built between then and 1932 are running on heritage railways today.

As a supplier of locomotives to many companies overseas, the firm expanded to also build engines for British main line companies, including 90 LMS 3F 'Jinty' 0-6-0Ts.

Several famous British locomotive builders such as Kerr Stuart and Avonside did not survive the depression of the 1930s, but Hunslet stood fast, and as its competitors failed, bought up their patterns, rights and designs.

The Jack Lane works closed in 1995 after supplying a batch of narrow gauge diesel locomotives for tunnelling on London Underground's Jubilee Line Extension.

HUNSLET REBORN

Eventually, by virtue of sales and mergers, the Hunslet Engine Company became part of the Burton-on-Trent-based LH Group Services, Britain's biggest independent remanufacturer of power train products.

The firm inherited the rights to locomotive manufacturers Andrew Barclay, Avonside, the North British Locomotive Company, Greenwood & Batley, Hudswell Clarke, John Fowler & Co, Kerr Stuart, Kitson & Co and Manning Wardle. That allowed the company not only to use those names, but to service and repair their products and supply replacement parts.

A mega enthusiast himself, LH Group chairman, Graham Lee, developed a multi-gauge private network at his farm near Tamworth, where the main crop is seed oil.

Graham regularly hunted across the world for redundant steam locomotives and repatriated them, rebuilding them to new condition in the Statfold Barn workshops.

One such locomotive was none other than *Trangkil No. 4*, which was returned to England in 2004. At Statfold, it was regauged from 2ft 6in to 2ft before being returned to steam.

However, Graham was not content merely with buying old steam locomotives, but in the Stafold Barn workshops, began building new ones that were badged under the Hunslet name.

The first emerged from the Statfold Barn workshops in 2005. Named *Statfold*, it was nothing less than a fully fledged Quarry Hunslet 0-4-0ST, and enough components for a batch of four were manufactured.

Statfold entered service in 2006, and worked on the revived Lynton & Barnstaple Railway while visiting other destinations.

The next was named *Jack Lane*. There were key differences between the two, although they were constructed to the same basic design. While *Statfold* has an enclosed cab, *Jack Lane* has an open footplate and a taller chimney to keep smoke clear of the footplate crew.

The pair were allocated works numbers 3903 and 3904 respectively, continuing the Hunslet steam locomotive numbering series from No. 3902 *Trangkil No. 4*.

◄

ABOVE: Hunslet's new Kerr Stuart Wren 0-4-0ST No. 3906 of 2009 which was supplied to London's Kew Bridge Steam Museum's Waterworks Railway. LES CHATFIELD

ABOVE: *Statfold*, the first of the heritage-era Hunslet new-build steam locomotives, approaches Woody Bay station with the 'Killington Kitty' on the Lynton & Barnstaple Railway on July 16, 2006. TONY NICHOLSON

ABOVE: New Hunslet *Statfold* at Woody Bay station on July 16, 2006. TONY NICHOLSON

ABOVE: New chimney caps for new Quarry Hunslets in the Statfold Barn workshops. ROBIN JONES

ABOVE: The boiler for No. 3905 of 2008 *Jennie* under construction at Statfold Barn. ROBIN JONES

The sale price quoted on the Hunslet website is £130,000. Of course, it is cheaper to restore an existing one, but if you are planning a theme park railway or private line and want an 'instant' steam locomotive, Hunslet is still a first port of call.

Next off the Statfold production line was a Kerr Stuart Wren 0-4-0ST, completed early in 2008 numbered 3905, and like the Quarry Hunslets, also a type already represented in preservation.

The first steam locomotive to be built and sold by Hunslet in 37 years, it is now privately owned and based at the 2ft gauge Amerton Railway in Staffordshire, where it is named *Jennie* and forms part of the regular service trains, easily hauling four-

ABOVE: The old sandwiched by the new: at the Statfold Barn Railway, modern Quarry Hunslets *Statfold* and *Jack Lane* stand either side of very much older sister No. 996 of 1909 *Edward Sholto*, which was repatriated from Canada by Narrow Gauge Railway Society member and book dealer Andrew Neale. ROBIN JONES

ABOVE: New-build Kerr Stuart Wren 0-4-0ST No. 3905 of 2008 *Jennie*, which is privately owned but kept at the Amerton Railway. Nearly an exact copy of the original design, the last one of which was built in 1941, it was built in the traditional way with a riveted boiler and has been fitted with driver's air brake controls. When built at Statfold, it was named *Howard*, but was renamed Jennie after the new owner's wife at a ceremony on Boxing Day 2008 at Amerton. It has also visited other heritage lines including the Leighton Buzzard Railway, Hollycombe Steam Museum and in 2013 crossed the North Sea to visit Belgium's Maldegem Stoomcentrum. AMERTON RAILWAY

coach rakes and being very economical on coal and water.

A second Wren, No. 3906, followed in 2009, supplied to London's Kew Bridge Steam Museum for use on its Waterworks Railway.

The museum's railway is inspired by the Hampton to Kempton Park coal railway built and operated by the Metropolitan Water Board between 1916-46. Coal was delivered by barge to the MWB wharf on the river Thames at Hampton and moved by three steam locomotives to the boiler houses of the Hampton and Kempton Park waterworks.

The engines were built by Kerr Stuart and named *Hampton*, *Kempton* and *Sunbury*. None of the engines have survived, but Kew Bridge Steam Museum has one locomotive headlamp and shunter's lantern in its collections. Some of the trackwork has now been incorporated in the museum's demonstration line.

A LOAD OF HOT AIR

Built in partnership with owner Roy Etherington, the Statfold Barn Railway workshops have replicated one of the most obscure steam locomotives of them all.

Issin' Sid is a new 2ft gauge Lishman & Young compressed air 0-4-0 mine locomotive built to the same design as those used at the Earl of Durham's Lambton Collieries towards the end of the Victorian age. This design was the world's first fireless underground locomotive, and so Roy's replica is of no small historical significance.

Before flame-proofed diesel and battery electric locomotives were developed for mining applications compressed air provided a safe form of underground motive power that could be recharged from the same power supply as was used to drive drills and other machinery.

When the price of animal feed rose, mine owners began looking at sources of motive power other than pit ponies. By 1887, about 25 compressed locomotives were in use in the earl's collieries but their use in British coal mines ceased before 1900.

The very basic design centred around a wooden frame having dumb buffers supporting an air receiver with a capacity of about 25cu ft. Each locomotive had a pair of cylinders, each 3in diameter by 6in stroke, mounted between the frames, which drove coupled 12in diameter cast-iron wheels with a wheelbase of 17in, to allow the locomotive to tackle curves of about 6-7ft radius. There were no springs on the suspension and the simple brakes were worked by hand at one end and by foot at the other.

These locomotives could haul up to four tons for up to 500yds on one charge of compressed air, provided that the gradient did not exceed 1-in-48. They could be driven from either end: when hauling empty tubs the driver sat in the first tub to work the controls, but when hauling full tubs, he sat on a small detachable seat.

Compressed air for the locomotives was piped down from the surface at a pressure of 210lb/sq in. Boys around 16 years old usually drove the smaller locomotives, and were able to undertake such work after a few hours instruction.

Six Lishman & Young compressed-air engines were exported to California in 1879 and became the first mine locomotives in the USA.

Roy found a copy of Young's 1881 drawings and realised that the construction of an accurate working replica of the small type of locomotive was possible, so he approached Graham Lee about building one. Statfold workshop staff, including Stuart Tomlinson and Richard Gooding, helped him build the locomotive from recycled parts. The frame was cut from the jib of a scrapped Smith steam crane and the cylinders, made by Holman of Camborne, were found by a dredger cleaning out the Kennet & Avon Canal in the 1970s!

ABOVE: Breaking surface: replica Victorian compressed-air mining locomotive *Issin' Sid* on a Statfold Barn turntable. ROBIN JONES

The eccentrics came from an aborted project to convert a canal boat to steam operation.

However, new wheels had to be cast and Hunslet produced the casting.

Few mine locomotives were named – a potentially appreciative general public would never see them in operation underground, so what would be the point of adding such prestige – but mining folk had a well-developed sense of humour and chalk was freely used underground, so Roy decided call it *Issin' Sid* after the distinctive noise it made, with Sid applied in genuine NCB chalk!

Issin' Sid was allocated Hunslet works number 9902 in the Statfold special projects series.

MORE HUNSLETS ON WAY?

Graham sold the LH Group to Wabtec, based at Barton-under-Needwood in Staffordshire on October 2, 2012, but retains all the rights to the Hunslet steam locomotive designs up to 1971.

So the Statfold Barn workshops, which today offer a service to build steam locomotives of any size, are likely to turn out more steam Hunslets in the future – and already have a stockpile of spares to make a head start.

The Statfold Barn Railway is open to enthusiasts by invitation on selected days, at which visitors can inspect the workshops, and see both restored repatriated steam locomotives in operation and others waiting in the restoration queue.

RIGHT: A 21st-century Hunslet maker's plate. ROBIN JONES

Chapter 15

The Steam Multiple Unit

It has been argued that there is no such thing as a new idea: each new concept has roots in one or a combination of two or more old ones. The steam railway locomotive itself was not a new idea: its inventor, Richard Trevithick, had earlier built a steam road engine, as had others before him.

'Modern traction', diesel and electric propulsion, has its origins in early self-propelled vehicles. So, where is the missing link between Stephenson's *Rocket* and the Virgin Pendolino, for instance?

The answer lies in the steam railmotor – a carriage with a steam locomotive built into it, with a driving cab at both ends, eliminating the need for a locomotive to be turned at the end of each journey.

Modern diesel and electric multiple units, which today comprise almost all passenger trains on the UK national network, can trace their ancestry back to the steam railmotor concept. It first appeared when engineer William Bridges Adams tested a handful of vehicles with the locomotive physically joined to the carriage section in the late 1840s. The Bristol & Exeter Railway's broad gauge steam carriage was trialled on the Clevedon and Tiverton branches, but the concept did not catch on.

However, a big breakthrough came when the GWR borrowed a London & South Western Railway railmotor for trials on its Golden Valley line at Stroud. It had the ability to stop at basic intermediate halts and generate additional local traffic far beyond the company's wildest dreams. The GWR was so impressed that it built two railmotors for this line. They entered service on October 12, 1903 and were so successful that the Swindon empire eventually had a fleet of 99. The public loved the local and convenient services they provided, and the railmotors were often packed to overflowing.

Many of them also hauled trailers, making them the first multiple units, and several other British railways followed suit.

ABOVE: GWR steam railmotor No. 93 on Somerset's Yatton to Clevedon branch in Edwardian times. GWS

ABOVE: GWR steam railmotors Nos. 40 and 93 at Stourport-On-Severn in the early 20th century. GWS
LEFT: GWR steam railmotor No. 93 and trailer No. 92 running over the Llangollen Railway on April 26, 2013. ADRIAN KNOWLES

ABOVE: One of the strangest steam locomotive movements ever seen on a British railway: the steam power bogie being taken for test runs on the Llangollen Railway without the railmotor body! ADRIAN KNOWLES

LEFT: The new-build boiler of No. 93 being lifted into the restored coach section at the Llangollen Railway.

However, the railmotors were the victims of their own success. They generated so much local traffic that steam bogies inside them struggled to pull extra vehicles, and so a 'halfway house' compromise was reached with the GWR's development of the auto train, a concept in which a tank engine could be controlled from a cab in a carriage at the far end of the train, a more cost-effective and flexible concept.

The first GWR steam railmotor was withdrawn in 1914 and the last in 1935.

In 1933, however, the GWR returned to the all-in-one concept with the introduction of the first of a successful series of diesel railcars, which started a path of technological evolution that led to the first-generation British Railways' diesel railcars and multiple units of the Fifties, luxury trains such as the Blue Pullman and later the InterCity 125 High Speed Trains, with many other designs following in their wake.

However, one steam railmotor survived by the back door.

GWR steam railmotor No. 93 was built at Swindon Works in 1908 and was allocated to Bristol, Croes Newydd, Chalford, Gloucester,

Stourbridge, Taunton and Yatton.

It was withdrawn in November 1934 and while its steam bogie was removed and scrapped, its body was converted into auto trailer No. 212. As a non-powered carriage it ran in passenger service until May 1956, when it was converted into a British Railways' work study coach and ended its days in service being used as an office in Birmingham.

Noting its historical importance as the sole-surviving example of a 'bridge link' between the steam age and modern traction era, the Great Western Society bought it in 1970.

In 1988, the society officially launched a project to rebuild the auto trailer into its original form as steam railmotor No. 93 – with a new-build steam motor bogie.

In November 2000 the main frame for the new power bogie unit was erected at Tyseley Locomotive Works under the supervision of chief engineer Bob Meanley. Driving wheels and cylinder blocks were cast and machined and other components made, and in 2003 a rolling chassis took shape.

Israel Newton of Bradford built a new boiler, and in March 2008 the bogie and boiler were moved to Didcot Railway Centre while

the remaining components were manufactured.

In January 2009, the bogie was moved to the Llangollen Railway's engineering workshops to be installed in the underframe of the coach body, which had been restored there with the aid of a £768,500 Heritage Lottery Fund grant, which also awarded for the restoration of a matching trailer car, No. 92.

This vehicle was built at Swindon in September 1912, and lasted in service until January 1957. It was then used as a mess room by GKN workmen in Cardiff Docks, and was bought by the GWS in 1969. The society also used it as a mess room until restoration started in 2006.

On November 17, 2010, the motor bogie ran separately up and down the railway without any hitches. Six days later, it was united with the body – and 75 years on, the heritage sector had a GWR steam railmotor once more.

No. 93 was painted in the largely forgotten GWR coach livery of 1912-22, crimson lake lined in gold with a white roof, which pre-dated chocolate and cream.

The railmotor entered traffic on March 21, 2011, carrying a party of project supporters from Llangollen to Carrog and back, before ▶

ABOVE: This unique line-up of modern traction at Didcot Railway Centre on May 28, 2011 illustrates the evolution of the diesel multiple unit concept from the steam railmotor. From left to right are No. 93, a GWR auto trailer, GWR diesel railcar No. 22, Class 121 'bubblecar' owned by Chiltern Railways, a First Great Western Class 166 Turbo train and a brand new Chiltern Railways Class 122 unit. FRANK DUMBLETON/GWS

ABOVE: Travellers in time: Railmotor No. 93 runs past broad gauge replica *Fire Fly* at Didcot.
FRANK DUMBLETON/GWS

ABOVE: GWR steam railmotor No. 93, which has an all-new steam bogie built into a restored original body, lined up alongside Peppercorn A1 Pacific No. 60163 at Didcot Railway Centre on June 11, 2011. FRANK DUMBLETON/GWS

taking part in four days of enthusiast photo charters. The standard of finish was incredibly high both outside and in, with even the finest details replicated.

Returned to Didcot, it ran there for the first time on April 29, 2011, and was officially launched into traffic on May 28 by Adrian Shooter, chairman of main line operator Chiltern Railways, who brought along his newest DMU, a Class 172 Turbostar, delivered just two days before and never used by passengers. A replica of the GWR railmotor shed at Southall was opened the same day.

On June 11, No. 93 proudly lined up at Didcot alongside the most famous new build locomotive of them all to date, No. 60163 *Tornado*.

In the 2011 Heritage Railway Association awards, the Great Western Society carried off the coveted Annual Award (Large Groups) for 50 years of excellence culminating in the restoration of No. 93 – acknowledging it as the priceless 'missing link' in the story of the evolution of rail transport. Not only was the railmotor restored, with an all-new steam bogie built, but a replica GWR railmotor shed was built at Didcot Railway Centre to house it; the judges commended.

ABOVE: The new-build replica railmotor shed at Didcot Railway Centre. ROBIN JONES

BACK ON THE MAIN LINE

There were more landmarks to come. In autumn 2012, No. 93 undertook a tour of the West Country, visiting the Bodmin & Wenford and South Devon railways – with a groundbreaking series of trips over Network Rail's Looe branch in-between.

The vehicle was given special dispensation to run over sections of the main line, from which wooden-bodied stock is otherwise universally banned.

On Sunday, November 11, the railmotor made four public passenger-carrying return trips along the GWR branch, operated by West Coast in conjunction with First Great Western. The £25-a-seat tickets for the 16-mile round trip were the most expensive in the history of the branch, but it proved a sell-out.

RIGHT: GWR steam railmotor No. 93 restarts after pausing before Terras crossing with the 3.20pm from Looe on November 11, 2012. BRIAN SHARPE

TWO'S COMPANY

The Llangollen Railway's 2013 spring steam gala marked a major landmark in the heritage sector – the first appearance of a steam multiple unit on public services in the UK in eight decades.

The day before the April 19-21 event, the Great Western Society launched its combination of steam railmotor No. 93 and newly completed railmotor trailer No. 92 to members who had contributed to the project.

The combination made two return trips between Llangollen to Carrog, where speeches were made and celebrations took place.

Its subsequent first gala appearance was a big thank you gesture to the Llangollen engineering workshops, which restored the bodies and underframes of both vehicles from derelict condition, the railmotor making its debut on the line two years ago.

ABOVE: The Steam Multiple Unit: railmotor No. 93 and trailer No. 92 at Didcot Railway Centre on May 4, 2013. FRANK DUMBLETON/GWS

NEXT STOP BRENTFORD

Just as in the early days of GWR railmotors, services were packed to capacity as GWR steam railmotor No. 93, minus its trailer, ran a series of trips on the freight-only Brentford branch over the weekend of October 18-19, 2014.

Promoted by the Great Western Society in conjunction with First Great Western, Network Rail and West Coast Railways, the event attracted an estimated 1000 passengers and large lineside crowds.

Capable of seating only 55 passengers, No. 93 made 20 round trips from Southall along the branch over the weekend.

The appearance of the railmotor at Southall reflected days when the GWR introduced the units on the Brentford branch in 1908, the first of which was allocated to a purpose-built shed at Southall.

LEFT: No. 93 passes the location of the former railmotor platform at Trumpers Crossing Halte while returning along the Brentford branch to Southall on October 19, 2014. In Edwardian times, the GWR added the continental 'e' to the normal Halt in a bid to make railmotor services sound more exotic and appealing. FRANK DUMBLETON/GWS

BELOW: A GWR railmotor stands in Trumpers Crossing Halte on the Brentford branch in the early 20th century. GWS

ABOVE: Steam railmotor No. 93 being serviced at Southall station during its Brentford branch trips on October 18, 2014. FRANK DUMBLETON/GWS

ABOVE: No. 93 passes through Reading station as it returns to Didcot early on November 8, 2014. On the main line, the railmotor travelled at 25mph maximum, in steam but hauled by West Coast Railways Class 47 diesel No. 47237. FRANK DUMBLETON/GWS

Building the 'perfect' new locomotive

The construction of a new British Railways Standard 3MT 2-6-2T is now filling a gap in locomotive history, but creating an 'ideal' locomotive for use on medium to long heritage lines.

RAISING THE STANDARD

Coming Soon - The New BR Class 3MT Tank For The Severn Valley Railway.

ABOVE: In Brunswick green livery, BR Standard 3MT 2-6-2T No. 82030 stands outside Swindon Works on October 18, 1959. RL COOK/82045 SLT

RIGHT: The 82045 Steam Locomotive Trust's promotional poster, painted by Stockport artist Stephen Millership, which is also available for sale to raise funds. 82045 TRUST

The best-known and arguably the most popular new-build is *Tornado*, and it may well be that its glamour and celebrity status will be eclipsed only by the new P2 *Prince of Wales*.

However, while *Tornado* is easily the most prominent new-build locomotive, is it the most useful?

A guaranteed crowd-puller and ticket seller, the economics of running it would be called into question if it was restricted to everyday use on the average heritage railway. The coal consumption and maintenance would hardly be met by the ticket price.

However, if an all-new medium-size tank locomotive were built from scratch, it would be a different matter.

The catalogue of British steam locomotives rendered extinct by the cutter's torch would easily throw up a sizeable shortlist of potential candidates for such a role. Yet, when selecting which type to build for the demands of the 21st-century steam sector, an excellent starting point would be a 'modern' type, that is modern in terms of the lineage of steam locomotive development.

It was back in 1998 that I received a call from South Devon Railway fireman, John Besley, who suggested the possibility of building a new British Railways 3MT 2-6-2 tank engine, and went on to launch the scheme.

Designed by Robert Riddles, the engineer responsible for most of the British Railways Standard classes, it was, like some of the other types, a hybrid.

On the creation of the Railway Executive in 1947 in preparation for the nationalisation of the railways in 1948, Riddles, who had been vice-president of the LMS, was appointed Member of the Railway Executive for Mechanical and Electrical Engineering.

Other countries by then were decades ahead in modernising their railway networks, replacing steam locomotives with diesels and electrics. Britain was still gripped by postwar austerity and could not afford to follow the example set by the USA and even Ireland, which had remained neutral during the Second World War.

Britain stuck with steam, but the 12 Standard classes that were produced post-Nationalisation were in effect a fort-holding exercise, replacing ageing types while the country recovered sufficiently from the ravages of war to modernise. A total of 999 standard locomotives were built.

A HYBRID CLASS

The BR Standard Class 3 2-6-2T was a hybrid design, the chassis being closely based on, and sharing a number of parts, with the LMS Ivatt Class 4, and having a boiler derived from a GWR No. 2 boiler as fitted to the GWR large prairie 2-6-2T and 56XX 0-6-2T.

The design and construction took place at the ex-GWR Swindon Works, along with the 2-6-0 tender engine version of the class, the 77XX.

Although the boiler shared flanged plates with the GWR No. 2 boiler, the barrel was shortened by 5$\frac{13}{16}$in and a dome was added.

In common with several other BR Standard Classes, the chassis design used a number of LMS-designed components including brake hanger brackets, flexible stretcher brackets and reversing shaft brackets. The LMS 'roots' of many of the Standard classes showed Riddles' very strong influence.

Although the chassis had many almost identical parts to the LMS Ivatt Class 4, the motion brackets were derived from the design of those fitted to the LMS Ivatt Class 2 2-6-0 and LMS Ivatt Class 2 2-6-2T.

A total of 45 Standard 3 tanks were built between April 1952 and August 1955. From new, they were based on the Western,

Southern, North Eastern and London Midland regions.

Excellent locomotives, with a design life span of 40 years, time was not on their side. In 1955, British Railways published its Modernisation Plan calling for the eradication of steam.

So, the class had a short life as most of the work that they had been built for soon disappeared with the branch lines; the closure of which had begun several years before Beeching, and the introduction of diesel multiple on shorter routes.

The shortest-lived example was No. 82043, which was only eight years and eight months old at withdrawal, while the longest-lived was No. 82019, two months before its 15th birthday.

The last two Standard 3 tanks in service were Nos. 82009 and 82029 at Nine Elms but four more survived until after the end of steam. Nos. 82000, 82003, 82031 and 82034 were transferred from North Wales at the end of 1966 to Patricroft shed in Manchester for use on local suburban trains. They were not really required there, however, but lingered until the shed's closure in 1968. One of these four had run very few miles since its final overhaul, and enquiries were made about saving it, but the price being asked (£1500, a fortune in those days) was too high and despite the establishment of a handful of standard gauge heritage lines by that date, the four went for scrap at Cashmores in Newport, South Wales; being broken up as late as October 1968. All of their mogul sisters in the 77XXX class were also scrapped.

A MIDLANDS MOVE

John Besley's scheme was subsequently taken under the stewardship of Severn Valley

ABOVE: BR Standard 3MT 2-6-2T No. 82009 on May 27, 1959 at Bridgnorth, where the new one is being built.
R HAMILTON//82045 SLT

Railway enginemen Tony Massau and Chris Proudfoot in the summer of 2003.

In those pre-*Tornado* days, it looked for a few years as if 82045 might prove to be just another pipe dream – and not a particularly glamorous one at that!

It took off of in the late autumn 2008 when the finished frame plates for the new engine were delivered to the group's site at Bridgnorth on the SVR, one of the class's BR-era stamping grounds. Since then, progress on this most practical of new-build locomotives has been rapid.

The 82045 Locomotive Fund, as the group was initially called, was reconstituted as a company limited by guarantee in April 2009 and gained charitable status in January the following year, accompanied by a change of name to The 82045 Steam Locomotive Trust.

From the start its stated aim is to build the next member of the class (the BR engines finished at 82044) specifically for heritage railway use and with no plans to run on the main line, because the type would probably be considered too small to haul trains of sufficient length to make such a venture pay.

Project engineer, Tony Massau, who is also a professional engineer, had considered for many years that Standard 3 tanks would be an ideal engine for average-sized heritage lines, because of their economical size.

Around the original partnership has grown a multi-talented team of SVR volunteers, and the trust now boasts three skilled engineers (including an expert machinist), a Lloyds coded welder, a patternmaker and an enthusiastic weekly working party co-ordinator in Colin Williams, a Severn Valley veteran.

CHEAPER THAN FIRST THOUGHT

The 82045 project looks set to buck the general trend of cost predictions being over-run by considerable margins, in that it is likely the final cost of the new locomotive will be quite a lot less than the figure of £1,125,000 estimated in the early days by the late and much-missed Graham Nangreave, the SVR's mechanical foreman at the time.

Chris Proudfoot, who is responsible for raising funds for the Riddles tank, estimates that more than £600,000 has been raised since the engine's frames arrived at Bridgnorth, and he thinks that around £100,000 still needs to be found over and above what the group has in the kitty – or can rely on coming into the kitty over the next two years thanks to established secure income streams – in order to see the job through to completion.

This amounts to a figure of about £950,000. Project engineer Tony Massau has this explanation for what seems an unlikely, if welcome state of affairs: "The one thing we never foresaw when we took over the project was the superb team of volunteers it began to attract once we'd got metal on the ground.

"We had anticipated having to make heavy use of the cheque book, but instead we have the resources within our working team to do so much work ourselves that we have saved literally hundreds of thousands of pounds so far. This is not a random figure, but predicated on a calculation of man-hours paid at a low hourly rate. Our chaps could actually command far more than that if they were being paid, so the figure is conservative."

ABOVE: Easter 2015 saw the bunker of new-build BR Standard MT 2-6-2T No. 82045 fitted to the frames. 82045 TRUST

LEFT: The completed bunker for No. 82045, fabricated at the Ffestiniog Railway's Boston Lodge Works, as seen on December 15, 2014. JOHN WHALLEY, FR/WHR

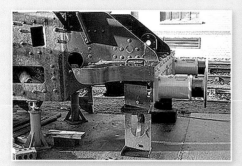
ABOVE: The completed front buffers on December 15, 2014. TONY MASSAU

ABOVE: Engineer, Bryan Clarke, checks the fit of one of No. 82045's left-hand leading hornguides. 82045 SLT

ABOVE: The newly shotblasted smokebox saddle awaiting machining. 82045 SLT

So, what is it that has united a powerful volunteer team, which includes skilled engineers and draughtsmen, a former BT office manager, a retired BR guard, an IT expert and a teacher of classical languages? Tony said: "Right from the start, we had only one aim in mind – to see No. 82045 running – and this aim has been shared by all the team members who have joined us down the years. Our team has earned an excellent reputation at Bridgnorth, where they simply knuckle down and get on quietly with the job, and work in harmony alongside the SVR paid staff. We have been amazingly lucky."

It certainly seems to be a winning formula. By the autumn of 2015, the engine's chassis was complete, bunker and cylinders in situ, cab, smokebox and side tanks well underway, and the coupled wheelsets ready and waiting at the South Devon Railway while the axlebox assemblies were completed in the West Midlands. The cab roof has been fitted to the cab side sheets and lifted into place on the locomotive frames, which, along with the temporary fitting of the smokebox, has given observers a good impression of how the finished locomotive will look.

BUILDING THE BOILER

The South Devon Railway was commissioned to build the firebox in kit form at its Buckfastleigh works, for delivery by April 2016. A quantity of copper for the inner firebox was ordered by the SVR to be stored until needed.

The plan is that it will be assembled by the SVR and that the engine will carry on its maker's plates the proud legend 'Built at Bridgnorth'.

The success of the trust's £300,000 boiler appeal, boosted by donations of £7000 during the Severn Valley Railway's four-day autumn 2015 steam gala after more than £200,000 was raised in 18 months, also led to an up-front payment to Black Country firm Barnshaws for rolling the boiler barrel, which has now been delivered to Bridgnorth.

The Ffestiniog Railway was booked to build the side tanks at Boston Lodge over the winter. They will be painted and lined out by the SVR volunteer team of Andy Williams and Gary Townley.

At the time of writing, the group has also started to raise funds for the motion, and so far has the forgings for the connecting rods, while sponsors have come forward to finance the coupling, return crank and radius rods.

There are, of course, myriad parts still to be made or purchased before 82045 takes its first train out of Bridgnorth, but the major unquantifiable items are now the front and rear pony assemblies; quite complex pieces of kit.

ABOVE: No. 82045's cylinders during machining at Tees Components of Saltburn, Cleveland. TEES COMPONENTS

The rear assembly is the same as that on the BR Class 2 tanks, and the group is working closely with the Bluebell-based Standard 2 group, which is recreating another extinct class by converting BR mogul 78059 to 2-6-2T No. 84030. The front pony assembly is common to both the 80XXX Class 4 tanks and the SVR's own mogul No. 43106.

The most frequently asked question is – as you would expect – when will the engine be ready? The reply from the group is cautious, not because of any internal hesitancy but because it is always an imponderable whether contractors will complete jobs on time. Two to three years, maybe 2017-18, is a reasonable estimate, but the group is reluctant to be too bullish.

COULD A BATCH BE BUILT?

Membership secretary, Barbara Massau, said: "We have always known that our engine would never be the belle of the ball, and it has never been our intention that this should be so.

"What we are aiming to do is to build a practical, no-frills but nevertheless attractive modern steam locomotive, which we hope will help take the age of standard gauge branch line steam forward for succeeding generations to enjoy."

LEFT: BR Standard 3MT 2-6-2T No. 82031 stands in Platform 3 at Bewdley after arriving on June 29, 1957. PJ SHOESMITH/SVR ARCHIVES

ABOVE: The chassis outside Bridgnorth Works in April 2015 with both cylinders fitted. PAUL APPLETON

ABOVE: The boiler barrel for BR Standard 3MT No. 82045 at Bridgnorth on November 2, 2016. TONY MASSAU

ABOVE: No. 82026 on station pilot duty at Waterloo in 1965. CHRIS WARD*

ABOVE: The white metal of one of the axleboxes being machined on November 2, 2015. TONY MASSAU

ABOVE: The pattern for the chimney of No. 82045. PETER LINE

ABOVE: The wheelsets of No. 82045 at the South Devon Railway on April 29, 2015. TONY MASSAU

ABOVE: Autumn 2015 saw the new 2-6-2T with a roofed cab at last. TONY MASSAU

And what about building No. 82046? The type has, after all, more than once been suggested as an ideal candidate for limited series production, in view of its perceived usefulness to heritage railways. However, the 82045 group itself is not proposing to build another.

Tony Massau said: "We can't really contemplate doing it all over again: average age is the ruling factor here. However, if another group was to come along wanting to build another 82 tank, we'd certainly be prepared to help with advice, hire of patterns etc, as much as we could."

And what is his advice for anyone else contemplating building a new steam loco?

"Make sure you have a good business plan, build a firm base of support so that you can generate solid income, and take no notice of the trolls and naysayers who are bound to have a go at you.

"Theirs is the problem not yours!" ●

■ If you would like to become involved with the 82045 project, please contact Barbara Massau, Membership Secretary, The 82045 Steam Locomotive Trust Ltd, Highlea, 4 Southfield, Prestbury, Cheshire SK10 4XF, telephone 01625 82045, email barbara.massau@ntlworld.com

RIGHT: The front end of No. 82045 as seen on September 14, 2015. TONY MASSAU

ABOVE: NER Class O (LNER G5) 0-4-4 tank engine No. 2084 pulls into Swalwell station. BEAMISH MUSEUM

Made in Darlington
– just like the first ones!

A type of tank engine once commonplace on lines in the North East but rendered extinct in 1958 is now taking shape once more in the town.

Another contender for the accolade of being the perfect size of new steam locomotive for use on a heritage railway is the North Eastern Railway Class O (LNER G5) 0-4-4T, a design that is decades older than the BR Standard 3MT tank.

On becoming NER Locomotive Superintendent, Wilson Worsdell switched the NER's passenger tank locomotive policy from his brother and predecessor Thomas William Worsdell's 2-4-2T Class A (F8) design, back to a design resembling Fletcher's 0-4-4T BTP class (G6), with his G5 design.

Compared with the F8s, the G5s had smaller driving wheels and greater coal and water capacities. A total of 110 were built between 1894 and 1901, across seven batches.

The later batches replaced many of the G6s, which were then converted to 0-6-0Ts (LNER J77) or push-pull locomotives.

The G5s were noted for being sturdy; working long and economical careers. They worked throughout the North-East area, and could be found on both branch line passenger trains and the heavier suburban trains.

Elegant, but simple in design and construction, a G5 had the capacity to handle four to five bogie coaches, unassisted, in an economic manner.

They regularly ran at 60mph on the Middlesbrough to Newcastle services, and

were transferred from these heavier suburban workings only with the arrival of the bigger A8s, V1s and V3s.

During the late Twenties and early Thirties, many of the G5s were replaced with steam railcars. In turn, the displaced G5s replaced withdrawn F8s and G6s.

In further attempts to economise on branch lines, 21 G5s were converted for vacuum-operated push-pull working from 1937.

All of the G5s passed into British Railways' ownership at Nationalisation in 1948.

The G5s survived pretty much intact to 1949. The first withdrawal was in 1950, but ▶

ABOVE: NER G5 0-4-4T No. 468 with a train at the now-closed Croft Spa station on the East Coast Main Line south of Durham. PHOTOMATIC/BEAMISH MUSEUM

ABOVE: Casting one of the cylinder blocks. G5LC

ABOVE: The still-warm cylinder casting on March 19, 2009.
JOHN LEWINS

ABOVE: A newly cast bogie wheel for the G5. G5LC

DOCTOR'S ORDERS

It was Durham GP, Dr Mike Wood, who dreamed up the idea of building a new example.

He approached Mark and Keith Ashton at Great Northern Steam in Darlington to discuss its feasibility, and commissioned a new fully welded boiler design, to be registered at Lloyds once it complied with all the current pressure vessel regulations.

Once the boiler design was fully registered, a small consortium of North East-based enthusiasts came together to form the Class G5 Locomotive Company Limited, with Mike as chairman.

The first component was cut at Great Northern Steam in Darlington on January 19, 2008.

It was fitting as all of the original G5s were built in the town.

most were withdrawn between 1955 and 1958 as they were replaced by diesel railcars and DMUs multiple units.

The last G5 was withdrawn in 1958, and none were preserved: had they managed to survive another decade, they would almost certainly have been of great interest to the fledgling standard gauge revival movement, if only for their versatility.

Great Northern Steam was chosen as it had a record over many years of building new traction engines, and miniature steam railway locomotives were followed by *Ant* and *Bee*, full-size replica 19in gauge steam locomotives for the Great Laxey Mines Railway on the Isle of Man.

A previous proposal to construct a full-size replica of one of the smallest standard gauge main line steam locomotives, a North Eastern Railway Y9 0-4-0T, had come to nothing. However, the G5 group was a different matter.

Unlike several other new-build projects that chose to manufacture an 'easy' bit from sheet steel, such as a cab or front footplate and steps, to act as publicity for the project, the group had the bulk of the finance in place and paid for the big bits of heavy engineering to be built first.

The company acquired more than 130 of the original drawings for the class, while further extensive redesign and updating of existing drawings has been undertaken.

David Elliott, who played a key part in the successful completion of A1 Peppercorn Pacific No. 60163 *Tornado*, assisted with the design specification and certification required for the new G5, and became the project's chief engineer.

The group aimed from the start to build a replica, not a new addition to the class, and the engine selected was No. 1759, which was withdrawn from West Auckland shed in 1958.

It is being built in distinct units; i.e. boiler, bogie, cylinders, wheelsets, frames and so on. Each unit has been paid for on completion. This policy has minimised the risk to both the company and its suppliers. The bogies, followed by the boiler, were the first units to be completed: with most schemes, the boiler comes last, because it is the most expensive part.

The incorporation of an all-welded steel boiler will not detract from the external appearance of the locomotive, which will appear as built in the 1890s, apart from the location of the 'Westinghouse' pump, on the front of the tank, rather than in the cab.

There will be steel bufferbeams, rather than the original wooden ones. The locomotive will be fitted with robust group-standard buffers, rather than those originally fitted, which were of NER design.

In addition, the bogie design was redrawn and updated to modern main line standards, as has been the case with the frames and wheelsets.

GOING MAIN LINE

In February 2009, the company board took the major decision to build the locomotive to main line standards, allowing it to obtain certification to run on the national network. However, this aim doubled the original estimate for the final build cost, which in 2009 was pencilled in at £900,000. In early 2010, a £500,000 share issue was launched.

In March 2012, the G5 project moved out of the Great Northern Steam workshops after the company announced that it was is moving much of its manufacturing operation from Darlington to India in a bid to cover costs.

The components for the new G5, including the frames, boiler, bogie and a number of castings were moved out of the Darlington workshops in mid-March to Rail Restorations North East's premises in Shildon.

Rail Restorations North East took over the detailed management of the assembly work, advised by David Elliott.

RIGHT: A test fitting of the boiler and outer firebox on March 11, 2009. JOHN LEWINS

ABOVE: A view inside the all-new G5 boiler. ROBIN JONES

ABOVE: The G5 frames erected at Rail Restorations North East at Shildon on March 21, 2012. G5LC

ABOVE: The first driving wheel cast at Boro' Foundry on April 13. G5LC

ABOVE: The first driving wheel cast at Boro' Foundry on April 13. G5LC

On May 12, 2012, the newly completed boiler was unveiled. It was the largest standard gauge steam engine boiler to be built in this country for the last 45 years.

The erection of the chassis, the casting and machining of the four driving wheels at Boro' Foundry in Lye, the manufacture of the welded cab and bunker were soon followed by the casting of the cylinder blocks and a steady stream of other components.

October 2014 saw the cylinder blocks and the front bufferbeam bolted into position, along with all of the horn guides.

MOVING ACROSS THE ROAD

Early February 2015 saw the project on the move again, after principal contractor Rail Restorations North East Ltd went into liquidation. The G5 moved to new premises in Hackworth Park, Shildon, directly opposite the unit occupied by Rail Restorations.

A statement issued by the G5 company said: "This is the last phase in the construction of the locomotive and will see the frames turned over ready to accommodate the bogie and wheel assemblies. The new unit has much more space and will allow us to work on the construction and store all the assembled parts safely."

Since then, the project has held several open days at its new premises.

Ultimately, it is intended to run the locomotive on historically appropriate heritage lines in the North East, such as the Weardale, Wensleydale and Aln Valley railways. ●

ABOVE: The machined pair of cylinder blocks. G5LC

ABOVE: The components of the new G5 in the group's premises in Hackworth Park on April 1, 2015.

ABOVE: A driving wheel after machining at Boro' Foundry. G5LC

Chapter 18

Island fever

The Isle of Man and its unique collection of historic railways boasts three new-build steam locomotives with a fourth on its way, and one of the lines has replicated its entire original fleet.

ABOVE: The original Lewin engine *Ant*, about to return to the mine workings with empty ore wagons, in a view taken before First World War. GLMR

One of the trademark images of the Isle of Man is the great wheel at Laxey, the *Lady Isabella*, built in 1854 to pump water from the Great Laxey Mine.

With a diameter of 72ft 6in, this striking masterpiece of Victorian engineering still turns today and is the largest working waterwheel in the world.

The Great Laxey Mine was one of the richest and successful lead and zinc mines in Britain. It opened in 1780 and in 1875, the year of its greatest output – more than 11,000 tons of zinc was extracted – accounting for half of the total British output of the metal. Mine shafts had been sunk to depths of more than 2000 feet deep and nearly 1000 men worked there, but as with underground workings elsewhere, water was a constant problem. Hence the need for the great pumping wheel.

Like most other mines of the day, Great Laxey was also served by its own railway.

A widespread but largely hidden application of railways has been their use inside mines. They were mostly narrow gauge lines with locomotives vastly reduced in height, and in most cases battery-electric types because steam with sparks and smoke would be totally unsuitable in a confined space.

The main level of the mine was known as the Adit Level and was nearly one-and-a-half miles long. It entered the hillside beneath the wheel and linked with each of the mineshafts deep underground.

A narrow-gauge tramway ran along the entire length of the Adit Level and was used to carry the extracted ore out of the mine to the 'washing floors' where the ore was prepared for sale.

Ponies were originally used to haul the

tramway wagons, but in 1877 they were replaced by two tiny 19in gauge steam locomotives built by Stephen Lewin & Company of Poole in Dorset. Lewin was far better known for building steamboats: his firm turned out only a few locomotives.

They were 4ft 9in tall, 3ft wide and could each haul up to seven of the mine's 200 wagons.

Named *Ant* and *Bee*, the diminutive Laxey pair remained in use until the mine closed in 1929 and were broken up for scrap a few years later.

The Isle of Man once boasted an extensive network of public passenger-carrying railways. Of the 3ft gauge steam network, sadly only the Douglas to Port Erin section survives, while the Manx Electric Railway from Douglas to Ramsey via Laxey, and the similar Snaefell Mountain Railway survive. There is also the

ABOVE: The 19in gauge Great Laxey Mine Railway's replica diminutive Stephen Lewin locomotive *Bee*, with sister *Ant* behind, and three replica ore wagons. *Ant* and *Bee* had no cabs, and because of the low clearances in the mine tunnels, drivers had to remain seated.GLMR

Douglas Horse Tramway, which runs from the steam railway station along the island capital's promenade (although this is currently under threat), and the 2ft gauge Groudle Glen Railway, as described below.

Over the decades, there have been many calls for the Douglas to Port Erin line of the old steam network to be rebuilt. However, a surprising choice for another revivalist group was none other than the Great Laxey Mine Railway, which had never carried passengers.

In 1999, the Laxey and Lonan Heritage Trust began the restoration of the surface section of the former tramway, with the aim of having it running again by 2004 to mark the 150th anniversary of *Lady Isabella*, which had been named after the Island governor's wife.

The brainchild of the trust's Richard Booth and Captain Stephen Carter, funding for the revival came from many sources, the largest

share from the estate of Island resident Lt Col Randolph Glen.

One stumbling block to any previous revival of the tramway was the fact that the line runs beneath the main Laxey to Ramsey road and the Manx Electric Railway through what, at 100ft, is the longest railway tunnel on the Island. Up to 1999 it housed a generator for the Manx Electric Railway, but when that was relocated it paved the way for the mineral line to be rebuilt.

It might have been content to build a basic horse-drawn line, or relay it to the commonplace 2ft gauge, rather than the unusual 19in of the original, which had been dictated by the cramped loading gauge along the route.

However, the trust decided that nothing less than a recreation of the original line would suffice.

A fully working replica of the original *Ant* was ordered from Great Northern Steam

Ltd of Darlington, a firm with an established reputation for building model steam engines. *Ant* cost just £30,000 – a bargain when compared with the £3-million A1 Pacific No. 60163 *Tornado*.

No original drawings survived, and because Lewin had manufactured so few railway locomotives, very little was known about them.

So, a new set had to be compiled; from drawings for replacement boilers, safety valves and regulators supplied by Bagnall in 1905. Some dimensions had been given in a 1902 edition of The Locomotive Magazine and contemporary photographs.

However, during construction of *Ant*, a decision was taken to build a replica of the second one, *Bee*.

Two tiny carriages were built by modern-day rolling stock manufacturer and restorer,   ▶

Alan Keef Ltd of Ross-on-Wye, so that passengers can now ride along the line where loaded wagons of ore were once hauled from the mine.

The restored Great Laxey Mine Railway was officially opened on September 25, 2004. Five years later, a refurbished Clayton battery locomotive was obtained from Alan Keef and in keeping with the insect theme, was given the name *Wasp*. The railway also has six replica ore wagons, which were made by the Laxey blacksmith.

In 2006, the Laxey Mines Research Group, in conjunction with the heritage trust, completed the restoration of the former Snaefell Mine 50ft waterwheel at Valley Gardens, the terminus of the rebuilt railway.

From Valley Gardens, the railway runs for a quarter of a mile up the valley to the Adit Level entrance where there is a picnic site, footpath and information boards explaining the mining features. The *Lady Isabella* wheel is just a five-minute walk away.

Apart from the appearance of the two Lewin locomotives, the railway is unusual in running beneath another heritage line in the form of the Manx Electric Railway, and having replicas of its entire original steam fleet.

ANNIE THE THIRD

The Groudle Glen Railway, a short 2ft gauge coastal line north of Douglas, was built in the late Victorian era in response to increasing demand for transportation down to the beauty spot of Groudle Glen brought on by the introduction of the Manx Electric Railway. The headland was developed, with a zoo being created and the railway laid.

The line opened on May 23, 1896 and started with Bagnall 2-4-0T *Sea Lion*, and three coaches, and became so popular that a further engine, *Polar Bear*, and additional coach stock were purchased in 1905.

The zoo closed at the start of the Second World War and never reopened, and without it, the railway's postwar popularity declined, until it closed after the 1962 season.

Twenty years later the Isle of Man Steam Railway Supporters' Association launched a plan to restore the line and in December 1983 a short section from the old lime kiln to the headland had been rebuilt for the launch of a Santa train operation. Eventually, the line was relaid to the glen terminus of Lhen Coan and a station was created at the headland with runround facilities. The railway was officially re-opened on May 23, 1986 by Carolyn Rawson as part of the Manx Heritage Year and a tree planted to mark the event in Lhen Coan station, and in September 1987, *Sea Lion* returned, after it was rebuilt by nuclear energy company BNFL at Sellafield in Cumbria as an apprentice training project.

A further extension, restoring the line to its original three-quarter mile length, was opened on July 23, 1992.

Volunteer, Richard Booth, then decided to locally build a second steam locomotive for the line from scratch.

He chose the design of a Bagnall class 'E' 0-4-2T tank locomotive named *Annie*, which was built in 1911 and shipped to New Zealand to operate the Gentle Annie Tramway near Napier. The original *Annie* later ended up at a quarry at Motuhora along with another Bagnall engine from the tramway, and was buried on the site by a landslide in the late 1950s/early 1960s.

Re-excavated in the late 1970s, the remains of *Annie* passed through several owners, and are now owned by the East Coast Museum of Technology at Makaraka near Gisborne, which prepared what remains of the engine for static display.

The replica *Annie* was built using working drawings. It is mechanically identical to *Polar Bear* but with a 0-4-2 wheel arrangement. The cylinder mould was obtained from the Bennett Brook Railway in Australia, where another replica *Annie* had been built. The two replicas are both 2ft gauge whereas the original *Annie* was built to 2ft 6in gauge.

Completed in 1998, the new *Annie* was officially launched as part of the Steam 125 event that year.

Despite having been 'built from new', the locomotive can claim some original components; the water tank lid on one of the side tanks is an original one from *Sea Lion*, new ones having been fabricated as part of her 1987 rebuild.

The locomotive carries a deep Tuscan red livery, the same as that carried by 3ft gauge Manx Northern Railway locomotive *Caledonia* on its return to Isle of Man Railway service in 1995.

ABOVE: *Sea Lion* about to depart from Lhen Coan station, with a Groudle Glen Railway evening service to Sea Lion Rocks. The new *Polar Bear* will be a sister locomotive. BAHNFRIEND*

A THIRD BAGNALL ON THE WAY

A replica of *Polar Bear* now is being built. Around 2012, volunteers of the 2ft gauge Isle of Man pleasure railway decided to build a new Bagnall 2-4-0T to supplement the existing *Sea Lion*.

When the original railway was scrapped in the Sixties, both engines were sold to enthusiast groups, with only *Sea Lion* permanently returning to the Island.

Polar Bear survives as part of the Amberley Museum collection in Sussex, which has a 900yd running line on which a number of narrow gauge steam and diesel locomotives are used to transport visitors around the 36-acre site. It received a new boiler in 1993 and since then has returned to the Isle of Man on three occasions to run on its 'home' railway, but, it is unlikely that it will ever make a permanent comeback.

The railway, a registered charity, found itself in a similar situation to the Corris Railway, which built a new Kerr Stuart Tattoo 0-4-2ST, No. 7, to replace its original No. 4, which was sold to the Talyllyn Railway revivalists in 1951 and is now part of that line's fleet, and is now replicating its original No. 3, which went the same way.

Accordingly, the new locomotive will not fill a historical gap by recreating an extinct class; the primary reason for most new-build projects today. The line needs an additional locomotive in order to maintain services while *Sea Lion* is under overhaul or repair.

The new *Polar Bear* will be called *Brown Bear*, following the tradition of naming locomotives after animals that were once housed in the zoo served by the original line.

An appeal to supporters to raise money to build *Brown Bear* was launched. No money was borrowed to fund its construction, and no parts will be ordered until they can be paid for. It is estimated that it will cost £50,000 to build the engine.

In January 2013, the railway took delivery of the frame plates for *Polar Bear*, which were subsequently assembled in the line's workshop.

The original chimney from *Polar Bear* (which now carries *Sea Lion's* original chimney) will be restored and incorporated into the new locomotive to create a historical link with the past.

Another milestone in the construction was passed in autumn 2015 with the delivery of a pair of fully machined cylinders, having been machined at the workshops of the Isle of Man Steam Packet Company in Douglas.

The valve gear eccentrics were made by North Bay Engineering in Scarborough, and two newly cast smokebox doors have been delivered, one destined for *Brown Bear* and the other for Bagnall replica 0-4-2T *Annie*, which is also resident on the GGR.

It is now estimated that *Brown Bear* will run in 2018.

*If you would like to help the Groudle Glen's new-build scheme, donations are invited online at www.ggr.org.uk or by post to Groudle Glen Railway, 8a The Village Walk, Onchan, Isle of Man, IM3 4EA. ●

ABOVE: Annie on shed at Lhen Coan on the Groudle Glen Railway. GORDON ASTILL*

ABOVE: The frames of *Brown Bear* after being delivered to the Groudle Glen Railway after being cut by the Isle of Man Steam Packet workshops. RICHARD BOOTH/GGR

ABOVE: Artists impression of the locomotive.

Chapter 19

Beachy Head reborn at the Bluebell

Many people remember the London, Brighton & South Coast Railway because of the number of brightly coloured A1X 'Terrier' tank engines that run in preservation. Yet the company also produced some storming express locomotives – and in 2018, we may see one run again!

ABOVE: The original No. 32424 *Beachy Head* leaving Victoria Station on its last-revenue earning run, April 13, 1958.
ALAN CHANDLER/ATLANTIC GROUP

Furthermore, Marsh also rebuilt many of his predecessors' locomotives with larger boilers thereby creating the A1X, B2X, C2X, E4X, E5X and E6X classes. In 1907 he introduced an example of the Schmidt superheater on one of his I3 class tanks, with superb effect.

However, during his time in office Brighton railway works a serious backlog of locomotives built up awaiting repair, and by 1910, nearly a third of the locomotive stock was unusable. Marsh was widely blamed for this predicament, but the fact that Brighton works was snowed under with work did not help.

Never popular with the workforce at Brighton Marsh resigned on the grounds of ill health in July 1911, following accusations of a number of irregularities in his accounting. He died in Bath in May 1933.

In 1911, while Marsh was on sick leave, his assistant Lawson Billinton was given the green light to build six Atlantics similar to the Marsh H1 class but incorporating the Schmidt superheater.

Built at Brighton, they appeared between June 1911 and January 1912 and were an immediate success. With the H1s, they shared the London to Brighton express trains including the heavily loaded Pullman services the 'Brighton Limited' and the 'Southern Belle' marketed by the LBSCR as 'the most luxurious train in the world'.

Douglas Earle Marsh (1862-1933) was the Locomotive, Carriage and Wagon Superintendent of the London, Brighton & South Coast Railway from November 1904 until his early retirement on health grounds in July 1911.

His locomotive classes included the H1 4-4-2 or Atlantic class and four designs of 4-4-2 tank engines, the I1, I2, I3, and I4. In 1910 he designed two 4-6-2T tank locomotive types, the J1 and J2 classes.

BELOW: LBSCR Atlantic No. 32424 at Newhaven on April 13, 1958. ATLANTIC GROUP

ABOVE: David Jones guides the rear of the piston by hand to line up with the crossheads on November 23, 2014. FRED BAILEY

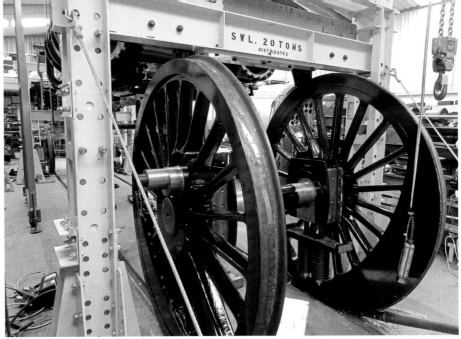

ABOVE: The main driving wheels passing under the front bufferbeam. FRED BAILEY

ABOVE: Finishing one of the connecting rods. DAVID JONES

ABOVE: A crosshead wedge complete. FRED BAILEY

They were gradually replaced on the London-Brighton express trains in 1925-26 by the King Arthur and River classes. Nonetheless, they still found use on other Southern Railway expresses, including boat trains connecting with the Newhaven-Dieppe ferry service. At the same time they were all named after geographical features of the south coast: Marsh had removed names from locomotives during his time in office.

The Nazi invasion of France caused the stoppage of the cross-channel ferries after 1940 and so the H2s became somewhat redundant, members being either replaced in storage or relegated to general duties in southern England.

However, the H2s returned to the boat trains after the end of the war and continued until the mid-Fifties.

One member of the class was withdrawn in 1949, but the remainder continued in regular use until 1956. The last survivor, No. 32424 *Beachy Head*, was withdrawn in April 1958, and no H2 was preserved.

Had it lasted two years longer, it may have come to the attention of the nascent Bluebell Railway, but it was not to be, and when *Beachy Head* was scrapped at Eastleigh in May 1958, the class became extinct.

Making up for lost time, on October 29, 2000, the Bluebell Railway announced its intention to build a new H2 Atlantic based on *Beachy Head* as it appeared in the Southern Railway/British Railways period.

The project was kick-started by the discovery and purchase in 1987 of one of the two Great Northern Railway Class C1 Atlantic boilers which had been used for heating in a woodworking factory at Maldon in Essex, along with the acquisition of a tender underframe from a Class B4, and a set of tender wheels from a Class C2X; both original LBSCR locomotives.

The LBSCR Atlantics were built to drawings modified from the GNR design, and so the boiler is entirely correct for the new locomotive.

The C2X tender had been based for some years at Guildford where it served as sludge carrier DS 70183 until being purchased by Barry scrapyard owner Dai Woodham around 1981.

ABOVE: The wheeled chassis of the new *Beachy Head* inside Atlantic House on June 13, 2015. The patterns for the wheels are displayed on the walls – maybe, JUST MAYBE, they might be used for another locomotive in the future? PHIL BARNES

He felt that some of the locomotives in his scrapyard would have a better chance of being sold if tenders were available, but this particular tender was sold to Madame Tussauds for its Royalty & Empire Exhibition at Windsor Central station, where it was made to look Great Western behind a full-size dummy GWR Achilles class 4-2-2 that had been built at Swindon works around the same time. When this attraction closed, the tender was cut up and the replica locomotive was left on display at the station.

The first parts made for the new *Beachy Head* were the hornguides, spring hangers and supports for the tender as the initial plan was to finish that first before embarking on the engine itself. Two Bluebell volunteer pattern makers asked if they could help, so their efforts enabled the front bogie wheels to be cast followed by many further parts thus saving an enormous amount of money.

By arrangement with the National Railway Museum, many original LBSCR drawings were made available. ▶

ABOVE: An end-on view of the chassis of the new No. 32424 taken on June 13, 2015. PHIL BARNES

In 2002, a site in the yard at the Bluebell's Sheffield Park headquarters was identified for the construction of a dedicated building to house the project, planning permission was obtained and a lightweight steel building, appropriately named Atlantic House, was officially opened by railway historian Richard Gibbon OBE on June 11, 2006.

On that day, *Beachy Head*'s new steel driving wheels from Norton Cast Products in Sheffield, which had been cast the year before, and the newly delivered blank main frames, supplied by Corus, were on display.

Financial support came initially from the Bluebell Railway Trust, which provided a start-up fund to launch the scheme and has also contributed 80 per cent of the cost of the building. Regular income is mainly from Bluebell Railway Preservation Society members who contribute £25,000 per year by standing order around, or through individual donations. A successful sponsorship scheme raised more than £150,000 and enables supporters to identify 'their' parts and receive a certificate.

In 2006, the original regulator handle from the first *Beachy Head* was donated to the project.

A major milestone took place on October 1, 2007 when the completed main frames were lifted upright and braced together – thereby officially creating the new No. 32424. Since then many parts have been cast, machined and fitted including cross members, hornguides and brake gear.

The bogie wheels and the trailing wheelset were delivered at the beginning of 2011, while the main driving and coupled wheelsets had their crankpins fitted at the South Devon Railway's Buckfastleigh works.

The cylinder and valve chest components were delivered in July 2008 and the first motion parts were cut by water jet from forged blanks the following April.

In the spring of 2010, the valve chest assembly was welded together and the main axleboxes delivered. That autumn saw the bogie and trailing wheelsets assembled at Ian Riley's workshop in Bury from the castings, and the cylinders fabricated.

The valve and cylinder liners were fitted in early 2012, and by that summer, the frames were supported on the bogie and trailing truck. That year, the valve chest and cylinders were fitted to the frames and pressure tested.

In March 2013, the main wheelsets were completed and delivered, and in December that year, the last major valve gear components were delivered.

The axleboxes were metalled, machined and fitted in February 2014, with the eccentric rods fitted the following month.

Most work between the frames, such as the valve and reversing gear, pipework for brakes and steam heat was completed in time for the new *Beachy Head* to be completed that May. In August that year, the cylinders were clad, crossheads fitted and superheater-header casting patterns completed.

Autumn 2015 saw ultrasonic testing of the boiler stays find no broken ones, and the intricate work on lubrication runs, and piping up the drain cocks is also underway.

The splashers have been completed, riveted to the running plate and completed. Painting of the splashers and cab is also progressing.

The connecting rods are now on and the coupling rods will follow in 2016, after which the main work will be on the boiler.

Castings for the superheater header, safety valve housing and its shield will be delivered in 2016.

Even before it is ready to steam, the new Brighton Atlantic has become an attraction in itself. Visitors to the Bluebell Railway's Giants of Steam weekend of October 31-November 1 were able to visit Atlantic House and see the rapid progress being made.

A target date for 2018 has been set for the debut of the new *Beachy Head* on the Bluebell Railway, which is certain to be in demand for high-profile galas and loan visits to other heritage lines.

■ For more details about how you can help the Brighton Atlantic Project, contact Terry Cole at tcole@steyning.fsbusiness.co.uk ●

ABOVE: The front of the new Brighton Atlantic with the cab in the background as seen on September 29, 2015. ATLANTIC GROUP

ABOVE: The connecting rod of the new *Beachy Head* in place on December 13, 2015. ATLANTIC GROUP

ABOVE: The pattern for the header of the new Atlantic. FRED BAILEY

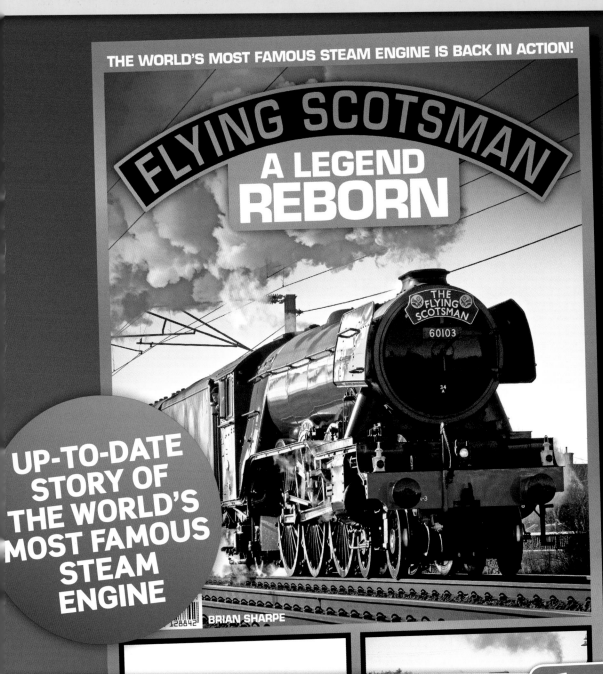

Chapter 20

Not the final whistle
for the B17s

Sadly, none of Sir Nigel Gresley's LNER B17 4-6-0s survived into preservation, but two separate groups are now building their own, one becoming the next in the Sandringham class, the other named after the world's most famous football club.

By the mid-Twenties, the power requirements of the GE District of the LNER (former Great Eastern Railway) were becoming critical. There was a particular shortage of suitable locomotives for hauling express passenger services, which had become heavier with the introduction of heavier vacuum-braked coaches and increasing traffic. The limitations of the GER loading gauge meant that suitable locomotive types could not be transferred from other parts of the LNER system.

The initial specification was for a three-cylinder 4-6-0 with a tractive effort of about 25,000lb and axle loading restricted to 17 tons. The Doncaster design office had problems satisfying this specification and the contract was handed to the North British Locomotive Company in late 1927.

Early the next year, two designs were offered with neither meeting the 17-ton axle-loading requirement. However an 18-ton axle loading was chosen with the LNER accepting the restrictions to the B17's route availability and an order for 10 locomotives was placed.

The final B17 aesthetic borrowed many features from the LNER family of locomotives to negate the need for a totally new design. The cab, cylinders and motion, and the raised running board were similar to the existing A1 (A3) design, the latter to facilitate access for the 6ft 8in driving wheels that were also used on the D49.

The boiler design had a history with the K3 and O2 locomotives and the cranked outside steam pipes design was visually similar to the V1 and V3 2-6-2T.

The one (though externally invisible) design peculiarity is the divided drive. It was impossible for all three cylinders to drive the middle coupled axle, so the middle cylinder powered the leading axle and was positioned forward above the front bogie.

The locomotives were specifically designed for lines in East Anglia to haul the increasingly heavier trains. However, small GE tenders were initially required because of the short turntables then extant in the area. Tender designs were already available at Stratford for the smaller tender for use on the GE section.

Aesthetically there is not one obvious feature that is peculiar to the B17 design. It was designed in a similar way to the GWR family of locomotives using, as we saw earlier, common parts and designs wherever possible. However, it is clearly one of the

BELOW: B17 4-6-0 No. 61629 *Naworth Castle* at Doncaster works in British Railways' days. Built in April 1931, it was scrapped in September 1959. B17SLT

ABOVE: B17/6 4-6-0 No. 61666 *Nottingham Forest* at Colchester in 1958. Built in February 1937, it was disposed of in March 1960. B17SLT

LNER family, and it could be argued that it inherited all the best features from the parental designs at its conception.

The first B17 was delivered by North British on November 30, 1928. Subsequently between 1930-36, Darlington produced 52 locomotives and Robert Stephenson & Co built a final batch of 11 locomotives in 1937. Small modifications were made to successive batches, resulting in four variants (B17/1 to B17/4).

Later, two locomotives were rebuilt with streamlining and classified B17/5. The final variant was known as B17/6 and these were locomotives from the previous classes rebuilt with diagram 100A boilers.

The B17 'Sandringhams' were all named after country houses, football clubs and local county regiments associated with the former LNER. The first of the class, No. 2800, was

ABOVE: B17 No. 61662 *Manchester United* at Liverpool Street station in 1957. RC RILEY/61662

named *Sandringham* after the Royal Family's Norfolk residence. Thereafter the whole class became known as Sandringhams.

Twenty-five B17s were named after Football League clubs. Known as 'Footballers', they each carried appropriate club colours and brass footballs.

Probably the most famous of the 'Footballers' was No. 2862 (later 61662) *Manchester United*, which was built in January 1937, and ran nearly one million miles in traffic before withdrawal at the end of 1959.

The last survivor, No. 61668 *Bradford City*, was scrapped at Stratford in September 1960.

ABOVE: No. 61653 *Huddersfield Town* heads a Broxbourne to St Ives service in January 1951. B 17SLT

OPERATION AND PERFORMANCE

ABOVE: B17/6 No. 61668 *Bradford City* at Stratford in 1950. Outshopped in April 1937, it was the last of its class to survive, being scrapped in August 1960, just as the standard gauge preservation movement had started with the volunteer-led takeovers of the Middleton and Bluebell railways. B17SLT

The first B17s ran the Cambridge services, where they were popular with both the public and railway men. The services from London to Ipswich and beyond were not such a great success as this route had gradients that caused problems for the heavier trains.

The initial batch (B17/1) had teething problems with cracked frames, so a second batch (B17/2) was built with lighter springing on driving axle boxes and stiffer bogie springing. Frame problems continued so the later (B17/3) locomotives were fitted with horn blocks for the middle driving axle rather than guides. Although the spring arrangement was further amended, and the axle box lubrication mechanism changed, the B17s would always have a reputation of being rough riders.

Later designs with draughting improvements, plus the larger LNER tenders, were introduced as B17/4s for use on heavier

trains both within and outside of the East Anglian restrictions.

This included the cross-country boat train services from Ipswich to Manchester, and when East Anglia's infrastructure was improved the heavy boat trains from London Liverpool Street to Harwich.

From 1936 B17s with the larger LNER tenders were allocated further afield to Leicester, Sheffield, Neasden, and Gorton replacing older Great Central Atlantics. The B17s continued to operate on the original LNER, and later Eastern Region network, across the routes of the eastern counties and between Marylebone and Manchester up to 1960.

The first three B17s were withdrawn between 1952-53. With the planned replacement of steam the remaining B17s were withdrawn between 1958-60 before the preservation movement was established and none survived.

▶

SPIRIT OF SANDRINGHAM

The B17 Steam Locomotive Trust was formed as an organisation with charitable status in 2011, with the mission to recreate the first of the class. The Gresley design fills the evolutionary gap between the B12 and B1 4-6-0s in the history of East Anglian express passenger steam locomotives.

The trust has clear objectives and programmes, with an associated and appropriate management structure, to deliver an operational B17 for heritage railway and main line use.

It is to be known as *Spirit of Sandringham* to represent the history of the entire class and will take the next number in the series of 61673.

It will be designed and constructed using both original and modern design and manufacturing technologies as well as providing educational and training opportunities for young people in formal training schemes.

The build standard is that of the final B17/6 design plus the necessary improvements required in performance,

reliability and maintenance to meet current Railway Group Standards.

It will be capable of operating with either the GE tender or the larger LNER Group Standard tender a both historically used with B17s – and an example of both are owned by the trust. Appropriate certification will be progressively obtained in conjunction with the Vehicle Acceptance Body and railway authorities.

Many original drawings have been sourced from the National Railway Museum library and detailed designs/CAD conversions: new designs where necessary are being created for appropriate and available manufacturing techniques.

Assembly of the locomotive has been delegated to the Llangollen Railway Engineering Services group, which has experience of three other new builds and the necessary proven capability.

ABOVE: Tim Godfrey, a grandson of B17 designer Sir Nigel Gresley, starts the process to cut the frames for *Spirit of Sandringham* at Boro' Foundry in Lye. B17SLT

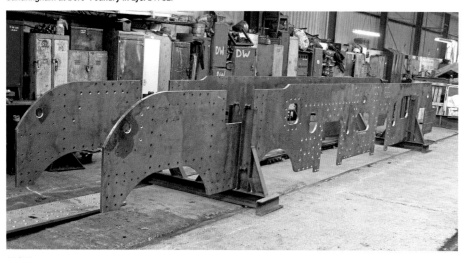

ABOVE: The frames for *Spirit of Sandringham* erected and on display at Llangollen in September 2015. B17SLT

PROGRESS TO DATE

The year 2015 saw significant progress on the manufacture of the locomotive.

In April the material for the frames and bufferbeam was rolled and the frames profiled by TATA steel. They were then delivered to the Boro' Foundry at Lye near Stourbridge, West Midlands, for machining during August.

Both the profiling and machining operations were initiated by Tim Godfrey, grandson of Sir Nigel Gresley; the original designer of the B17.

On completion, and following successful dimensional checks, the frames and front bufferbeam were transported to the Llangollen Railway where the frames are aligned ready for construction.

To ensure that correct alignment and orientation of the frames is achieved adjustable support stands and spacers are being used to effectively comply with defined dimensions and tolerances for the mainframe assembly. This will be a temporary arrangement until correct frame stays are manufactured and become available for assembly.

The trust has a funded programme of work to complete the design definition of the dragbox and fabricated frame stays in preparation for manufacture. This funding also covers the cast frame stays, which will be manufactured to the original drawings obtained from the NRM. The manufacture of the dragbox and frame stays will progressively build up the static mainframe assembly at Llangollen throughout 2016.

Two cast brass *Spirit of Sandringham* nameplates have been ordered for delivery to Llangollen, for temporary mounting in the correct position and orientation above the centre axle to give the locomotive its unique identity.

■ Further information about the *Spirit of Sandringham* project and the B17 Steam Locomotive Trust may be obtained from the website at www.b17steamloco.com (including email contact) or telephone 07527 670436.

LEFT: The nameplate for *Spirit of Sandringham* takes pole position on a promotional stand for its builders at the big Barrow LMS-themed gala on September 25-27, 2015.
ROBIN JONES

OLD TRAFFORD BACK ON WHEELS

In late 2011, around two million supporters of Manchester United across the world were asked to contribute to a separate £1.8-million project being promoted by the North British Locomotive Preservation Group to recreate No. 61662 *Manchester United*.

This scheme aims to have the locomotive built to main line standards as an ambassador both for the steam movement and the football club itself.

The origins of the project lay in the group's previous scheme to build not one, but two, B17s, unveiled in 2008. At that time, several enthusiasts joined the NBLPG to support it, and eventually the Sandringham Locomotive Company was formed. Renowned steam engineer Kim Malyon was a leading light of the company but passed away before much progress could be made.

Early in 2010, some members within the Sandringham Locomotive Company proposed the idea of forming a new trust to take over the project, and this came into being in 2011, as described above, when they took over most of the assets of the company.

The NBLPG retained its 'half' of the scheme, to build a new 'Footballer', but held back with relaunching its Manchester United scheme so that the new B17 Trust could become established in its own right.

Engine 61662 Appeal project leader, Ken Livermore, said: "There are an estimated two million Manchester United supporters worldwide and if each one would be prepared to make just a £1 donation we will be well on the way to success.

"Any funds we raise for No. 61662 will not be at the expense of the B17 Trust and indeed, if middle-of-the-road enthusiasts contact us we will be happy to point them in the direction of the trust."

One of the group's members found an original LNER tender in Balby scrapyard at Doncaster where it had been hidden under old lorries and cars for more than 20 years.

The tender, No. 041249, is of a type that ran with many locomotives built by North British for the LNER including K3s, B1s and K1s, and the B17s. The scrapyard had bought it from Thornaby depot where it saw many years' use as a waste oil tank.

The group duly bought it for £6000, and had it moved to the Mizens Railway at Knaphill Woking for restoration.

Members also built a replica B17 cab to promote the project at enthusiast events.

Initial estimates placed the cost of the new *Manchester United* in the region of £1.8 million.

■ Anyone who wants to donate to the *Manchester United* project or become involved is asked to visit www.engine61662appeal.co.uk or send donations to: Engine 61662 Appeal, Engine 61662 Appeal, 22 Delta Road, Audenshaw, Manchester, M34 5HR.

ABOVE: The end: on a snowy day in Doncaster, Class B17 'Footballer' No. 61662 stands in the work's scrapyard after its withdrawal in December 1959. The 1937-built 4-6-0 still carries its left-hand nameplate, football, smokebox numberplate, and 30E (Colchester) shedplate, but not its worksplate. It was cut up at the works in January 1960. GORDON TURNER

ABOVE: The North British Locomotive Preservation Group's project to replicate LNER B17 'Footballer' 4-6-0 No. 61662 *Manchester United* has seen its tender's BR identity restored. Mick Strickson of Trackside Ltd supplied its crest and BR number transfers free of charge as a donation to the project appeal. The tender is housed at the Mizens Railway at Woking. NBLPG

Chapter 21

Building Gresley's mighty
Mikado

How do you follow a soaraway steaming success like Tornado*? By building an even more powerful locomotive to take the main line of the future by an even bigger storm! Graham Nicholas, quality and certification director of The A1 Steam Locomotive Trust, outlines the story of the world's fastest-growing standard gauge new build project – the seventh member of Sir Nigel Gresley's P2 class.*

On September 16, 2010, at a star-studded, glittering reception in London's Grosvenor House Hotel, The A1 Steam Locomotive Trust was presented with a special commendation in the 'project of the year' category at the annual rail industry awards. It was a highly deserved and fitting celebration of the remarkable work that had seen A1 Peppercorn Pacific No. 60163 *Tornado* enter service on the main line the year before.

In 1934, there were no annual awards ceremonies, or not in the way we'd recognise them today, but if there had, there would have been only one contender for the 'locomotive of the year' category that year – the LNER's express passenger 2-8-2 No. 2001 *Cock O' The North*.

What they did have in 1934 were voracious publicity machines, none more so than the LNER. In the pre-jet age, railways were big

news and at the forefront of technological developments, so when the LNER unveiled its latest creation at a formal press launch at King's Cross station on June 1, 1934 it was big news.

The locomotive was a leviathan of the rails, as big and impressive as anything seen up to that point on Britain's railways. It was immediately in demand for publicity exhibitions, which were interspersed with

BELOW: Dream pairing: artist Chris Ludlow's depiction of No. 2007 *Prince of Wales* racing No. 60163 *Tornado.* A1SLT

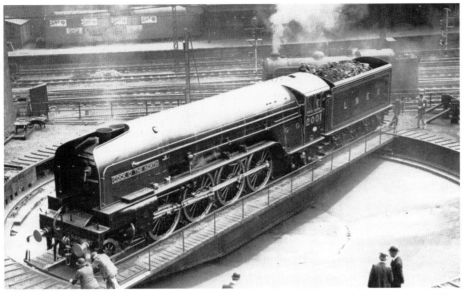

ABOVE: The original P2, No. 2001 *Cock O' The North*, being turned at King's Cross on its first day in service. Designed to haul 600-ton trains on the arduous Edinburgh to Aberdeen route, following Gresley's death in 1941, all six P2s were rebuilt as Pacifics by his successor Edward Thompson in 1943-44 and scrapped by 1961, leaving a major gap in the UK heritage steam fleet. The project to build No. 2007 will demonstrate how the design can be fully realised through use of modern computer design and modelling techniques, enabling it to deliver its full potential hauling passenger trains at high speed across today's national network. A1SLT

ABOVE: P2 No. 2007 *Prince of Wales* as it will be seen from above. A1SLT

ABOVE: No. 2001 *Cock O' the North* on rollers at the Vitry testing centre in France. A1SLT

ABOVE: P2 No. 2001 *Cock O' The North*: the development of the class was cut short after Gresley's death… until now. A1SLT

testing and initial service running. In these trials No. 2001 showed the capabilities of the type by taking 19 coaches (total weight 65 tons) over Stoke summit at 56.5mph on a dynamometer test run. The LNER clearly had a potential world-beater on its hands.

Yet when the six members of the class settled into everyday service on their intended route (Edinburgh to Aberdeen) this early promise was never truly fulfilled. Though not everything that was said can ever be substantiated, (an early search of the records at Kew provided scant information), the locomotives gained reputations variously for

spreading the track and consuming prodigious quantities of coal. Additionally, although there were no main line derailment incidents per se, there were several recorded examples of premature crank axle failures – an undesirable attribute for any locomotive.

What is known is that, with the attention of Gresley and his LNER design team turned to new streamliner trains by 1935, little if any development of the P2 class was done, other than the abandonment of the Lentz valve gear of the prototype for conventional Walschaert. History records that the six original class P2s had all been rebuilt as ungainly looking

Pacifics by 1944 under the Thompson regime. From that time to the present day, the enigma of the 'what might have been' P2 has endured.

Meanwhile, what of that feted A1 project team? Basking in their glory? Resting on their laurels? No. With a huge credibility factor established, based on a proven formula it was a foregone conclusion that the team would wish to build a second locomotive (irreverently referred to as 'Lot 2') And what more iconic a challenge than to pick up the baton from the 1930s Gresley design team and realise the full potential of the P2 by creating the next member of the class – No. 2007 *Prince of Wales*.

THE NEXT GIANT NEW-BUILD STEP

The choice of the giant Gresley Mikado nevertheless represents a significant step forward from the work done to create *Tornado* and this is reflected in the subtle differences in the mission statement for the P2 project (compared with that for *Tornado*): "To develop, build and operate an improved Gresley class P2 Mikado steam locomotive for main line and preserved railway use".

As a starting point for the project the trust made good use of the years following the introduction of *Tornado* by commissioning a feasibility study into the proposed new P2. Indeed, preparatory work had quietly been going on in the background for some time, even before the completion of *Tornado*.

Central to this was work done to evaluate the ride performance of the locomotive, this being a key area to get right if permission is to be gained for operation at speed on the mainline railway. Realising at an early stage that, owing to the reputational issues and the limited service experience (compared with the A1), a

Grandfather Rights argument was unlikely to succeed, the trust firmly embraced modern railway design technology from the outset. Industry specialist Delta Rail was engaged to harness the power of the internationally recognised vehicle dynamics computer modelling package VAMPIRE®.

As well as being able to provide some totally fresh analysis on the issue, adoption of a computer modelling approach will considerably smooth the way to the eventual certification and approval of the locomotive, being a recognised modern technique to support the introduction of any new rolling stock.

TORNADO LEADS THE WAY
A particular area for study has been the original swing-link design of the leading pony truck. Although there are no known mainline derailments of P2s attributed to this feature, there were no fewer than four affecting the V2 2-6-2 locomotives as originally fitted with

the same type of pony truck. The entire V2 fleet was subsequently fitted with pony trucks fitted with side-control springing instead.

Here is where *Tornado* has been able to lend a massive helping hand. During the original commissioning programme in 2008, the A1 Trust was tasked with undertaking some track force tests as part of the approvals for the A1. Although this was unexpected and required additional effort, it was quickly realised that here was an opportunity to get some steam locomotive ride test data 'in the bank' to validate any future computer modelling assumptions.

It was therefore a satisfying thought that, as it roared through the night between York and Newcastle on that memorable evening of November 18, 2008, festooned with measuring devices as part of its own testing, *Tornado* was also helping to pave the way for its future stablemate. An intimate bond between the two locomotives was thus formed.

The work has resulted in a fully validated computer model within Vampire for *Tornado*. This work has then been extrapolated to derive computer models of the P2 as originally designed and as proposed (with the side-control spring bogie). A tweak on a spring rating here, a slice off a clearance there and the ride characteristics of the new P2 have been evaluated and optimised. So much easier – and far less heart-breaking – than the traditional (and nowadays largely frowned upon) method of 'trying it and see if it works'.

The study showed conclusively that the myths and legends that have surrounded the original locomotive type were probably just that. An improved P2 design, featuring the developments mentioned should produce a ride performance at least as good as *Tornado*.

Other aspects affecting the 'should we; shouldn't we?' decision were also being considered.

It has always been a slightly uncomfortable truth that the particular route that influenced the original P2 design was its very undoing. The twisting, sinuous nature of the Edinburgh-Aberdeen run was by no means the kindest for an eight-coupled machine. Among the many unanswered questions from the story of the original P2s is why they were never transferred to the southern end of the East Coast Main Line during the darkest hours of the Second World War when their prodigious haulage abilities would have been invaluable.

Transfer this thought forward to the 21st century, however, and this becomes the perfect raison d'être for recreating such a powerful machine.

The trust has always regarded the ECML route north from King's Cross as a 'core' route as far as it is concerned, being the spiritual home of the LNER Pacific. With modern charter train operations often dependent on the ability to fill a large train and keep to 75mph paths to minimise running times, the high performance attributes of the P2 would appear perfectly suited to the modern world.

THE MEANS TO THE END

Overall, the output of the feasibility study was a resounding 'yes', allowing the trust to turn its attention to the formal launch of the project. Despite the undoubted success of the business model that supports *Tornado*, the P2 project team led by Mark Allatt was determined to learn lessons to ensure an even slicker approach second time around.

One radical idea was the concept of a 'racing start' to capitalise on the credibility factor and show some significant early progress.

The idea was simple – to seek 100 people to donate £1000. The response was extraordinary – when the P2 founders' club was – reluctantly – closed down, an incredible £460,000 had been raised in just 10 months, largely through a series of road shows that took the P2 project team along the East Coast route from London to Aberdeen. No. 2007 was off to a meteoric start and the exercise demonstrated emphatically the obvious hunger for 'Lot 2' to be turned into reality.

As with the A1 project, it was off to the National Railway Museum to seek the drawings. This time though, the trust benefited enormously from the York museum's commendable Search Engine project, implemented during the intervening 20 years since their original visits. The key frame and wheel drawings were readily identified and copied along with the mouth-watering General Arrangement drawing (interestingly, there never was one of these for the A1).

A distinct difference this time though has been the adoption of a full 3D computer drawing package on David Elliott's laptop.

With the degree of alterations to the original design that were required this was an obvious application of modern technology. As well as being able to quickly and efficiently amend the physical details of the design, the program can produce elegant publicity pictures of any aspect of the locomotive, from a traditional full three-quarter view down to the tiniest minutiae of a fitted bolt, images that can easily set pulses racing and hopefully wallets opening.

Equally importantly, the 3D software knows where each component is relative to another and can easily detect when an 'impossible' juxtaposition has been proposed (something that was not so easy with the previous traditional two-dimensional drawings and which caused a few headaches with *Tornado* when it came down to some of the final pipe run details). Furthermore, once the details of a component are finalised, the 3D software can be easily translated into manufacturing drawings and/or linked to a supplier's computer-driven manufacturing tools, offering further efficiencies and a high degree of reproduce-ability of components.

Some aspects of the creation of No. 2007 have been surprisingly similar, however.

Once again the Tata (formerly British Steel) Scunthorpe manufacturing plant rolled and cut the frame parts and once again William Cook Cast Products took on the challenge of casting all the wheels for the locomotive. Meanwhile, having hosted the interim project of creating *Tornado*'s new support coach (former BR Mk.1 BCK No. E21249), Darlington Locomotive Works was given a thorough spring clean and prepared for the delivery of the first P2 frame components. So the trust can look forward to creating the new P2 entirely within its very own facility. It is even being built the right way round this time so when the inevitable launch day comes, *Prince of Wales*

ABOVE: The cutting of the mainframes at Tata Steel in Scunthorpe. ROBIN JONES

RIGHT: Ben and Tim Godfrey, the grandsons of Sir Nigel Gresley, began the cutting of the mainframes for what will be the next of the LNER Chief Mechanical Engineer's masterpieces to be built – P2 2-8-2 No. 2007 *Prince of Wales*. On May 21, 2013, the pair pressed the green button at Tata Steel in Scunthorpe to begin the profiling of the 21-ton frames, which were rolled at the plant's plate mill two days later. The profiling of the frames marked the start of the construction of *Prince of Wales*, which when finished will be Britain's most powerful steam locomotive and the seventh member of the P2 class.

will be able to emerge from its birthplace smokebox first in the traditional manner.

With much of the founders' club funds already committed to the frame and wheel components, further funding efforts are continuing. The ever-popular covenant scheme has been adopted for the P2 project and already enjoys 90% of the support of the total *Tornado* take up.

There is one difference though. A pint of beer is no longer £1.25 (even in the North East!) so it is now based on a minimum £10 per month. A separate boiler fund has already been started, this time more along the lines of the general covenanter scheme – the aim here is for the locomotive to be 100% funded at the point of completion.

At the trust's Silver Jubilee annual covenanters' convention in October 2015, it was announced that £2 million of the anticipated £5-million price tag had already been raised or pledged.

JAMES MAY BUILDS FIRST P2 COMPONENT!

TV presenter James May manufactured the first component of the new £5-million Gresley P2 2-8-2 No. 2007 *Prince of Wales*; the smokebox dart, which is the component that keeps the smokebox door securely closed.

The celebrity spent the best part of February 20, 2013, patiently crafting the component at the works where *Tornado* was completed in 2008. It's estimated that it will take around 100,000 man hours to build the P2.

James said: "Not many man-made machines stir the soul, but a full-blown steam locomotive is right up there, and we invented it. However, over the decades we've lost so much of the talent, skill and knowledge needed to build them.

" That's why it's such a thrill to work alongside the team building No. 2007 *Prince of Wales*, determined to not only resurrect this monster from the past, but to improve it using modern wizardry.

"The whole spectrum of manufacturing brilliance will be represented in the P2. At one end, boffins will program computerised plasma-cutters to produce – more accurately than could have been imagined originally – the massive frames of the engine's chassis.

"At the other, someone might produce a small control handle at a bench, using just a vice and a few simple files in a scene that has gone largely unchanged for two centuries."

The A1 Steam Locomotive Trust's chairman, Mark Allatt, has known James since the Top Gear team raced *Tornado* from King's Cross to Edinburgh on April 25, 2009. James drove a Jaguar XK120 of similar vintage to the original Peppercorn A1s, while Jeremy Clarkson acted as fireman on *Tornado*.

ABOVE: The A1/P2 team and James May with the finished smokebox dart and the *Prince of Wales* nameplate. A1SLT

LEFT: Top Gear's James May manufacturing the first component for the new Gresley P2 on a lathe inside Darlington Locomotive Works on February 20, 2014. A1SLT

A MODERN MIKADO

Further development work has been continuing in parallel with the first phases of manufacture.

Foremost among this has been the valve gear arrangements for the locomotive. As is well known, the original No. 2001 was fitted with Lentz rotary valve gear, which the LNER had been trialling on other locomotive types, notably the D49 4-4-0s. The first version, fitted with infinitely variable cams soon gave trouble and a simplified arrangement with six stepped positions was substituted. However, this led to loss of efficiency and so No. 2001 reverted to conventional Walschaerts form, as fitted to the other members of the class.

The Lentz arrangement was not therefore considered a suitable basis to go forward with for No. 2007 and, for some time, the favoured route was to fit the visually similar, but technically different Caprotti rotary cam gear (as fitted to unique BR Pacific No. 71000 *Duke of Gloucester*).

However, when David Elliott started to research this in detail, two coincident factors emerged. Firstly, having studied in detail the arrangement fitted to No. 71000, when he came to try to graft this on to the virtual 2007 on his computer, it was by no means straightforward, requiring some considerable contortions to orientate it correctly into the frame and cylinders of the P2.

Secondly, some further development work on the original Lentz design came to light – this had been undertaken in the USA and the name of Franklin was attributed to an arrangement fitted to a Santa Fe 4-8-4 No. 3752. Patient but persistent work corresponding 'across the pond' was ultimately rewarded when a set of drawings was delivered to David Elliott from one Charles Smith, whose father had an archive of ▶

ABOVE: The frames for new £5 million Gresley P2 2-8-2 No. 2007 *Prince of Wales* were dedicated at a VIP ceremony in Darlington attended by the town's mayor Coun Gerald Lee on July 19, 2014. The ceremony marked the formal start of construction of what will be Britain's most powerful steam locomotive. Pictured is the rear end of the frames where the Cartazzi wheelset will fit. PAUL DAVIES/P2

information on the Franklin valve gear – there were even operating instructions and a parts catalogue.

Crucially, the Lentz-Franklin valve gear (as the trust now refers to it) includes infinitely variable cams and it transpires that a considerable and largely successful service history of locomotive No. 3752 was amassed while fitted with this arrangement.

Even more remarkably, the design is based around a fabricated set of cylinders, which the trust was considering in any case, having first been put on to the idea by work done at Meiningen. It does therefore seem that a sound way forward has been found to fit a valve gear arrangement that will deliver the performance and efficiency requirements while retaining the classic, aesthetic look of the Gresley original.

ABOVE RIGHT: Former King's Cross shedmaster, Peter Townend, meets the mayor and mayoress of Darlington on July 21, 2014. A1SLT ABOVE LEFT: P2 engineering director, David Elliott, (far left) discusses the first driving wheel to be cast with the mayor and mayoress of Darlington while trust chairman, Mark Allatt, (far right) looks on. William Cook Cast Products of Sheffield, the principal sponsor of *Tornado*, was commissioned to produce the P2's eight 6ft 2in diameter driving wheels on 'very advantageous terms'. The commercial price for the eight driving wheels is in excess of £100,000. A1SLT

SHARING THE BOILER DESIGN

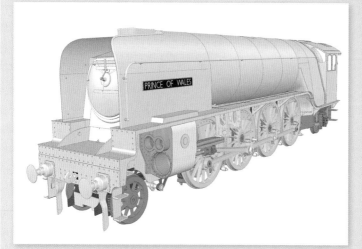

One of the massive areas of commonality with *Tornado* is the boiler.

Although the boiler barrel of the original P2 was a little longer than that of the A1, the discrepancy can be compensated by a larger smokebox; all hidden beneath that distinctive cladding. Seven years' operational experience with the boiler type as fitted to *Tornado* has shown it to be a prodigious steam raiser but not without some weaknesses that have meant some unplanned repairs in that time. However, likely causes behind these issues have been identified with corresponding remedial work undertaken on *Tornado*'s boiler (most recently during the A1's first intermediate overhaul at the beginning of 2015).

LEFT: The locomotive and frames as visualised in 3D Solidworks in September 2015. A1SLT

All this means that a boiler to the refined design can be ordered from Meiningen straight off the current plans. Not only will this therefore be a significantly simpler operation than with *Tornado* but the advantages of having two fully interchangeable major components are obvious.

Eventually, the trust would like to have a third boiler of the type, fully overhauled and ready to go in order to maximise the availability of both locomotives.

SUPERIOR CRANK AXLES

Meanwhile, what about those broken crank axles that beset the original P2s? In common with all Gresley three-cylinder designs (but unlike *Tornado*) all three cylinders act on the same driving wheelset. Additionally, with an increased number of driving wheels providing adhesion compared with a Pacific type, the P2s were less prone to slipping so, with the full 43,000lbs of tractive effort bearing down on this one component, particularly when starting away, its potential to be the achilles heel is all too obvious.

Fortunately, a priceless record of one of the axle failure incidents has been unearthed (that which befell No. 2005 in July 1939 while starting away from Stonehaven with a heavy southbound train), including a crucial photograph of the fracture. From a study of this photograph, coupled with the details of the LNER drawing, the shortcomings of the crank axle design are all too obvious to the contemporary rail vehicle engineer, with all the benefit of hindsight that 80 years of intervening research and greater understanding of fracture mechanics can provide.

However, in order to full quantify and optimise the design, the trust has engaged industry consultants Mott MacDonald to undertake a full structural analysis of the complex crank axle design, including use of state-of-the-art finite element analysis. This should ensure that the best possible arrangement can be derived to give a long and trouble-free life for this most critical of components. At the time of writing, this work is well advanced and will enable the orders to be placed for the axles themselves (the wheels already nearing completion).

While work such as the above may appear to have delayed the ordering of main components, this is not regarded as an undue problem. One lesson the trust is determined to learn from 'Lot 1' is not to under-estimate all those little detail components that are required in the final push to completion. Therefore any slack time is being put to good use by quietly building up the necessary valves and other control fittings that will be required at the end of the project. Not only will that streamline the final run in but, with many parts in common, it also ensures that there are spares for *Tornado* sitting on the shelf if required in the interim.

With a sound pedigree behind them, coupled

ABOVE: The eight proof-machined coupled wheels delivered by William Cook Cast Products to Darlington Locomotive Works. The builders are aiming to have a rolling P2 chassis in 2016. A1SLT

with the learning experiences from *Tornado*, it can be seen that the team behind the construction of No. 2007 stands every chance of delivering its second project on, or around, the projected completion date of 2021.

Given that, by that date, there will be only a tiny proportion of people able to remember the original machines; most of us will be experiencing something entirely new.

With the design developed and finely honed to suit the world of 21st-century mainline steam, Gresley's mighty Mikado class P2 should be an enigma no more.

By June 2015, less than two years since the project to build a new Gresley P2 2-8-2 was launched, a third of the £5-million locomotive was complete by weight. The milestone was passed with the delivery of the 12 tyres.

PROGRESS TO DATE

• Engine's frames erected at Darlington Locomotive Works with several cast frame stays permanently fitted
• Footplate angles made and fitted, footplating profiled and fitted
• All 20 wheels for engine and tender cast; eight 6ft2in driving wheels proof-machined
• Engine tyres delivered and axles and crank pins ordered
• Roller bearings for all engine and tender wheelsets ordered and most delivered
• All major engine frame stays, brackets, horn blocks, axle boxes and buffers cast and machined – 64 in total
• More than 1000 fitted and driven bolts delivered
• Preliminary discussions held with boiler manufacturers and forged foundation ring corners manufactured and machined
• Vampire study into ride and suspension completed and Finite Element Analysis of crank axle underway to ensure locomotive complies with modern standards
• Assessment and notified body appointed to oversee certification
• Profiles for cab delivered – assembly under way
• The Gresley Society Trust to sponsor the manufacture of the smokebox and distinctive 'face', smokebox door pressing and door frame manufactured, smokebox barrel plates delivered, pattern for chimney in manufacture
• More than £2 million already pledged
• Nameplates delivered and chime whistle ordered

VOLUNTEERING

There are many ways in which you can help build No. 2007 *Prince of Wales*.

The trust is always on the lookout for volunteers to help with the building of the locomotive at Darlington Locomotive Works. Experience is useful but many jobs on the locomotive require the services of a fitter's mate so qualifications are not essential.

The trust has established a successful fundraising team, which attends events to promote No. 2007 *Prince of Wales*, but more people are needed, wherever they live.

HELP COMPLETE NO. 2007 *PRINCE OF WALES* IN RECORD TIME

The trust estimates that No. 2007 *Prince of Wales* will cost around £5 million to build over a seven- to 10-year period. As with *Tornado*, funds will be raised through regular monthly donations, donations dedicated to specific components, The Boiler Club and commercial sponsorship.

Regular donations: a monthly payment made by standing order in units of £10 – "a P2 for the price of a pint". In recognition of your support, you will receive:
• The opportunity to buy ticket (seat already reserved) on one of the first trains hauled by No. 2007.
• Reasonable access to No. 2007 at all times
• A print of the launch painting of *Prince of Wales* by Jonathan Clay
• The opportunity to join one of the teams building No. 2007
• Monthly e-newsletter Mikado Messenger and quarterly newsletter The Communication Cord
• An invitation to the annual convention and other exclusive events
• A covenanter card and opportunity to buy exclusive tie and annual team photograph
• The opportunity to take part in the trust's awards scheme
• Your name inscribed on the Roll of Honour at Darlington Locomotive Works

The Boiler Club: following the success of the Founders' Club, which was designed to get to the P2 Project to the point of cutting No. 2007's frames, the trust decided to establish The Boiler Club to fund the construction of *Prince of Wales*'s boiler.

The trust set an initial target for the Founders' Club of at least £100,000 from 100 'Founders' but thanks to the overwhelming generosity of supporters, more than £450,000 was raised from 360 donors. The trust aims to leave No. 2007 *Prince of Wales* debt free on completion and seeks to raise at least £600,000 for The Boiler Club from 300 supporters each donating £2000 to the project in up to 40 payments of £50 by standing order.

Special benefits for members of The Boiler Club include:
• The opportunity to buy a ticket (seat already reserved) on No. 2007's first main line train
• Reasonable access to No. 2007 at all times

• The opportunity to buy exclusive Boiler Club badge
• The opportunity to join one of the teams building No. 2007
• First choice of other components to sponsor
• Special limited-edition version (signed/numbered) of the first official painting of No. 2007 *Prince of Wales* with No. 60163 *Tornado*
• Special Boiler Club day with *Tornado*

Dedicated donations present a unique opportunity for supporters to be associated with a component of No. 2007. Just as with *Tornado*, supporters will have the satisfaction of pointing to the part they paid for when No. 2007 enters service.

Those who subscribe to the scheme will have their names inscribed on the official Roll of Honour at Darlington Locomotive Works listing the component/s sponsored, receive a certificate recording the sponsorship and a copy of the drawing of the component.

Components available range from a fitted bolt and associated nut at £25 to a driving wheel casting and proof machining at £12,000 (monthly payments available). Would-be participants are invited to contact the dedicated donations team on dedicated.donations@p2steam.com to secure their chosen component.

For further information on any aspect of the new P2, visit www.p2steam.com, email enquiries@p2steam.com call 01325 460163 or write to P2 Construction Fund, Darlington Locomotive Works, FREEPOST RTJS-XECR-XARL, The A1 Steam Locomotive Trust, Hopetown Lane, Darlington DL3 6RQ.

ABOVE: A cab at last! The cab was displayed inside Darlington Locomotive Works on December 18, 2015. A1SLT
RIGHT: Trial fit of cab side with spectacle plate to the roof on December 8, 2015. A1SLT

ABOVE: The front end of *Prince of Wales* as seen on November 30, 2015. A1SLT
ABOVE RIGHT: The trial fit of a frame stay and the front boiler support on December 14, 2015. A1SLT

BELOW: Artist Jonathan Clay's impression of the finished product. A1SLT

Chapter 22

The Clan is rising again!

A commendable project to recreate another lost class of Pacific, that of a British Railways Standard Clan 72XXX, is very much a slow burner that has visibly lacked the fundraising machine of The A1 Steam Locomotive Trust, but continues to make steady progress.

ABOVE: A rare working saw BR Clan Pacific No. 72005 *Clan Macgregor*, one of a small class that normally worked in Scotland, alongside Chester 3A signalbox at Chester General with a freight working on August 29, 1964. BEN BROOKSBANK

After British Railways came into being on January 1, 1948, chief engineer, Robert Riddles, was appointed to design a fleet of standard locomotives, coaches and wagons, which were economic to run, easy to maintain, with a high availability and shared interchangeable, standardised parts and fittings.

His BR Standards eventually comprised 12 classes and 999 locomotives, but not all of them ended up being represented in preservation.

In the case of the Clan Pacifics, increased loads over secondary routes were frequently being doubleheaded by regional Class 5 types, and a more powerful, more economic locomotive with a similar route availability was required. Riddles and his team decided to use a modified Class 7 chassis, fitted with a smaller boiler, creating a mixed traffic Class 6. The additional build and maintenance cost was offset against the savings on coal, and it was planned to build 117 in all.

Designed at the Derby Works drawing offices, the new class was constructed at Crewe between 1951-52. The initial order was for 25 locomotives, but such was the immediacy of demand regarding a smaller version of the Britannias that a batch of 10

was rushed through construction before teething problems had been ironed out at the BR Rugby testing station.

The first Standard Class 6MT was turned out in 1952 at a cost of £20,426 and carried the number 72000. The initial batch, numbered 72000-72009, was allocated to the Scottish Region, and named after Scottish clans, No. 72000 becoming *Clan Buchanan*.

Tests carried out by the Scottish Regional Executive reported that the Clan was a fast, economical engine, light on both coal and water, able to run to, and make up time, "the steaming capacity of the boiler a revelation".

Locomotive crews, especially those at Carlisle Kingmoor shed, thought the Clans to be fine machines. They operated daily over some of BR's most testing routes, encompassing Beattock, Shap, Settle & Carlisle, and the tortuous 'Port Road' to Stranraer.

An impressive run timed over the Settle & Carlisle was made by No. 72005 *Clan MacGregor* on the 12-coach 'Thames-Clyde' relief. A total of 141.5 minutes from Carlisle and over the Pennines to Leeds including temporary speed restrictions gave an average speed of 45mph: today's quickest schedule,

using modern diesel units is 149 minutes.

However, no more Clans were constructed owing to the steel shortages of the 1950s, and after the publication of the 1955 Modernisation Plan, all orders for new express passenger locomotives were cancelled. Sadly, none of the 10 Clans made it into preservation.

THE 11TH CLAN

In the early Nineties, Paul Burns, a modern-day main line steam locomotive fireman and driver, who had worked the first and similar but larger BR Standard, No. 70000 *Britannia* on main line specials, found himself admiring the Clan not only from an aesthetic point of view, but also from a design and work aspect.

He and like-minded enthusiasts launched a project to build a new one, filling in a void left by what they saw as a very underrated and overlooked locomotive, under the banner of the Standard Steam Locomotive Company Limited.

It would be numbered 72010 and named *Hengist* after what would have been the next in line at Crewe, adopting all the improvements outlined in Lot 242. In 1995, the first of what has been a steady stream of components was found.

ABOVE: Impression by artist Steve Lucas of how BR Clan Pacific No. 72010 *Hengist*, the 11th member of its class, will look.

Initially components were stored all over the country, until a small space at the Swanage Railway's Herston Works was offered. There, many parts were manufactured, culminating in the front bufferbeam, apron, valance and smoke deflectors being displayed at Barrow Hill in 2002.

The bogie frames, main frames and the frame extensions were all cut, machined and drilled. The smokebox barrel, door and ring were made and the cab structure was almost completed.

However, the space at Herston had to be vacated, and the project moved to the nearby Shillingstone station project in Dorset, it leading a somewhat nomadic existence until a new base was agreed in June 2012. Once the frames of the locomotive have been erected, tested, and certified as fit for future main line operation, at Riley and Son (E) Ltd's Bury workshops, (where other parts have been stored) the components will be moved to the Great Central Railway's workshops at Loughborough, raising the profile of the project at a stroke.

Being located on Britain's only double-track heritage trunk line is an attractive proposition when it comes to testing the completed locomotive in the future.

On November 14, 2003, members of the Standard Steam Locomotive Company had travelled to the Corus plant at Lye in the Black Country on November 14 to watch *Hengist's* frames being cut out from a steel sheet by use of a computer-controlled profiler, for a bargain four-figure sum. It was the project's first major component. Sadly it was a false start.

An inspection of the frames carried out several years later found that the plates and hornguides had been incorrectly manufactured, and there was no possibility of correcting the faults.

Thankfully, a project member came forward and donated sufficient funding to enable new plates to be ordered. These have since been finished, new hornguides being manufactured and welded in, using the correct procedures, and all work has been tested, passed, paperwork completed, and the completed plates have been moved to Rileys for storage. The original plates were scrapped at the same time.

Since then the project has been making steady progress. All the major castings that go between the frames have been ordered and delivered.

Other frame stretchers, the trailing keep feet, bogie bolsters and the frame cross stay, have been either machined, or manufactured and machined.

It is hoped that the erection of the frames' parts will take place during 2016, 50 years since the last of the original class, No. 72006 *Clan MacKenzie*, was withdrawn in May 1966.

Away from the frames, other work recently has concentrated on refurbishing the cab structure, and assembling the smokebox. At the start of 2016 these were displayed in the station yard at the GCR's Quorn & Woodhouse Station, Great Central Railway.

While progress has not been on the spectacular scale of other new builds, nonetheless it is being made, steadily and surely. The project currently has components to the value of £500,000 in storage, many of which can be utilised once the frames are completed.

Once finished, there is little doubt that a new Clan will be a magnificent addition to Britain's heritage steam fleet.

■ For details of how to help *Hengist* become reality, visit www.theclanproject.org ●

ABOVE: The smokebox and cab displayed at the Great Central Railway's Quorn & Woodhouse station. RICHARD HENLEY/CLAN PROJECT

ABOVE: The replacement Clan frameplate in slings. KEN HORAN/CLAN PROJECT

ABOVE: A line-up of new *Hengist* castings and parts outside Ian Riley's Bury workshops. BOB IFE/CLAN PROJECT

Chapter 23

A new tank engine for Ongar

A new steam engine for the line that London Underground did not want to keep is now taking shape in Birmingham.

ABOVE: An illustration of GER F5 2-4-2T 789 by Eddy Dodwell who produces artwork for the Holden F5 Steam Locomotive Trust's merchandise. HFSLT

While the British Railways' network was destroyed by closures following Nationalisation, before, during and after Beeching, very little of the London Underground system was axed.

However, one section to close was the Central Line's 6½-mile former Great Eastern Railway branch from Epping to Chipping Ongar, which was electrified as recently as 1957 and lost its passenger services owing to low uptake on September 30, 1994.

Shortly after the branch closed, the Ongar Railway Preservation Society was formed to take over the line, but the Labour government instead awarded it to a private company, Pilot Developments, a move that sparked great controversy among enthusiasts, especially when the promised commuter services failed to start. Famously, Pilot said that it would have

incoming charters running in from outside, and when it was pointed out that *Flying Scotsman's* chimney would not fit beneath the M11 overbridge, the answer was that it would be hinged back.

Undeterred, ORPS members bided their time, while planning for a day when they might yet take over the redundant route. Looking at the progress being made on *Tornado*, in 2001 several of them opted to recreate a GER F5 24-2T, a class that had formed the mainstay of services on the branch before electrification. The National Railway Museum Record held a huge amount of drawings, including some of the F4/F5 on microfiche.

After several private attempts to reopen it, the line is now the multiple award-winning Epping Ongar Railway, which has been

returned to its steam-era grandeur by owner Roger Barker, and one day it may well see an F5 running over it.

The type was designed by GER Locomotive Superintendent, James Holden, as a development of his predecessor William Worsdell's M15 2-4-2Ts. At first, the M15s were modified into F5s by fitting Stephenson valve gear as a major improvement on the poorly performing Joy's value gear. A second batch, the P55s was built new to this design between 1903-09.

Stephen Dewar Holden followed in the footsteps of his father in 1908 and built a batch of 20 larger versions of the M15 with a boiler of higher pressure and increased water and coal capacity, which raised the overall weight by three tons. Twenty of these engines were built by the GER and could be distinguished by the side cab windows; they later became the LNER class F6. Some P55s were rebuilt with the higher-pressure boilers from 1911-20 and became classified as M15R. After Grouping in 1923, classes M15/M15R became LNER F4 and F5 respectively.

At Nationalisation, 37 F4s and all 30 F5s passed into BR ownership and all were given the prefix '6' to their number. Soon after, in 1949, seven F5s were fitted with vacuum push-pull gear. Of these, Nos. 67193, 67200, 67202, 67203 and 67213 were based at Epping to work the Ongar shuttle while Nos. 67199 and 67218 were based at Yarmouth. The Epping-based locomotives were also fitted with trip-cock apparatus for safe working between Epping and Leyton. No. 67218 later came to Epping and joined 67200 and 67212 to operate the last steam trains on the branch on November 16, 1957.

OPRS pioneer members Graham Rowland, Stephen Cooper and Ian Strugnall saw that the F5 would not only be the most suitable to work over a revived Ongar branch but also on heritage railways anywhere as it weighed just 16 tons. The new engine could legitimately run in Great Eastern blue and grey liveries, LNER, BR black, with or without push-pull gear, and with or without trip cocks.

It was decided to number the new F5 No. 67218. To start the project, a 30A Stratford shed plate was bought from Procast of Cleckheaton, followed by the sourcing of various minor components.

In June 2002 the Holden Steam Locomotive Trust was granted charitable status, and in autumn 2003 it located a suitable workshop at Ovington in North Essex.

The trust was granted corporate membership of the Heritage Railway Association in March 2004.

During 2004 and 2005 the valances and bufferbeams were completed and assembled, with patterns made for the non-driving wheels.

Over the years, steady progress has been made. By late 2013, other parts fabricated includ the bunker, main frame plates, the complete smokebox, chimney, valances, rail guards, frame plates, mid-frame stretcher, bufferbeams, as well as leading and trailing wheel patterns. It was in December that year that the trust announced that its new locomotive will run as GER No. 789 in Prussian blue, rather than as No. 67218 in BR black as originally planned.

ABOVE: F5 2-4-2T No. 67202 at Epping shed in 1950. EPPING ONGAR RAILWAY SOCIETY

ABOVE: Seen in 2005 is the non-driving wheel pattern and core box with the Holden F5 Steam Locomotive Trust's Graham Rowland (far left) and chairman Steve Cooper (far right) with Dave Harriman and John Hazlehurst of South Lincs Patterns. HFSLT

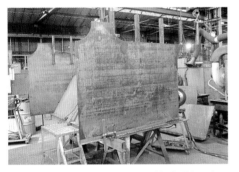

ABOVE: The bunker being built at Hunwicks in Halstead, Essex, in March 2010. HFSLT

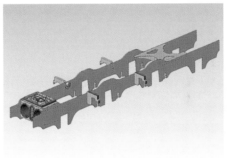

ABOVE: A CAD drawing of the F5 frame assembly. HFSLT

ABOVE: The frame plates for GER 789 were profiled by Tata Steel on March 13, 2012. HFSLT

The project later moved to Mangapps Railway Museum in Essex, but in October 2013 was given notice to quit because of maintenance work needed on the building in which it was based. The trust found a new home at Tyseley Locomotive Works in Birmingham.

In November 2011, the cylinder halves were cast at Harco Engineering of Brierley Hill, and united the following July.

It has been estimated that the F5 can be completed for around £550,000, including the boiler, as the cost of patterns has plummeted through the innovation of CAD and the advent of polymer. Whereas throughout the steam era wooden patterns were made for castings, the user of polymer – which dissolves when the hot metal is poured – can cut the

cost significantly. The disadvantage is that if you get it wrong, you will need another polymer pattern, but they are so cheap by comparison that it is still by far the most cost-effective method today. All engineering is now being overseen by West Steam Design and Tyseley itself.

Trust chairman and co-founder, Steve Cooper, said: "The sight of GER No. 789

operating on the Epping-Ongar branch, or the Mid-Norfolk or North Norfolk railways, would be a sight to behold for both enthusiasts and visitors alike." ●

■ Find out more about how you can help the project by visiting www.holdenf5.co.uk or emailing: info@holdenf5.co.uk or write to The Holden F5 Steam Locomotive Trust 49 Beech Avenue, Halstead, Essex.

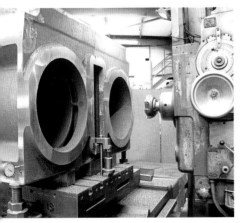

ABOVE: The F5 cylinder block halves united at Harco Engineering, Brierley Hill, on July 5, 2015. TERRY FLAVELL

ABOVE: The smokebox and bufferbeam of the new F5, No. 67218. The door handles and dart are also in place and lock against the crossbar temporarily bolted to the doorplate of the smokebox. HSLT

Chapter 24

Recreating a Victorian
Great Central train

One day, the Great Central Railway will be Britain's first inter-city heritage trunk line, running between Nottingham and Leicester, and a new-build project could ensure that the journey can be made in a fully fledged pre-Grouping wooden-bodied train.

ABOVE: Manchester, Sheffield & Lincolnshire Railway Class 2 4-4-0 No. 567 freshly outshopped at Gorton works in January 1891. JOHN QUICK COLLECTION

LEFT: The GCR 567 Locomotive Group's logo: the Manchester, Sheffield & Lincolnshire Railway Class 2 features on the GCR crest. GCR567LG

GCR 567 Loco Group

In 2009, a project was launched to recreate an example long-extinct class of Great Central Railway locomotive at an estimated cost of half a million pounds.

Great Central? Actually, the chosen locomotive, Class 2 4-4-0 No. 567, was built for the GCR's predecessor the Manchester, Sheffield & Lincolnshire Railway, and once hauled express trains across the trans-Pennine Woodhead route.

The original No. 567 was one of a class of 31 locomotives built between 1887-94 at Kitson Works in Leeds and Gorton Works in Manchester. Popular and economical locomotives, they survived into the LNER era where they became Class D7. The last was taken out of service and scrapped in 1939.

The project is being run by the GCR 567 Locomotive Group, with the aim of running the locomotive on the Great Central Railway, Britain's only heritage double-track main line. At the time of going to press, serious moves were underway to tackle arguably the biggest obstacle in the heritage sector – the missing bridge over the Midland Main Line at Loughborough, the replacement of which will allow the modern-day GCR to link with its northern sister, the Great Central Railway (Nottingham). Once the lines are joined together, there will be a unique inter-city heritage line between the outskirts of Leicester and Nottingham.

At the GCR(N)'s Ruddington base, excellent progress has been made with restoring MSLR/GCVR wooden-bodied coaches – ideal for running behind No. 567 and adding a major new dimension to our heritage portfolio.

Group chairman Andrew Horrocks-Taylor said: "These elegant 4-4-0s were the pride of the MS&LR and then contributed towards the nascent GCR's slogan 'Rapid travel in Luxury'. Indeed the GCR's legendary first chairman Sir Edward Watkin was so pleased with his Class 2, it was immortalised as the locomotive that features in the company crest.

"While we'll incorporate some minor changes, the new No. 567 will be externally indistinguishable from its predecessors.

The funding plan envisages 567 supporters signing up to give £5.67 a month for 10 years. At the close of 2015, there were 140 regular donors, a £95,000 funding commitment against a budget estimated at £400,000.

A suitable cylinder block has been found and an original GCR tender, the frames of which are suitable for reuse, has been obtained from the Midland Railway-Butterley and taken to Ruddington, while original Kitson drawings for the class have been located at the National Railway Museum.

Progress has bene such that the frames for No. 567 were cut in July 2015, and at the time

ABOVE: The frames of No. 567 were cut at PP Profiles of Bury, Lancashire in July 2015. GCR567LG

ABOVE: The frames of No. 567 in main contractor Ian Howitt's Wakefield workshops. GCR567LG

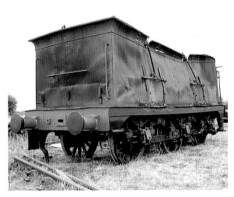

ABOVE: The group's original Great Central tender pictured at Ruddington on May 2011. GCR567LG

ABOVE: Newly constructed sandboxes, the first new components from the project team displayed in a mock-up of the locomotive installation in June 2014. GCR567LG

of writing, they were awaiting machining before erection.

A set of Austerity 0-6-0ST connecting rods (a fortunate coincidence means they fit with minor strap adaption) is being cleaned up and shotblasted before painting.

Design work also progresses with frame manufacture queries. Frame stretchers, front and rear buffers, front and rear dragbox are the priority to finish, but work to progress the bogie truck is also underway. As funding is still showing a surplus, bogie wheel castings are also out for quotation.

Andrew said: "The objective is to recreate a Victorian main line express on the only preserved Victorian-built main line. We have the line, Victorian/Edwardian theme stations, restorable and operational carriages; the missing element is an 1890s built express locomotive.

"No. 567 fits the bill nicely and should help to bring the era of Queen Victoria, Sherlock Holmes, Kipling, The Railway Children and the railway magnate, Edward Watkin, back to life in a most spectacular way."

As well as running on the GCR, No. 567 will be available for hire to other heritage lines.
■ Donation and supporter forms are available at www.GCR567Loco.co.uk or by post at GCR 567 Locomotive Group, c/o Mrs Dawn Bullock, 19 Hartridge Walk, Allesley Park, Coventry, CV5 9LF. ●

ABOVE: John Quick's OO gauge model of 567 in early GCR livery of chocolate frames, mid-chrome green lined-out in yellow, pictured on the Ruddington model railway layout hauling a GCR six-wheeler carriage. GCR567LG

ABOVE: The cylinder block, an unused machined spare for a Robert Stephenson and Hawthorns Corby class industrial locomotive confirmed fit for use. GCR567LG

Chapter 25

From George the Fifth to
Prince George

The London & North Western Railway fared extremely badly in the preservation stakes, with no 20th-century design express passenger locomotive surviving into preservation. However, a charity formed in 2012 is well on the way to rectifying matters.

ABOVE: The pioneer engine George the Fifth with a full brake coach. The LNWR George the Fifth Steam Locomotive Trust has already secured a similar vehicle from the Chasewater Railway to place its locomotive in its proper historical context.

In the spring of 2012, a group aiming to build a new LNWR George the Fifth 4-4-0 announced that it had been given a £50,000 boost towards getting the project started.

Three members of the LNWR Society, Bruce Nixon, Paul Hibberd and Derek Buckles, had just set up the LNWR George the Fifth Steam Locomotive Trust to undertake the £1.5-million project.

The trust had been offered financial backing from an anonymous donor, in the form of £50,000 in five-year tranches of £10,000 provided that the group first matches these sums.

The group, which has acquired registered charity status, plans to run the locomotive on both the national network and heritage lines, and will introduce technical improvements to overcome known deficiencies in the original Charles Bowen Cooke design.

The group had already established the presence of sufficient drawings at the National Railway Museum.

The class, which appeared in 1910, was not only Bowen Cooke's debut passenger

design but the first Crewe locomotive to use superheaters. He fitted them to several of the Precursors, which formed the basis of his George the Fifth design, as well as to his own designs.

A total of 90 members of the class were built between 1910-15. The LNWR reused names and numbers from withdrawn locomotives.

The George the Fifth class retained traditional features (notably the Joy valve gear) but was in front of its time and looked forward to much later designs through the use of high-temperature superheat and long travel piston valves.

These features produced spectacular performances. The pioneer locomotive achieved faster than 'even time' with an express train load from Euston to Crewe and a recent run by LMS Princess Coronation 4-6-2 No. 46233 *Duchess of Sutherland* from Carnforth to Shap summit was but two minutes faster than a performance by a George, *Deerhound*, with a similar load. The class worked principal expresses on all the routes out of Euston.

The Georges were followed in 1911 by the Prince of Wales class 4-6-0, a development of the earlier Experiment type.

All of the Georges passed into LMS ownership at the Grouping in 1923. The LMS gave them the power classification 3P. Withdrawals of the George the Fifth class began in 1935, and by 1939 only nine were left. The last three examples remained in service until 1948. No. 25321 was withdrawn in February that year, and Nos. 25350 and 25373 were allocated the BR numbers 58011/2 but never carried them as both were withdrawn that May.

The George is a classic example of an LNWR express engine of 20th-century design, of which no example survived into preservation. Therefore, the trust aims to fill another big gap in preservation, remedying a great wrong. The objective is to build a highly successful 4-4-0 of pre-First World War design.

In July 2013, the trust approached the Duke and Duchess of Cambridge to name their locomotive after their newborn son, Prince George. The royal couple accepted, and the

the locomotive was given the number '2013', the year of his birth, and named *Prince George* on July 22, 2014, in honour of his first birthday, when the project was officially launched.

As the prototype locomotive was named George the Fifth, therefore it is fitting therefore that the new build (with royal approval) carries the name of a future king, Prince George.

Construction of No. 2013 began with the smokebox door followed by a 20ft section of the side of the locomotive, enabling the name to be unveiled on the little prince's first birthday.

On July 22, 2014 the unveiling of name, cabside and splasher assembly took place at Quorn & Woodhouse station on the Great Central Railway.

As only one 20th-century LNWR locomotive exists, there are virtually no spare parts in existence; the whole locomotive must be built from scratch.

However, the trust has acquired genuine auxiliary fittings including an LNWR whistle, which came off a 0-6-2T. A presentation of the whistle took place on the footplate of LNWR 2-4-0 No. 790 *Hardwicke* at Railfest 2012 at the National Railway Museum in York.

The trust has stated it will cost between £1.5 and £2 million to complete *Prince George*. Funds are being raised through private donations and sponsorship of parts. Raising the necessary capital is being achieved through having a presence at events, giving talks and generating publicity through the media.

Corus Steel at Cradley Heath in the West Midlands was contracted to cut the front frames and bufferbeam, and the full smokebox has been riveted together. The trust has, at the time of writing, gone out to tender for the pattern and casting of the four bogie wheels.

Trustee Paul Hibberd said: "The aspiration throughout has been for main line operation with clearance for 75mph running. In this way we seek to recreate something of the past glories of pre-Grouping rail travel and those of the old LNWR in particular.

"The LNWR really is the sleeping giant, being the largest joint stock company in the British Empire and a company with a fiercely loyal and proud work force (they even had their own fashion style). Their many achievements are often overlooked."

■ Donations can be sent to Paul Hibberd, LNWR George the Fifth Steam Locomotive Trust, at 62 High Street, Buntingford, Hertfordshire SG9 9AH. If you send an email to paulhibberd@gmail.com a gift aiding form will be sent to you, which is also suitable for regular contributions. Alternatively it can be downloaded from lnwrgeorgevtrust.org.uk ●

ABOVE: George the Fifth 4-4-0 No. 5000 *Coronation*, was the 5000th locomotive to be built at Crewe. THE RAILWAY MAGAZINE

ABOVE: The parts for No. 2013 made to date. LGTFSLT

ABOVE: At the time of writing, the builders had invited tenders for the casting of the bogie wheels. LGTFSLT

ABOVE: The riveted smokebox for the new George the Fifth. LGTFSLT

ABOVE: The bufferbeam for No. 2013. LGTFSLT

ABOVE: The smokebox door for *Prince George*. LGTFSLT

ABOVE: The splasher with nameplate unveiled on the first birthday of namesake Prince George. LGTFSLT

ABOVE: The trust took the splasher and cabside of No. 2013 to Sir William McAlpine's private Fawley Hill Railway in Buckinghamshire for a private members' day in July 2014. LGTFSLT

ABOVE: The new 'Bloomer', No. 670, under construction inside Tyseley Locomotive Works, with progress taking place as time and money permit.
ROBIN JONES

One day it will be blooming marvellous

A longrunning project to recreate a locomotive which grabbed the headlines in more ways than one in Victorian times is underway at Tyseley.

Birmingham's Tyseley Locomotive Works has in the modern day taken over the mantle of Swindon as the centre of excellence for running GWR locomotives on the main line.

Its Vintage Trains' railtours arm has an extensive year-round itinerary using locomotives of the ilk of GWR 4-6-0 No. 4965 *Rood Ashton Hall* and Castle class No. 5043 *Earl of Mount Edgcumbe*, plus its Swindon-built pannier tanks. In summer, it runs the 'Shakespeare Express' on Sundays, taking passengers from Birmingham to Stratford-upon-Avon and back, along the very unspoiled North Warwickshire line via Shirley and Henley-in-Arden.

However, lurking inside its extensive modern workshops is a project, which aims to capture the glories of main line running from the century before last, and from one of the GWR's rival companies too.

In the late 1980s, Tyseley drew up a scheme to build a fully working London & North Western Railway 'Bloomer' 2-2-2.

This powerful express type was designed in 1851 by Southern Division locomotive superintendent James McConnell and built at the LNWR's Wolverton Works.

Around 160 locomotives are believed to have been built at the works, the last in 1863, after which new construction was transferred to Crewe. Locomotive repairs continued at Wolverton until 1872, the works then switching entirely to the construction and maintenance of carriages, eventually becoming the largest carriage works in Britain. It currently houses the Royal Train.

Developed from a design of McConnell's predecessor Edward Bury, the 'Bloomers' were considered ahead of their time, with high boiler pressure, hopper grates and experimental fireboxes. So, why the nickname?

American Amelia Jenks, married a lawyer, Dexter C Bloomer, and by the age of 33 in 1851 she had been editing and publishing a pioneering fortnightly magazine for more than two years.

She shocked Victorian society by wanting to reform contemporary female clothing so that underwear could be glimpsed.

When a handful of young women appeared on the streets of London in loose knee-length frocks and lightweight pants down to the ankles, as she recommended, as opposed to tight-laced corsets with yards of flannel petticoats and crinolines, it caused a sensation.

At first the girls who were wearing bloomers ran the gauntlet of ridicule, but the fashion quickly caught on, in the year of the Great Exhibition at the Crystal Palace, and the word quickly passed into common usage. London theatres staged Bloomer farces, while one brewery clad all its barmaids in Bloomer costume.

Anything novel and striking was likely to be labelled Bloomer, and when an example of McConnell's new 2-2-2 – also highly unusual in appearance as it unashamedly showed all of its wheels – arrived at Camden shed, the choice of nickname was a no-brainer as far as the footplate crews were concerned.

The nickname caught on so fast that it was soon used in LNWR official correspondence.

Their design was reflected in the evolution of other LNWR classes although the last was

ABOVE: One of the first new 'Bloomers' to appear in 1851. ILLUSTRATED LONDON NEWS

ABOVE: A LNWR postcard of 'Bloomer' No. 1007 *President*, which was built in 1861.

withdrawn in 1888. Despite their success, none was preserved.

Tyseley, however, decided that such a magnificent type should not be permanently consigned to the pages of history.

Its new-build project kicked off when two McConnell tender underframes completely authentic to the 'Bloomers' were discovered at the closed British Rail motive power depot at Northwich.

A third, which despite the passage of time still had the brake gear complete with wooden blocks, was found at Machynlleth.

With the 150th anniversary of the opening of the London & Birmingham Railway approaching in 1988, a £40,000 grant to begin work was obtained from Birmingham City Council.

An all-welded steel boiler was completed in 1987 for around £25,000, while Goodwin Foundries of Stoke-on-Trent cast the six steel wheels. The driving wheels were 7ft 4in in diameter and weighed around 1.6 tons.

Precision Machinery Ltd of Lye in the Black Country manufactured the cylinders, while a neighbouring firm built the smokebox, and a new tender tank was constructed at Tyseley.

When one of the tender frames from Northwich was stripped down for renovation following acquisition of the pair, it was found to have the number 603 stamped on the steps, pairing it with 'Small Bloomer' No. 3, which was built at Wolverton in 1859 and scrapped in 1884 after being based locally at Nuneaton.

ABOVE: Amelia Bloomer, whose name was taken by both women's underwear and crack LNWR express locomotives. Remembered mostly for women's fashion, she was also an important contributor to the women's rights movement. Her efforts have been remembered in an annual booklist: The Amelia Bloomer Project honours the top feminist books for young readers.

Sadly, the early impetus was lost with the development of Tyseley's core business; that of rebuilding, overhauling and maintaining locomotives to run on the national network.

There were more pressing claims on Tyseley's income stream, so progress on the 'Bloomer' took a back seat, and progress is made when time and funds permit. Such an occasion came in 2008-09, when donations and a legacy from Ffestiniog Railway architect, Michael Seymour, totalling £20,000, were used to manufacture components for the motion of the Bloomer, which by then was 90% complete.

The project team has been working steadily in the background to both produce more components and to raise funds; the hardest part of any new-build scheme.

When complete, the new 'Bloomer' will be numbered 670, the works' postal address in Warwick Road, following the LNWR practice of not having a numbering sequence for ▶

ABOVE: The non-working 'Bloomer' on static display outside Milton Keynes Central station.

ABOVE AND BELOW: New non-ferrous components for the motion of No. 670 waiting to be fitted in the Tyseley workshops. ROBIN JONES

ABOVE: Tyseley Locomotive Works is today best known for the restoration of GWR locomotives and their operation on today's national network. Pictured left to right at an open day in June 2009 are No. 4936 *Kinlet Hall*, No. 7029 *Clun Castle* and No. 4953 *Pitchford Hall*. ROBIN JONES

locomotives but often taking them from works numbers.

A non-working replica 'Bloomer' numbered 1009 and named 'The Wolvertonian' was commissioned by Milton Keynes Development Corporation for display in the new town's Station Square.

It was constructed in 1991 by engineering students with assistance from craftsmen in nearby Wolverton Works.

Its official unveiling was performed by actor Jon Pertwee, the third Dr Who, who once came out with a classic bloomer by referring to 'Wolverhampton's' illustrious railway history. The 'Bloomer' has since been returned for display at Wolverton works, which at the time of writing was faced with redevelopment, so its future destination remains unclear.

Tyseley's chief engineer, Bob Meanley, said that the new 'Bloomer' will not be built to current main line specifications, but for use on heritage railways, and is likely to prove very popular as a guest at galas and special events.

In any event, its appearance will not only provide a new window into an era of railway history, which has by circumstance been largely bypassed by the preservation sector, but might also well give a reminder of an aspect of Victorian social history and women's rights. ●

ABOVE: The under-construction new 'Bloomer' and tender inside the Tyseley workshops. ROBIN JONES